Intentionality: A Study of Mental Acts

INTENTIONALITY:

A Study of Mental Acts

Richard E. Aquila

The Pennsylvania State University Press
University Park and London

Library of Congress Cataloging in Publication Data

Aquila, Richard E   1944–
  Intentionality : a study of mental acts.

  Includes bibliographical references and index.
  1. Intentionalism.   I. Title.
BF311.A65   153.8   76-15160
ISBN 0-271-01228-5

Copyright © 1977 The Pennsylvania State University
All rights reserved
Designed by Richard Villastrigo
Printed in the United States of America

To my Mother and Father,
To Pier and Ellen,
and
To Marienne

Contents

Preface

At least some of the states which people sometimes are in are those which we call "mental" states. Among these are states which involve a person's having an awareness or a conception of some object or kind of object, or of some state of affairs involving some object or kind of object. To discuss the "objects" of mental states is, of course, ambiguous in at least one important way. For I may—speaking *"de re"* of some actually existing object—report that *it* is the object of some particular mental state; or I may—speaking *"de dicto"* of some particular mental state—merely report that it is, or involves, an awareness or a conception of some object. The first usage clearly implies that if there is an awareness or a conception of some object, then there actually is an object of such an awareness or conception; it is not, however, at all clear that the second of these usages implies this. It is certainly possible, for example, to be perceptually aware of all sorts of purely hallucinated objects, and to deal, at least in one's thoughts, with objects and states of affairs which are purely imaginary and which do not comprise any part of the actual world. I shall follow the practice of some philosophers by using the term 'intentionality' to designate the phenomenon of awareness or conception when it is construed in the second sense; mental states which exhibit this feature will be known as "mental acts."

My purpose is to provide a critical and analytical survey of the major attempts, in modern philosophy, to interpret the phenomenon of intentionality. The earlier philosophers whose views I deal with at some length are Descartes, Brentano, Meinong, Husserl, Frege, and Bertrand Russell, and the contemporary philosophers are Gustav Bergmann, Roderick Chisholm, and Wilfrid Sellars.

My concern with the problem of intentionality is primarily an ontological or metaphysical one. It is therefore neither primarily a *phenomenological* concern with describing the various worlds (and "subworlds") that present themselves as objects (whether "real" or not) to consciousness, nor primarily a *linguistic* concern with describing the various sorts of things that one ordinarily says about the consciousness of such objects. My concern is with the nature of awareness and the nature of the "relation" (if there is one) that unites awareness and the world (or worlds) of objects that confront it. Nevertheless, it will of course be important to review, at least to some extent, both of these other concerns as well. In particular, it will be necessary to examine the view, most recently defended by Roderick Chisholm, that certain purely linguistic considerations lead directly to the conclusion that the mind occupies, in virtue of its intentionality, an ontologically unique position in what might otherwise be a purely material universe. I shall also attempt to show how my own view does more justice than could otherwise be done to the phenomenological data.

With respect to the metaphysical issues raised by intentional phenomena, two general lines of approach have inevitably reappeared throughout the history of philosophy—together, perhaps equally unavoidably, with the attempts of those such as Descartes, who have become almost hopelessly entangled in an attempt to have it both ways at once. The first of these emphasizes the *object* of awareness and supposes that some unique sort of *relation* between mental acts and their objects is necessarily involved in the fact that we have awareness and conceptions *of* such objects. The main difficulty in this approach is of course posed by the fact that awareness of objects seems not necessarily to be of objects that *really exist*. In the face of this difficulty, one might continue to maintain a relational theory of mental acts only by also maintaining (with Meinong) that a relation with objects of awareness does not in fact *require* that there be any such objects for one to be related to; or (with Russell) that we do not really have an awareness or conception of various sorts of objects of which we at least *seem* to have some awareness or conception; or (with Bergmann) that the realm of "real existence" comprises only a vanishingly small *part* of the total realm of being; or, finally (with Frege and the later Husserl), that we are always in fact aware of objects of a sort that we might ordinarily never *seem* to be aware of (Meanings, Propositions, Senses, etc.) and which are at least simply overlooked in any purely materialistic dealing with reality. The second line of approach to the phenomenon of intentionality emphasizes the *act* rather than the object of awareness or conception, and it attempts to account for the awareness or conception of objects solely by appealing to the internal *contents* of such acts. Despite appearances and frequent opinions to the contrary, Brentano and the early Husserl provide examples of this sort of view. Contemporary "linguistic" accounts of intentionality, such as Sellars', can also be considered as offering a viable form to this approach.

The correct view, I believe, involves elements of both approaches, although without, of course, falling into the Cartesian confusion of simply attempting to regard objects of awareness, insofar as they are objects of awareness, as *themselves* forming an actual part or content contained "within the mind." (What I call the "content theory of awareness," in Chapter 1, is this Cartesian view which Brentano, and later the early Husserl, made every effort to reject, without at the same time being willing to accept a *relational* account of mental acts, and yet without themselves being able to provide the details for a viable alternative.) The intentional properties of *some* mental states, namely those which I call "non-intuitive" acts, are wholly due to the presence of certain quasi-linguistic contents in those states; and at least *part* of the intentional character even of properly intuitive acts is attributable to the same feature. But the very *notion* of "mental content" which, by virtue of its quasi-linguistic character, is capable of performing these functions, can itself be explicated only by presupposing the existence of certain primitive relations of immediate apprehension of objects given to consciousness.

My interest in the problems of this book, and the philosophical approach which I have adopted, originally developed in the course of my graduate studies at Northwestern University. I must especially acknowledge the invaluable encouragement and inspiration that I have received, both at that time and since, from Professor M.S. Gram. I must also extend my appreciation to those journal editors and publishers who have granted permission for the use of materials previously published. A portion of the first part of Chapter 1 originally appeared as "Brentano, Descartes, and Hume on Awareness," *Philosophy and Phenomenological Research* 35 (December 1974): 223–29, and an argument in the second part of that chapter was originally contained in "Perceptions and Perceptual Judgments," *Philosophical Studies* 28 (July 1975): 17–32. Some material in Chapter 2 originally appeared in "The Status of Intentional Objects," *The New Scholasticism* 45 (Summer 1971): 427–56. Chapter 3 contains material from "Intentionality and Possible Facts," *Nous* 5 (November 1971): 411–17. Chapter 4 contains material from "Husserl and Frege on Meaning," *Journal of the History of Philosophy* 12 (July 1974): 377–83.

1

Brentano and the
Problem of Awareness

The philosopher and philosophical psychologist Franz Brentano is chiefly responsible for placing the problem of intentionality in its contemporary philosophical setting. Brentano maintained two theses concerning intentionality. First, every mental state possesses the feature of intentionality:

> Every mental phenomenon is characterized by what the scholastics
> of the Middle Ages called the intentional (and also mental) inexis-
> tence of an object, and what we could call, although in not entirely
> unambiguous terms, the reference to a content, a direction upon
> an object (by which we are not to understand a reality in this case),
> or an immanent objectivity.[1]

Second, no physical phenomenon possesses the feature of intentionality: "This intentional inexistence is exclusively characteristic of mental phenomena."[2] In this chapter I introduce the problem of intentionality by contrasting Brentano's approach to the problem with certain classical alternatives.

Brentano's claims about intentionality might be viewed in a number of ways. They might, for example, reflect on the issue raised by the so-called identity theory of the mental, that is, on the question whether mental states can be identified with physical states. However, as Brentano himself considered the matter, the two theses which he presented do not have any immediate bearing on this issue. Brentano clearly distinguishes between physical objects, entities, or states and what he calls physical "phenomena." Physical phenomena are, for Brentano, the immediate objects of sensory awareness. But our awareness of physical phenomena depends upon a system of external causality which is grounded in a domain of three-dimensional existence that is at best analogous in its structure to the order of the physical phenomena themselves. This external causal system, which is distinct from the system of physical phenomena, is the ultimate concern of investigation in the physical sciences.[3] It follows, then, that the claim that no physical phenomenon possesses the property of intentionality is compatible with the claim that intentionality is a feature which is to be found in the ultimate objects of investigation in the physical sciences, for example, with the claim that mental acts are identical with states of the brain. Thus Brentano's theses are not incompatible with the "identity theory" of the mental.

The distinction between physical "phenomena" and physical "reality," however, does point to what is most significant in Brentano's claims. Consider a case of "direction upon" some object, where the object in question is not one which we would say is, in the same sense, *also* "directed upon" an object. Consider a case of visual awareness of an object, where the object itself exhibits no features of "mental reference." Then, according to Brentano, the object must be a "physical phenomenon." This claim of Brentano's may strike us, initially, as rather inconsequential. When we recall, however, that on Brentano's view the phenomenon of "direction upon an object" does not require that the object in question "really exist" in the physical world, two alternatives to Brentano's view immediately present themselves. Both have, in the history of philosophy, exhibited a strong attraction for philosophers, and it is Brentano's achievement to have resisted both of these. Supposing that I am aware of something (e.g., a visual hallucination) which has no material reality, two alternatives may suggest themselves to me. First, I might regard the object in question as possessing some sort of merely "mental" status. Brentano rules this alternative out by insisting that, unless the object exhibits the feature of intentionality, the object in question must have a purely *physical*, and not a mental, status. Second, I might regard the object in question as being an object that really exists, but simply one that fails to be identical either with anything mental or with anything physical. Brentano excludes this alternative as well, by insisting that the objects of intentional reference need not really exist *at all*. Brentano's philosophical predecessors, as well as many of his contemporaries and successors, mistakenly thought that these were the only alternatives for dealing with cases of awareness of the (apparently) non-existent. Brentano offers a third alternative: awareness of objects may be of objects which do not exist in *any* (literal) sense, either "in the mind" or elsewhere.

I shall endeavor, in Chapter 1, to emphasize the force of this claim by contrasting it with specific instances of contrary claims. In Chapter 2 I shall discuss the ontological *implications* of Brentano's view about the status of intentional objects. In this connection, therefore, it is important to see that there are *two* distinct ontological issues which Brentano raises, in addition to the problems posed by the "identity theory" and to what Chisholm calls Brentano's "psychological thesis," which is an attempt to characterize the domain of mental phenomena in unique terms. One issue concerns the ontological status of objects of awareness (*qua* objects of awareness), which is the concern of Chapter 1. The other concerns the ontological account of our awareness *of* such objects (whether, e.g., it involves some special sort of "relation"). This will be our concern in the next two chapters.[4]

A Classical Theory of Awareness

One classical instance of the sort of view against which Brentano's polemic is directed is what I shall call the "content theory" of awareness. In Chapter 3, I argue that we do require a notion of "mental content," as something distinct from the *objects* of mental acts. On the view against which Brentano's polemic is directed, however, the objects of mental acts are *themselves* regarded as the contents of those acts. Brentano rightly rejects such a view.

The fullest expression of the "content theory" of awareness is perhaps found in the philosophy of Hume, although its roots are deeper than is generally acknowledged in the philosophy of Descartes. All of the objects directly apprehended in sensory awareness are, according to Hume, impressions: "properly speaking, 'tis not our body we perceive, when we regard our limbs and members, but certain impressions, which enter by the senses."[5] Thus, for example, any philosophical question concerning the "distinct and continued existence" of perceptual objects will be settled only once we have discovered "those peculiar qualities in our *impressions*, which makes us attribute to them a distinct and continu'd existence."[6] Impressions, however, are mental entities. Impressions, together with the ideas which resemble them, exhaust the class of perceptions, and "the true idea of the human mind, is to consider it as a system of different perceptions."[7] Impressions and ideas are literally "contents" or constituents of the human mind, and all of the objects of sensory awareness are therefore mental phenomena.

There are, to be sure, numerous passages in which Hume also speaks in a very different way about impressions. There are passages in which sense impressions do not appear to be regarded as the proper *objects* of perceptual awareness at all, but only as our perceptions *of* such objects. It is only, for example, by making this assumption that Hume could maintain that "all impressions are internal and perishing existences, and appear as such."[8] If at t_1 I am engaged in the perception of a colored spot which I cease to perceive at t_2, then it is clear that my perception of the spot was a merely "perishing existence." But there is nothing at all which should lead me to assume, or even to suspect, the same regarding the spot which I have perceived. There is no sense in which the spot itself even *appears* to be a merely "perishing existence." Hence perceptions in general, and sense impressions in particular, would appear to be, at least on some occasions on which Hume considers them, awarenesses of objects rather than objects of awareness. If this is the case, then Hume's claim that the mind is a bundle of impressions and ideas would not after all imply that the objects of sensory awareness are necessarily contained in the mind which is aware of them. To maintain that the mind itself is nothing but a collection or series of awarenesses of such objects (i.e., a collection or series of impressions) is compatible with denying the claim that perceptual objects are necessarily contained in the mind.

The force, however, of this distinction between two senses of the word 'impression' is not as great as the above remarks may suggest. Suppose that we call all of the objects of immediate sensory awareness *impressions*$_1$ and all occurrences of the *awareness* of such objects *impressions*$_2$. (I restrict myself to the case of impressions, though the point may be extended to the case of "ideas" as well.) Then *impressions*$_2$ turn out to be a particular class of events, the class of perceptual events. But the claim that the human mind is merely a collection or series of perceptual events, that is, of *impressions*$_2$, is not incompatible with the view that the mind also contains all *impressions*$_1$. The latter, I would maintain, is in fact the view to which

Hume is committed. He is committed to the belief that every event which is an *impression$_2$* just *is* the event of some *impression$_1$* coming to be contained in some mind—in other words, in some collection or series which also contains many other *impressions$_1$*.

Consider the alternatives to this view. First, an *impression$_2$* might consist in some person's coming to apprehend an *impression$_1$* where the apprehension of an object in perception is not a matter of the literal containment of some entity *in* the thing which is said to be apprehending that object. This clearly cannot be Hume's view, since it is incompatible with the claim that the mind is just a collection or series of perceptions. Second, an *impression$_2$* might consist in the event of some awareness of a given *impression$_1$* occurring in a collection or series which also contains many other such awarenesses. Awarenesses are construed on this view as particular entities; they are not events which, like *impressions$_2$*, merely *involve* particulars. Here, then, the mind is viewed as a collection or series of particular awarenesses. If it is viewed in this way, then the conception of the mind as a collection or series of some sort is compatible with the view that perceptual objects are never contained in the mind. But this cannot be a view which is acceptable to Hume. It is no easier to grant that introspection reveals, in addition to the particular colors and sounds which are apprehended by sense, a series of particulars which are the awarenesses *of* these colors and sounds than it is to grant that introspection reveals a permanent and abiding *subject* of awareness. Hence the same empirical considerations which lead Hume to reject the classical conception of the mind as a "substance" of some sort seem to apply with equal force to the conception of an "awareness" as a particular sort of entity distinct from, but standing in some relation to, the objects of perception.

Moreover, even if there were such particular awarenesses distinct from *impressions$_1$* and we were in fact aware of them, we could only introspectively identify them by *relating* them to *impressions$_1$*. The awareness, for example, that I am perceiving red at t_1 and green at t_2 could only be an awareness that my mind contains a particular which is an awareness of red at t_1 and a particular which is an awareness of green at t_2. There is nothing besides the fact that they are awarenesses of red or green and that they occur at one moment or another that I could introspectively determine concerning the particular awarenesses which are in question. But there is nothing at all in these facts which implies that the particular which is an awareness of red at t_1 is not strictly identical with the particular which is an awareness of green at t_2. Thus I could have no reason to infer, as Hume does, that my perceptions are constantly changing, hence that I am not introspectively aware of some particular entity which is *never* changing. There is no contradiction in the claim that while my awarenesses are never, from moment to moment, awarenesses of just the same objects, the particular which *is* the awareness of these objects is always the same particular. Hence there is nothing to prevent this second alternative from collapsing into the first and thereby undercutting Hume's own argument for a conception of the mind as a collection or series of some sort. We must, therefore, take Hume's view to be that *impressions$_2$* are simply the events of *impressions$_1$* occurring in a group which contains many other *impressions$_1$*. The only collection or series, then, with which the mind could possibly be identified is a collection or series of *impressions*₁ (and the ideas which are "copies" of them), hence the mind is an entity which contains as its constituent parts perceptual objects and not simply the awarenesses of such objects.

The Humean account of awareness is an instance of what might be called a "content theory" of awareness: to say that a person is aware of some object is to imply that some object is contained in the mind of the person who has the awareness of it. Hume does not, in one sense, deny a distinction altogether between mental states and their objects. *Impressions*₂, for example, are awarenesses of objects, hence they are distinct from the *impressions*₁ of which they are the awarenesses. But while awarenesses for Hume are not identical with their objects, nevertheless they *contain* those objects as constituents. Furthermore, the mind which "has" these awarenesses is nothing but a *sequence* of such awarenesses. Accordingly, all objects of awareness are literal constituents of the perceiver who is aware of them. Therefore, Hume fails after all to draw the sort of clear distinction between awarenesses and their objects which characterizes Brentano's account of awareness. He fails, that is, to capture the notion of mental activity as awareness directed toward something *beyond* itself.

It was the influence in philosophical psychology of the Humean account of awareness which led many of Brentano's contemporaries to describe all the immediate objects of awareness as mental "contents."[9] It was against such an account of awareness that Brentano was reacting when he insisted that all perceptual objects are physical phenomena, not mental. There is a sense in which, even for Brentano, all of the objects of awareness are "in" the mind which contains the awareness of them. But this is only a metaphorical sense:

> When Aristotle said the *aistheton energeia* is in one's experience, he was also speaking of what you call simply "object." But because we do use the word "in" here, I allowed myself the term "immanent object," in order to say, not that the object exists, but that it *is* an object, whether or not there is anything that corresponds to it. Its *being* an object, however, is merely the linguistic correlate of the person experiencing *having* it as object.[10]

To say that actual objects of sense are "in" one's sensory awareness is *just* to say that there is some awareness of them; it is not to say that those objects are, in any literal sense, in the mind at all. Furthermore, the same point must be applied to the case of nonperceptual phenomena as well. "What are experienced as primary objects, or what are thought universally as primary objects of reason, are never themselves the objects of inner perception."[11] On the Humean account of awareness, however, the objects which I contemplate in a thought are the very "content" of that thought, in precisely the same way that sense impressions are the very contents of sensory awareness. If we are to take this in any literal sense, then the object of nonperceptual acts ought to be accessible to the process of introspection. It ought to be, as it is for Hume, a mere "idea" in the mind. This Brentano rightly denies.

Brentano's attack upon the content theory of awareness must of course also be considered in the context of the problem of non-existent objects. Brentano, as we have seen, not only insisted that every mental state has an object, but he also insisted that it was a mistake to assume that the object which every mental state has is a "reality." It follows, however, from the content theory of awareness that we are never, strictly speaking, engaged in mental activity directed toward non-existent objects. Since the objects of awareness are, on that theory, a literal constituent of awareness itself, the very existence of an awareness assures the existence of its object. There is thus no problem for Hume about the awareness of non-existent objects. But the price to be paid for the Humean solution is great; it is just the admission that we are never aware, and never could become aware, of anything besides impressions and ideas, and these are just the contents of our own minds.

We may deepen our grasp of the structural connections among these points by considering the following argument which might in fact *lead* from a concern with the problem of non-existent objects to the Humean account of awareness: It is possible to contemplate in thought the nature or essence of objects which have no existence apart from the mind. The "content" of any thought about objects or kinds of objects will be the same whether or not such objects do in fact exist apart from the mind. Therefore, every thought is, in its inner nature, directed toward an object which exists *in* the mind; that is, every thought is properly directed only toward an "idea." An instance of this type of argument appears to have been offered by Descartes:

> If someone asks what feature in the sun's existence it is to exist in my mind, it will be quite right to reply that this is a merely extrinsic attribute which affects it. . . . But if the question be, what the idea of the sun *is*, and the reply is given, that it is the object thought of in so far as that exists objectively in the understanding, he will not understand that it is the sun itself, in so far as that extrinsic attribute is in it . . . but that it is in the mind in the way in which objects are wont to exist there. Hence the idea of the sun will be the sun itself existing in the mind, not indeed formally, as it exists in the sky, but objectively, i.e., in the way in which objects are wont to exist in the mind.[12]

Descartes distinguishes here between the sun "as it exists in the mind" and the sun which exists in the sky. Though the latter entity may in some way be a causal determinant of the former, it is not, Descartes argues, identical with it. We do not need to consider what exists in the sky in order to know what our idea of the sun *is*, that is, to be assured of the "content" of that idea. Descartes uses the word 'idea' to stand for those entities which form in this way the content of the thoughts which we have. However, he also uses the word in a very different sense:

> In this term *idea* there is here something equivocal, for it may either be taken materially, as an act of my understanding, and in this sense it cannot be said to be more perfect than I; or it may be taken objectively, as the thing which is represented by this act,

which, although we do not suppose it to exist outside of my understanding, may, none the less, be more perfect than I, because of
its essence.[13]

The distinction between an idea in the "material" sense and an idea in the
"objective" sense should not be confused with another, related distinction. In
taking any idea which is considered materially "as an act of my understanding,"
there are two different sorts of things which we may say about it. First, we may
observe that it is an event or "act" which occurs at a particular moment and to
a particular person. But we may say something else about it too: this particular
event or operation is also an event which possesses some specific "representative
character." Like every idea, it must be an idea *of* a specific object or kind of
object. About this distinction Descartes says the following:

> Since ideas themselves are forms, and are never composed of any
> matter, when we take them as representing something, we regard
> them not in a material guise but formally; but if we were to con-
> sider them not in so far as they represent this or that other thing,
> but in the respect in which they are operations of the intellect, it
> might be said that they were taken materially, but then they would
> have no reference to the truth or falsity of objects.[14]

Thus Descartes distinguishes between an idea considered materially and an idea
considered *formally*. This is a very different distinction from the distinction which
Descartes also draws between an idea considered materially and an idea considered
objectively. The material/formal distinction is a distinction between two different
ways in which we might regard any operation of the understanding. We might
regard it either with respect to its feature of occurring at some particular moment
and to some particular person, or we might regard it with respect to its very
different feature of representing some particular object or kind of object.

The material/formal distinction, therefore, is one which applies only to ideas
when they are being considered "materially" (as distinct from ideas considered
objectively). It applies to ideas only as "operations of the intellect." Let us then
distinguish ideas as considered $materially_1$ (as contrasted with ideas considered
objectively) from ideas as considered $materially_2$ (as contrasted with ideas considered formally). To draw the distinction between ideas considered $materially_2$ and
ideas considered formally commits us to the existence of operations of the intellect
as occurrences which are regarded as at least occasionally present "in" the understanding. To draw the distinction, however, between ideas considered $mate-
rially_1$ and ideas considered objectively appears to require the further admission
that something may exist in the understanding in addition to its own operations. It
appears to commit us to the existence of such entities as the sun considered, not "as
it exists in the sky," but as it is "wont to exist in the mind."

The distinction between the $material_2$/formal distinction, on the one hand, and
the $material_1$/objective distinction, on the other, comes, not surprisingly, to be

blurred by Descartes himself when he introduces what he terms the "objective reality of an idea":

> By the objective reality of an idea I mean that in respect of which the thing represented in the idea is an entity, in so far as that exists in the idea. . . . For whatever we perceive as being as it were in the objects of our ideas, exists in the ideas themselves objectively.[15]

Two very different things might be meant by the "objective reality" of an idea. By speaking of the objective reality of an idea, Descartes might simply be referring to whatever feature an idea possesses in virtue of which it is an idea of one particular object or kind of object rather than another. On this interpretation, to consider the objective reality of an idea is just to consider an idea as it is taken formally rather than *materially*$_2$, and to speak of some object or kind of object as existing "in" an idea would then be merely a loose way of describing the idea itself as an idea of such a thing.[16] But something quite different might also be meant by the "objective reality of an idea." In considering the objective reality of an idea, one might examine not merely some general feature of some possible mental act but rather the very *object* itself of some possible mental act. This would then be to consider an idea as it is taken "objectively," or as "the thing which is represented *by*" some particular mental act, although of course not as that object might exist *apart* from the way in which it is represented by that act. If this interpretation differs in any way from the first, then it implies that objects may exist "in" the understanding in something much stronger than the sense that there are acts in the understanding which *refer* to those objects, and this is in fact what Descartes himself appears to be granting when he draws the *material*$_1$/objective distinction in the first place.[17]

Now it might be argued that Descartes could only have been speaking loosely and metaphorically when he drew the distinction between ideas considered *materially*$_1$ and ideas considered objectively, and when he spoke of objects which "we do not suppose to exist outside of my understanding." For one thing, it might be urged, Descartes himself is intent upon insisting that the mind is a thing which is utterly incorporeal. We would, then, be attributing to Descartes the sheerest of contradictions if we attributed to him the view that contemplated bodies might exist "in the mind" in anything more than the sense that such objects are objects of some of the activities of the mind:

> Here you ask, "how I think that I, an unextended subject, can receive into myself the resemblance or idea of a thing which is extended." I reply that no corporeal resemblance can be received in the mind, but that what occurs there is *the pure thinking of a thing*, whether it be corporeal or equally whether it be one that is incorporeal and lacking any corporeal semblance.[18]

Here, one might argue, Descartes certainly says that all that the mind contains are just its own operations or acts and that it never contains any of the *objects* of those acts. But this does not, strictly speaking, follow from the passage which I have quoted.

All that Descartes is in fact claiming in this passage is that no mind could contain either corporeal substances or the actual resemblances of corporeal substances. But corporeal substances and their resemblances are not the only possible objects of an understanding which may be occupied with thoughts about the corporeal. We are capable of contemplating, by means of operations of the intellect, not only specific corporeal substances, but the nature or essence of corporeal substance in general, or of particular kinds of corporeal substances. Since the nature or essence of corporeal substance, which is a possible object of the intellect, is itself neither a corporeal substance nor the resemblance of a corporeal substance, there would at least be no contradiction in the claim that the "pure thinking" of some corporeal nature is just the event of a certain corporeal *essence or nature* coming to be present in the understanding. If this suggestion were accepted, then the difference which Descartes has drawn between the sun considered as it exists in the sky and that same sun considered as it exists within the understanding would just be that the object of the former consideration is the solar "nature" as it exists outside of our mind, while the object of the latter consideration is that same solar nature as it exists *within* our mind. Of course, the scholastic notion of the natures, or "intelligible species," of things coming to reside in the mind which contemplates them, apart from their matter, could not possibly have been a notion with which Descartes was unacquainted.[19] In any case, it can be shown that Descartes is in fact *committed* to that notion, and to the view that objects may come to exist in the mind in something more than the sense that there may be acts in the mind which grasp them.

Descartes introduces the "objective reality of an idea" in order to prove the existence of God. He introduces it, that is, in order to prove that an infinitely perfect nature exists outside of the understanding which contemplates it. But Descartes could not have supposed his proof to have any force at all unless he had already been prepared to suppose that an infinitely perfect nature does at least exist *in* the understanding which contemplates it in something more than the sense that there exist mental *acts* by which such a nature is contemplated. Descartes' first proof, in the Third Meditation, makes use of the axiom that there must exist at least as much reality in the total cause of any object's existence as there is present in the object itself. There are, however, two very different ways in which we might consider an *idea* to possess some particular degree of reality.

> If ideas are only taken as certain modes of thought, I recognize
> amongst them no difference or inequality, and all appear to pro-
> ceed from me in the same manner; but when we consider them as
> images, one representing one thing and the other another, it is
> clear that they are very different one from the other.[20]

This, of course, is Descartes' distinction between ideas considered *materially$_2$* and ideas considered formally. Descartes is thus claiming that while all of our ideas possess the same reality when they are considered *materially$_2$*, nevertheless they differ greatly with respect to their formal capacity for representing objects: ideas which represent objects possessing some higher degree of reality than others will themselves possess a higher degree of reality than the ideas which represent those objects. Accordingly, the amount of an idea's "objective reality" will be equal to the least amount of reality which must be possessed by any total and sufficient cause of an idea's representing the object which it does represent.

It is clear that if this in fact is all that we mean by the degree of "objective reality" which an idea possesses, then Descartes' causal axiom, when it is applied to the idea of infinite reality or perfection, will not help us in any way to prove the existence of God. All that it could help us to do is to establish that there does exist some total and sufficient cause for an idea's being an idea of infinite perfection, and that this cause possesses at least as much perfection in itself as the cause of any other idea's being the idea of what it represents. In order to be able to infer, however, that this particular amount of perfection is infinitely great, we must also assume that an idea of infinite perfection is *itself* of infinite perfection, and we must assume that it is so in something more than the sense that it is an idea which merely *represents* infinite perfection. But there is no sense at all in which an idea considered *materially*$_1$, that is, as an operation of the finite intellect, could be of infinite perfection *except* for the sense that the idea is, when formally considered, representative of infinite perfection. Since the *material*$_2$/formal distinction is a distinction which applies only to ideas considered *materially*$_1$, it follows that Descartes cannot intend to introduce the notion of degrees of objective reality solely in terms of that distinction.

When Descartes speaks of the objective reality of an idea, he has, therefore, shifted from the material to the "objective" use of the term 'idea.' He has shifted from the consideration of ideas as operations or acts of the intellect to the consideration of *objects* which are represented by or "contained in" those operations:

> For there must be some definite cause of the fact that this idea of a machine displays this objective artifice rather than another, and its objective artifice bears to this cause the same relation that the objective reality of the idea of God bears to its cause. . . . We must note that every contrivance which in the idea has only objective existence, must necessarily exist in its cause, whatever that cause be, either formally or eminently. And we must apply the same rule to the objective reality which is in the idea of God.[21]

The cause of the objective reality of an idea is the cause of that idea's representing the object which it does represent only because it is the cause of that very object *itself*. At the very least it is the cause of that object as something which has an existence *in* the particular idea which is in question.

We must thus distinguish two very different senses of the word 'idea' in Descartes' argument. In one sense of the word, an idea is an act or an operation of the intellect, an event which occurs in the mind; we may call it an *idea*$_1$. But in another sense, *idea*$_2$, an idea is the very *object* of some act or operation of the mind. It is an object which exists, however, *in* some *idea*$_1$, though it might also happen to exist apart from an *idea*$_1$. The expression 'objective reality of an idea' is, accordingly, also an ambiguous one. It may simply designate that feature of any *idea*$_1$ in virtue of which it represents the object which it does represent. Or it may designate the object itself, though without any implication at all concerning that object's existence apart from the mind. In the latter case, the objective reality of an idea is just an $idea_2$. That, in other words, in virtue of which an $idea_1$ is able to represent the object which it does represent is just the containment *in* that idea of the object which it represents. It is only when objective reality is construed in this second way that Descartes' argument for the existence of infinite perfection, not only as the objective reality of any idea which contemplates it, but as existing apart from any idea altogether, is a valid argument:

> In this term *idea* there is here something equivocal, for it may
> either be taken materially, as an act of my understanding, and in
> this sense it cannot be said to be more perfect than I; or it may be
> taken objectively, as the thing which is represented by this act,
> which, although we do not suppose it to exist outside of my under-
> standing, may, none the less, be more perfect than I, because of its
> essence.[22]

There is, then, a sense of the word in which one of my "ideas" is not simply an act or an operation of a mind engaged in the contemplation of infinite per-fection, but rather is itself the very infinite perfection which is thus contemplated. It is only in fact *because* of this very infinite perfection, as an $idea_2$, existing in the understanding which contemplates it that there exists an idea, that is, an $idea_1$, which merely *represents* infinite perfection in the first place.

Therefore, all of the proper objects of mental activity are contained for Descartes in the mind itself, and to say that they are contained in the mind is not just to say that the mind contains mental acts which refer to these objects. In one sense, of course, there is nothing startling about this conclusion. Descartes' view has in fact often been taken as paradigmatic of "representative realism." On that account, a threefold distinction needs to be drawn between (a) an act of the mind itself, (b) the transcendent object which exists, possibly, in the external world, and (c) an *imma-nent* object which represents the transcendent object and which will exist, at least in the mind, whether or not the object which it represents exists in the external world. The distinction between (a) and (c) is Descartes' distinction between $ideas_1$ and $ideas_2$, but the claim which I have made goes much further than the claim that Descartes is a representative realist. My argument is that there is a sense in which the very distinction between (b) and (c) *collapses* for Descartes. Only if it does collapse could we suppose that the $idea_2$ which represents infinite perfection to the mind is *itself* infinitely perfect. The distinction between (b) and (c), therefore, cannot merely be a distinction between two different entities, one of which repre-sents the other. If the distinction remains at all, then it can only remain as a distinction between two different ways in which one and the same entity might exist. It might exist apart from the mind, or it might exist within the mind. The view with which we are left, then, is that the mind contains two very different sorts of things. It contains its own mental activity and also all the proper objects *of* that activity.[23]

But what sense can we make of the claim that the objects of ordinary, non-reflective acts, like those acts themselves, exist "in the mind" which apprehends them? All mental acts have, it would seem, the capacity precisely for pointing *beyond* themselves to objects. It is possible to suppose that both objects and the non-reflective acts which are directed toward them are something "in the mind" only if we adopt the "content theory" of awareness. By that theory, a mental act ($idea_1$) is *nothing but* the event of some object ($idea_2$) coming to exist in the mind. Consider what must be the alternatives to the claim that my becoming aware (my $idea_1$) of some object X is simply identical with that object's coming to exist in my mind. If these events are not identical, then the mere event of an object's coming to exist in my mind would not *in itself* be a sufficient condition for any awareness of an object. This leaves two possibilities. (a) The occurrence of an $idea_1$ is by itself a sufficient condition for an awareness of X, *apart* from the presence of X as an immanent object ($idea_2$). This alternative is ruled out by hypothesis, however, since we are supposing that the presence in the mind of $ideas_2$ is at least a *necessary* condition for any awareness of objects. (b) A sufficient condition for an awareness of X consists not merely in the presence of X as an immanent object ($idea_2$), nor merely in an $idea_1$ *apart* from any immanent object, but rather in the presence of an $idea_1$ directed *toward* an immanent object. But then all awareness would consist in one mental event directed toward another, or part of another, which is just what we mean by reflective as opposed to non-reflective awareness.

In order, therefore, that there be such a thing as non-reflective awareness, the event of an $idea_1$ being directed toward some object ($idea_2$) must not be distinct from the event of some object coming to exist in the mind. On the content theory of awareness, this condition is satisfied. With that theory the awareness of some object just *is* the event of some object coming to exist in the mind. Hence while awareness of an object does involve the coming to exist of that object in the mind, which is presumably a mental event, it does not involve the direction of one mental event upon *another*. Reflection alone would involve such an operation. Only, therefore, if Descartes accepted the content theory of awareness could he have been led to suppose in the first place that the object of any awareness must at least exist in the mind which is aware of it.

Now we may return, at last, to the specific problem of awareness of non-existent objects. It is precisely the possibility that we are aware of things which have no transcendent existence that apparently leads Descartes to the assumption that all of the objects of awareness must have at least an immanent existence. Since being certain in any case of what my awareness is an awareness *of* is compatible with being uncertain of what might exist apart from awareness itself, what awareness is properly awareness of would seem to be something which exists *within* that very awareness itself. Hence Descartes' views on reference to the non-existent may be represented as follows:

      I. Act-------Immanent Object-------Transcendent Object
        ($Idea_1$)   ($Idea_2$)
     II. Act-------Immanent Object
        ($Idea_1$)   ($Idea_2$)

Diagram II presents the case where an act of awareness apprehends an object which fails to exist apart from the awareness of it. In such a case as this, Descartes assures that my act yet has some object which it apprehends by providing that act at least with an *immanent* object. This picture must be contrasted with Brentano's approach to the problem of non-existent objects:

I. Act - - - - - - - Transcendent Object
II. Act - - - - - - - [Transcendent Object]

As Brentano insists, the proper object of an act is never itself an object of "inner perception"; hence there are no *ideas*$_2$. The awareness, nevertheless, which is depicted in diagram II is an awareness which, like any awareness, "has" an object. This is signified by the "presence" of an object in both of the two cases. The object in the second case simply happens to be a non-existent or a merely "ideal" object, hence the introduction of brackets. Brentano's achievement is thus that he succeeded in separating, in a manner in which some of his classical predecessors did not, the real/ideal distinction from the transcendent/immanent distinction. Some of the objects of human awareness may in fact be merely "ideal." They may, that is, have no existence apart from my awareness of them. (Brentano, as we shall see, maintained that all of the objects of perceptual awareness *are* in this sense ideal.) But to say that objects are in this sense ideal is not to call them "ideas," for while the objects of ordinary perceptual awareness may not exist apart from the mind which apprehends them, it does not follow that there is any sense in which they exist *in* the mind which apprehends them. It does not indeed follow that there is any sense in which they exist at all.[24] This point will be examined, in the following section, with respect to Brentano's account of perceptual awareness.

Non-Existent Objects and Brentano's Account of Perception

I attempted in the preceding section of this chapter to convey the force of Brentano's account of awareness and intentionality by contrasting it with a classical account of awareness which in fact had exercised an influence upon the contemporaries of Brentano. Our interest centered primarily around the notion of an "immanent" object of awareness. The notion of an "immanent" object is connected in an important way with the problem of non-existent objects of awareness. Brentano's views concerning non-existent objects will be further explored by contrasting his account of perceptual awareness with another "classical" theory, the sense-datum account of perceptual awareness.

Brentano includes as instances of mental phenomena the occurrences of mere "sensation," such as the hearing of sounds, the seeing of colors, and the sensing of warm and cold.[25] Since all mental phenomena, according to Brentano, possess the feature of intentionality, it must follow that mere sensations, like the pure conceptual operations of thinking and judging, bear in themselves a "reference to" or a "direction upon" some object in a way that will distinguish mere sensation from any non-mental phenomenon. A number of philosophers have taken issue with the claim that an act/object distinction is properly applicable to sensation in itself, without at the same time denying that sensation is a mental phenomenon.[26] In this respect, Brentano's position is like that of the sense-datum philosopher. On the sense-datum account we must in every case, including the cases of illusion and hallucination, distinguish between an act of sensation and the object which is apprehended by it. We must also, with this account, distinguish two very different uses for such mental verbs as 'sees' and 'hears.' What we may properly be said to see or to hear, even in the case of hallucinations, are merely such items as colors and sounds, while in another sense what we see or hear are just such concrete objects as colored balloons and sounding chapel bells. The latter are ordinary physical objects, while the former are, on the sense-datum account, at most the "appearances" of such objects. It might appear on the surface that Brentano does share the view of the sense-datum philosopher, since he does distinguish, as we have seen, between the "physical phenomena" which we apprehend by sense and the physical objects which we assume to exist independently of that apprehension. Therefore, he also distinguishes, at least by implication, the sense in which we see or hear physical phenomena from the sense in which we see or hear physical objects and events. We could be said to see or hear the latter for Brentano only in the sense that we might correctly judge that such objects exist as the causes of those sensations through which see or hear certain physical phenomena.

It would be a mistake, however, to count Brentano's theory of sensation as an instance of the sense-datum theory.[27] The sense-datum account construes sensation as a relation between two entities, an act and an object of sensation. Each of these entities is real or exists so long as sensation exists. But, according to Brentano, the physical phenomena which are apprehended by acts of sensation do not have any actual existence at all. They exist "only phenomenally and intentionally."[28] It might appear that this assertion fails to distinguish Brentano's account from the sense-datum account of sensation. The issue hinges upon what is meant by asserting that sensations have a merely phenomenal or intentional existence. Suppose that what it means to say that physical phenomena have a merely phenomenal existence is simply that physical phenomena exist only so long as they are apprehended in sensation. Then what Brentano would be saying about the ontological status of physical phenomena is precisely what most defenders of the sense-datum account also say about sense data. Consider, for example, C. D. Broad's comment in his statement of "the theory of sensa":

> The reader may be inclined to say, "After all, these sensa are not real: they are mere appearances, so why trouble about them?" The answer is that you do not get rid of anything by labelling it "appearance." Appearances are as real in their own way as anything else. . . . No doubt the kind of reality which is to be ascribed to appearances will vary with the particular type of theory as to the nature of sensible appearance that we adopt. On the present theory an appearance is a sensum, and a sensum is a particular existent, though it may be a short-lived one.[29]

On the theory of sensa too, it might be asserted, sensa or sense data have a merely phenomenal existence, and there is no clear distinction between that theory and Brentano's account of sensation. Brentano, however, does not simply mean, when he says that physical phenomena have a merely phenomenal existence, that physical phenomena exist only when they are apprehended by sense. This assertion about physical phenomena is compatible with the claim that physical phenomena exist, when they do exist, in the same sense that mental phenomena can always be said to exist. But Brentano maintains that mental and physical phenomena do not both exist in the same sense of the word. Only the former, according to Brentano, "truly and actually" exist.[30] We must, of course, be very careful to distinguish the claim that physical phenomena exist only when they are apprehended by sense from the claim that physical phenomena exist *only in the sense that* they are apprehended by sense. The former claim is compatible with the assertion that, when they do in fact exist, both physical and mental phenomena exist in just the same sense; the latter claim is not. In a precise sense, the latter claim implies that, even when they are in fact apprehended by sense, physical phenomena do not really exist *at all*. This, however, does not appear to be a claim which any philosopher has ever made who has stated or defended a sense-datum account of sensation. Though Broad, for example, in the passage above, seems prepared to claim that appearances or sensa do not exist with the same "kind of reality" as do other entities, he still insists that they do exist in the most general and ordinary sense of the word: both sensa and physical objects "are real in the most general sense that a complete inventory of the universe must mention the one as much as the other."[31] Broad's claim that sensa do not exist with the same "kind of reality" as other things seems simply to be a way of asserting that sensa are a very different *sort* of entity from any others.

There is another reason to conclude that Brentano's account of physical phenomena differs from all standard sense-datum accounts of sensation. This is simply that he equates the merely phenomenal existence of physical phenomena with a merely *intentional* existence. To say, then, that physical phenomena have a merely phenomenal existence is to say that physical phenomena "exist" only in the sense that unicorns and centaurs exist. But most philosophers who have argued on behalf of a sense-datum account have not been prepared to argue also for the existence of mythic creatures. This argument apparently demonstrates that Brentano's account of physical phenomena is not equivalent to the sense-datum account of sensation, which asserts that sense data do exist. Since unicorns and centaurs do not exist and since Brentano equates the ontological status of physical phenomena with that of such mythical beasts, we may conclude, in contrast with the sense-datum theory, that physical phenomena do not exist on his view.

It might be argued that Brentano thought that there *was* a sense in which intentional objects such as unicorns and centaurs do in fact exist. Brentano, for example, does say that "no real centaur exists; but a *contemplated* or *thought-about* centaur (*ein vorgestellter Zentaure*) does exist, and indeed it exists as often as I think of it."[32] Brentano appears to be saying that centaurs do exist at least to the extent that they are apprehended in thought. Since he also maintains that physical phenomena exist in the same sense that centaurs do, it would seem to follow that physical phenomena really do exist as well, although only to the extent that they are apprehended by sense. This conclusion would appear to be supported, furthermore, by the fact that Brentano speaks of the objects of awareness as "immanent objects," and even of their being "objectively" in me, or in my mind, whenever I am aware of them.[33] Brentano's view would then appear to be that physical phenomena do exist as long as they are apprehended by sense, but that they exist "in the mind" in that peculiar way in which immanent objects such as unicorns and centaurs also exist in the mind.

In assessing these assertions, we must compare them to some of Brentano's later claims about objects of awareness:

> 1. It has never been my view that the *immanent* object is identical with "*object of thought*" (*vorgestelltes Objekt*). What we think about is *the object* or *thing* and not the "object of thought."
> But the object need not exist. The person thinking may have something as the object of his thought even though that thing does not exist.
> 2. Because we do use the word "in" here ["things existing in the mind"] I allowed myself the term "immanent object" in order to say, not that the object exists, but that it *is* an object . . . Its *being* an object, however, is merely the linguistic correlate of the person experiencing *having* it as object, i.e., his thinking of it in his experience.
> 3. I have always held (in agreement with Aristotle) that "horse" and not "contemplated horse" is the immanent object of those thoughts that pertain to horses. Naturally, however, I did say that "horse" is thought or contemplated by us, and that insofar as we do think of it we have "horse" as (immanent) object.[34]

A centaur for Brentano is the "immanent object" of any thought which is a thought about centaurs. Also, he certainly asserted that a "thought-about" centaur *exists* as long as there are any thoughts about centaurs. It follows that, unless he can draw some distinction between a centaur which happens to be thought about (immanent object) and a "thought-about centaur" (*vorgestelltes Objekt*), Brentano is indeed committed to the existence of all centaurs which are thought about; apparently this is the distinction which he is attempting to draw in the above passages. Some of Brentano's commentators have simply seen in these passages a contradiction between his earlier and later positions. Out of enthusiasm for the later position, they have been prepared to grant that Brentano had forgotten the very point of his earlier position.[35] It is clear, however, that none of Brentano's earlier writings grants that whenever I am thinking about a centaur a thought-about (*vorgesteller*) centaur is the object of my thought (i.e., its immanent object). Brentano does of course argue that whenever I am thinking about a centaur a thought-about centaur *exists*. But this is not the same thing as saying that the *object* of my thought exists. Thus there is no contradiction between Brentano's earlier and later positions.[36]

What remains of course is to explain precisely what the difference *is* between a centaur which happens to be thought about and a "thought-about centaur." If this distinction cannot be explained satisfactorily, then we will have rendered Brentano's view consistent at the cost of rendering it implausible. However, a very simple explanation can be offered. The centaur which happens to be thought about is an object of somebody's thought; the "thought-about centaur," which Brentano distinguishes from the centaur which happens to be thought about, is simply the *fact* that a centaur happens to be the object of somebody's thought. Brentano, it is true, did not officially countenance "facts" in his ontology. But that this is nevertheless the sort of distinction which he intended is evident from the very passage which his critics cite as evidence for a change of view:

> In contrasting the A which is contemplated or thought about with the A which is actual, are we saying that *the contemplated A* is itself nothing actual or true? By no means! *The contemplated A* can be something actual and true *without* being an actual A. It is an actual contemplated A and therefore—since this comes to the same thing—it is an actual contemplated A which may be contrasted with a mere *contemplated* contemplated A. (One may think that someone is thinking about an A.)[37]

It has appeared to some that Brentano is granting in this passage that the object which I contemplate is always something actual, at least to the extent that it is being contemplated. But it is clear that Brentano is saying no such thing. For what Brentano says is not that the A which I contemplate is necessarily something actual, but that the "contemplated A" is necessarily something actual. What Brentano means by this is evident from his contrast between a "contemplated A" being actual and a "contemplated A" being something merely contemplated. In the latter case, someone is merely thinking that someone is contemplating A. In the former case, someone is *in fact* contemplating A. The "contemplated A" which necessarily exists and is actual whenever someone contemplates A, then, is simply the fact that someone is contemplating A. Thus Brentano never did argue, even during his early period, that whenever somebody thinks about centaurs, there is a centaur which is thought about. He simply argued that whenever somebody thinks about centaurs a certain fact obtains: somebody is thinking about centaurs. There is in fact a very good reason for Brentano to have insisted upon this apparently trivial assertion. The point that Brentano wishes to make is simply that it *can* be a fact that somebody is thinking about centaurs, even though there is no centaur. To say that a centaur is something thought about, or that it is the "immanent object" of a thought, is *just to say* that somebody is thinking about centaurs. This does not imply that centaurs exist in any proper sense at all. As Brentano formulates the point, "I allowed myself the term 'immanent object,' in order to say, not that the object exists, but that it *is* an object. . . . Its being an object, however, is merely the linguistic correlate of the person experiencing *having* it as object."

We may finally apply these results, then, to Brentano's account of sensation. Brentano makes it clear that he accords no more ontological status to the physical phenomena which we apprehend by sense than he does to a merely intentional or "immanent" object. We have seen, however, that there is *no* proper sense in which merely intentional objects such as unicorns and centaurs can be said to exist. Hence there is no proper sense in which physical phenomena, or sense data, exist on Brentano's view. Therefore, it cannot be the case that physical phenomena exist, but only when they are apprehended by sense. Nor should we say even that physical phenomena exist, but *only in the sense that* they are apprehended by sense. There is just no proper sense at all in which physical phenomena exist, even when they are apprehended by sense. It follows, then, that Brentano's account of our apprehension of physical phenomena is not exposed to all of the objections which have with justification been raised against the sense-datum account of sensation. For most of the objections that have been raised to that account have been directed against the existence of such entities as sense data in the first place, and there are no such entities as sense data in Brentano's ontology. It is true that we are immediately *aware* of such entities as physical phenomena. To this extent Brentano does share the viewpoint of the sense-datum account of sensation. But the fact that we do apprehend them by sense no more establishes the existence of physical phenomena than the fact that we do also imagine centaurs establishes the existence of centaurs, whether "inside" the mind or out.

There is one other respect, besides that which concerns the ontological status of physical phenomena, in which we might note that Brentano's account differs from the sense-datum account of perception. On the sense-datum account, at least as it is ordinarily represented, there is no sense in which we might apprehend a realm of concrete three-dimensional bodies *directly*. For what we directly apprehend are only the *appearances* of such bodies to our senses. The realm of physical phenomena for Brentano, however, *is* a realm of objects in three dimensions.[38] Brentano need not deny that we apprehend three-dimensional objects directly. In this respect, Brentano's view is much closer to the view which Roderick Firth has called the "percept theory" than it is to the sense-datum theory. "The direct and immediate experience of anyone who looks at the world about him, according to this interpretation of the Percept Theory, always consists of a number of full-bodied *physical objects.*"[39] Brentano, to be sure, does distinguish between physical phenomena and really existing physical objects, but then a similar distinction must also be made on the percept theory. In order to allow for the epistemological fact that perception might in any case be mistaken and no three-dimensional object might actually exist with the qualities of the object which I am given in experience, the percept theory must at least introduce a distinction between physical objects and *ostensible* physical objects.[40] The distinction parallels Brentano's own distinction between physical reality and physical phenomena.

There is, however, one important difference between the claim that Brentano makes concerning the relations between physical phenomena and really existing objects and the claim that Firth makes concerning the relation between ostensible physical objects and physical objects. According to Brentano, none of the phenomena which are apprehended by sense does in fact possess a real, as opposed to a merely intentional, existence. None, that is, is identical with some actually existing entity. But this does not *follow*, on Brentano's view, from the fact that sensation is intentional. To claim that sensation is intentional is just to claim that sensation is an act, and that it has an object which might or might not exist. That none of the objects of sensation does in fact exist is, according to Brentano, a merely contingent truth which stands upon the same epistemological footing as the fact that no unicorns or centaurs exist.[41] There is no *contradiction* in supposing, for example, that phenomenal colors exist apart from our apprehension of them. Scientific investigation simply gives us reason for thinking that they do not.[42]

Brentano, then, takes it to be a merely contingent truth that no physical phenomenon is identical with an actually existing entity. On Firth's view, however, there is a contradiction in the supposition that if ostensible physical objects are the immediate objects of sensory awareness, then some ostensible physical objects might be identical with some actual physical objects: "anyone who accepts the Percept Theory must admit that there is at least one important fact about an *ostensible* physical object which serves to distinguish it from a physical object—the fact, namely, that *some* of its properties, if not all, can be discovered by direct inspection of a single state of perceptual consciousness."[43] If I see something elliptical, then it follows that some ostensible physical object is elliptical. It remains doubtful, however, whether any actual physical object is elliptical. Since ostensible physical objects are in this way the subject of immediate certainty, while no physical object is, ostensible physical objects and physical objects are distinct sorts of objects, though there might be certain resemblances between them. This argument seems to be fallacious, since the property which Firth appeals to in order to distinguish ostensible from actual physical objects is an intentional one. Firth also claims that ostensible physical objects must be necessarily distinct from actual ones if any sense is to be made of the notion of illusory perception: "However naive the man in the street may be, his naivete does not consist in his failure to possess *some* concept of a physical object as distinguished from an ostensible physical object. To deny this, indeed, would be to deny that he possesses any concept of 'illusion.' "[44] But the concept of illusion will have an application just so long as it is not a necessary truth that *every* ostensible physical object is identical with an actual one. It is not evident, therefore, how granting an application to the concept of perceptual illusion in itself implies that no ostensible physical object is identical with any actual physical object.

The problem of illusion does, however, raise a difficult point of a different sort. It is clear that if some ostensible physical object is identical with a physical object, then it must have all of its non-intentional properties in common with some physical object. Accordingly, if I look at a penny and see something elliptical, the ostensible physical object which I see could not *be* (since it is elliptical) the penny at which I am looking. But neither could the ostensible physical object which I see be identical with the penny at which I am looking so long as it *lacks* any of the penny's actual qualities. Since it is impossible, however, to be given in a single experience all of the qualities of some object, an ostensible physical object could never be identical with a physical object.

This argument raises a serious difficulty for the claim that the failure of some object of illusion or hallucination, or of any sensory awareness at all, to be identical with some actually existing entity is a merely contingent matter. It is, however, a difficulty which arises only so long as "ostensible physical objects" or "physical phenomena" are construed as particulars. I shall argue in Chapter 3 that they might be viewed as universals of some sort. Brentano did in fact take physical phenomena to be particulars rather than universals, hence the objection does apply to Brentano. But it is important to distinguish Brentano's specific views about intentionality from other views which he held in combination with them. There is not any contradiction at all in the notion of sensory awareness as the apprehension of objects which might or might not *be*, and not simply resemble, actually existing objects, that is, in the notion of sensory awareness as an intentional phenomenon. Thus we may continue to explore in this section the general structure of Brentano's account of perception. Though we will presume, with Brentano, that physical phenomena are particulars which might or might not be identical (and which science instructs us are not identical) with actual physical objects, the points to be made do not depend on this presumption.

Brentano's notion of an intentional object of sense which may or may not be *merely* intentional seems to me to be required by some accounts of perception which other philosophers have offered, particularly those offered by philosophers inclined to identify, at least in the case of veridical awareness, the immediate object of sense with a part of the surface of some material object. The identification of those sense data which are apprehended in our veridical perception of some object with a part of the surface of that object is one which G. E. Moore once considered to be, though a rather doubtful view, at least not obvious nonsense.[45] The view has been most recently defended by Panayot Butchvarov in *The Concept of Knowledge.* Those things which, according to Butchvarov, we immediately apprehend by sense are "entities that are *at least* perceptual expanses but may also be parts of the surfaces of bodies."[46] This view appears to possess some advantages over ordinary sense-datum accounts. Like any sense-datum account, it does justice to the "phenomenological fact" that every perceiving has an object, without implying that any real *body* exists as the object of that perceiving, for the "perceptual expanse" which is apprehended by sense need not be identical with part of the surface of any physical body. On the other hand, the view also appears to possess all the advantages of direct realism. It does allow that the perceptual expanses which we apprehend by sense may in fact be identical with part of the surface of some body, hence that apprehension of such expanses may intelligibly be regarded as *evidence* for the existence of such a body.[47]

The main difficulty with this view is that it simply makes no sense to suppose that a part of the surface of some material body might exist and be apprehended apart from any such body. Hence it makes no literal sense to suppose, for any given expanse which I apprehend and which is not in fact a part of the surface of some material body, that this very entity *might* have been a part of the surface of some body. It is not at all clear, accordingly, how we are in fact to combine the phenomenological advantage of the sense-datum account with the epistemological advantage of direct realism. To do this we must suppose that the very same entity which I apprehend in the case of a sheer hallucination might possibly be identical with the surface of some body. But this, as Butchvarov grants, is something which is absolutely impossible, and impossible not simply in the sense that no perceptual expanse which I apprehend could possibly be a part of the surface of some body *while* it is the object of a pure hallucination, but impossible in the stronger sense that the very *sort* of entity which might possibly exist in the absence of any body is not the *sort* of entity which could be a part of the surface of some body.[48]

It seems to me that there is only one way to understand Butchvarov's suggestion. If the sort of object which I can apprehend in the case of illusion or hallucination is an object which might possibly be a part of the surface of some really existing body, and if this object could not possibly exist apart from any body, then it follows that what we are apprehending in that case could not possibly be any entity which really exists at all. Whatever in this case we are apprehending must be precisely a *non-existent* part of the surface of some (possibly non-existent) body. It must be a *merely intended* part of some bodily surface. The very clear sense in which what we thus apprehend might be, but is not, the surface of some material body must be precisely the same as the sense in which the unicorns and centaurs which we imagine might be, though they in fact are not, something real. Thus in order to combine the advantages of the sense-datum account of sensation with those of direct realism, in the way that Moore once considered possible and as others have recently attempted, it is necessary to construe sensation as intentional in Brentano's sense: sensation must be intentional not simply in the sense that we may always distinguish an act and an object of sensation but also in the sense that its proper objects may be such objects without really existing at all.

It might appear that this approach to perception is one with which no philosopher has ever in fact disagreed. What, after all, are we saying, when we distinguish between those sensory apprehensions which do, and those which do not, have objects that really exist? The claim that some of what we apprehend by sense does not really exist seems merely to state the very obvious fact that many beliefs which are based on the senses are mistaken. It is of course perfectly possible to believe that I am being presented with a part of the surface of some material body, when I am not in fact so presented, and no philosopher has thought to deny this. It is not clear, therefore, what philosophical issue is at stake in insisting that sensation is intentional. But this insistence that sensation is an intentional phenomenon is necessary to do justice to a very important fact: belief and judgment are simply not the only means by which objects are given to us "through the senses." If belief and judgment, and the more complex phenomena which are built upon these, were in fact the only means by which objects are "given" to us, then it could hardly be said that objects ever really *are* in fact given "through the senses." They would be given only through the understanding, while sensation itself would be, as some have argued, "blind." There is an important sense in which sensation is blind, but it is not blind in the sense that objects are apprehended in sensation only through distinct beliefs and judgments which are based upon sensation. If objects *were* apprehended only in this way, then it is hardly clear in what sense such judgments could be "based" upon sensation at all. Since no objects are then apprehended by sensation, there seems to be no way in which our judgment is based on evidence which sensation provides.

Most philosophers who have objected to the sense-datum account of sensation believe that the reference to objects which perception involves is solely a function of the fact that perceptions are complex states involving both sensations and (standing in the appropriate relations with them) judgments, and it is, properly speaking, only the latter which effect a reference to objects. This view seems mistaken. Even if the reference to objects which perception involves is an accomplishment only of some properly judgmental aspect of a perception, nevertheless, at least in the case of "basic" perceptions (e.g., seeing something as red), this judgmental aspect must *itself* possess an intrinsic "sensuous content" in virtue of which it is distinguished from any "non-sensuous" judgments. Hence, though the aspect in question is properly judgmental, it is also properly *sensory*, and the referential aspect of a (basic) perception will thus not involve the presence of "mere judgments" in perception.[49]

Suppose that, on a given occasion, I am "sensibly impressed" in a way which is typical of those occasions when I see something as red. Furthermore, suppose that my being sensibly impressed in this way causes me to judge that the object before me is green (and that there are no general beliefs of mine which bear on the case in question). Then, presumably, it would be incorrect to say that I am noticing or perceiving, or being immediately "aware of," anything at all about the color of the object before me. (For, if I were, then what could I be noticing? Would I be noticing that the object before me is red? Or would I be noticing that it is green? The choice appears purely arbitrary.) But suppose we consider a case which differs from the preceding one either in the respect that the judgment in question is that the object before me is red or else in the respect that I do in fact hold certain general beliefs, causally operative on this occasion, to the effect that objects appearing as red in such circumstances generally are actually green. Then, on the view that perception merely involves a judgment externally related to the properly *sensory* aspect of a perception, it would presumably be correct to say either (in the first case) that I am noticing that the object before me is red— that I am "aware" of it as red—or (in the second case) that I am noticing that the object before me is green—that I am "aware" of it as green. But this would mean that the difference between not noticing or perceiving *anything at all* on an occasion and in fact noticing or perceiving something about an object could be provided simply by a difference in the conceptual content of certain judgments or beliefs about that object (or about objects of that sort).

It is of course reasonable to suppose that a mere difference in judgmental content might make a difference in *what* I am noticing or perceiving about an object on a given occasion. But it seems to me unreasonable to suppose that a mere alteration in the content of certain beliefs or judgments of mine could be all that is required in order to change a state in which I notice or perceive absolutely *nothing at all* about an object into a state in which I finally succeed in noticing or perceiving it (and not merely in believing something about it). It does seem reasonable to conclude, then, either that perceptual states do not merely involve judgments which stand in certain external relations with an appropriate sensuous content or that the sorts of "judgments" that perceptual states involve *also* contain a certain intrinsic sensuous content.

There is therefore a real philosophical issue at stake in insisting upon the intentionality of sensations, and this is just to draw the very important distinction between a purely judgmental and a properly sensuous apprehension of objects in perception. But, we might now inquire, is it not misleading to identify the latter with mere sensation? Though I have argued that we must distinguish judgmental from non-judgmental awarenesses of objects "through the senses," it is nevertheless clear that the ability to be thus non-judgmentally aware of objects is not independent of our abilities to make judgments about objects. Being presented in hallucination with a merely hallucinated knife is admittedly not at all the same thing as judging, or having a tendency to judge, that there is a knife before me, yet it would seem to require the kind of "recognition" which is possible only for an individual who is in possession of certain concepts and knows how to use them in judgments. But surely our ability to have sensations is not dependent upon any of our conceptual abilities. Hence we ought to distinguish mere sensations from any non-judgmental apprehension of objects through the senses. The latter should be called not "sensation" but rather "sensible intuition."

Although this objection is entirely sound, it does not require the admission that perception involves a merely external connection (a causal connection, for example) between sensations and thoughts or judgments. We may make a threefold Kantian distinction between mere sensation, sensible intuition, and thought or judgment.[50] The sense-datum philosophers have blurred the distinction between sensation and sensible intuition. They have drawn a distinction between being "given," or "immediately" apprehending, objects and making judgments concerning material bodies. But they have wrongly concluded from this that the apprehension in question must consist in the apprehension of objects, the recognition of which is completely independent of judgmental abilities. But if the sense-datum philosophers have blurred the distinction between sensation and intuition, most of their opponents have made the equally serious blunder of blurring the distinction between intuition and judgment.[51] Sensible intuition involves both sensation and recognition, but its "conceptual content" is not reducible to the distinct presence of thought or judgment in addition to sensation. The "conceptual content" of intuition is rather something introduced *into sensations themselves* in intuition. A more sophisticated notion of "mental content" than what we encountered in Descartes and Hume will permit the elaboration of this view. I examine that notion in Chapter 4.

Having made these distinctions, we are finally able to see in what respect the senses are "blind" and in what respect we are given objects *through* the senses. Sensation, as a capacity of ours which is independent of conceptual abilities, is not the apprehension of an object; in this sense, sensation is blind. Sensible *intuition* is, however, the apprehension of an object. Regarded as "sensible intuition," therefore, sensation is not blind at all. Thus while Kant is correct when he claims that "intuition without concepts is blind," granting that intuition necessarily involves concepts is not conceding that intuition is merely a species of judgment or thought. Accordingly, when he asserts that "sensation" is, like any other mental phenomenon, an intentional phenomenon, Brentano is simply calling attention to the important distinction between sensations, intuitions, and the judgments and thoughts which may be connected with them.[52] Moreover, he is adding the important observation that sensible intuitions having the objects which they have does not imply that there really *are* any such objects.

Conclusion

We have considered in this chapter some questions concerning the concept of awareness and the status of the objects of awareness. I have attempted to show that the major force of Brentano's conception of intentionality lies in its challenge to two different approaches to the problem of non-existent objects. An instance of the first is what I have called a "content theory" of awareness. On that theory there is, in the final analysis, no such thing as awareness of a non-existent object. For all objects of awareness, on the content theory, at least exist "in the mind" of the subject who is aware of them. The content theory of awareness must be rejected because it fails to do justice to the fact that awarenesses of objects which do not exist apart from the mind may nevertheless be awarenesses of transcendent objects—of objects which do not and could not possibly exist in the mind. The content theory fails to distinguish the real/ideal dichotomy from the transcendent/immanent dichotomy. The awareness of non-real, that is, of merely "ideal," objects provides just as adequate an example of the mind's ability to transcend and to point beyond itself as is provided by awarenesses of objects which in fact exist apart from the mind. Awareness is always awareness *of* something, and it is to this mere "of" that Brentano is drawing our attention when, apart from any concern at all for the reality of intentional objects, he insists that they are "physical phenomena" and in no sense contained in the mind which apprehends them. Since, as Descartes clearly saw, all awareness is in its internal structure the same, whether its object really exists apart from the mind or not, the consequence of a failure to grasp the transcendent nature of awareness of the non-existent must be an ultimate failure to grasp the transcendent nature of awareness altogether. In this respect, the Humean doctrine of mental contents is a necessary consequence of the so-called representative realism of Descartes.

An instance of the second approach to the problem of non-existent objects is the sense-datum account of perceptual awareness. Since it need not be part of the sense-datum theory that sense data exist only "in the mind" which apprehends them, the sense-datum theory does not necessarily fail to do justice to the transcendent nature of awareness. It is this point, of course, on which G. E. Moore had insisted when he "refuted" idealism by exposing the ambiguity in the notion of "contents" of awareness.[53] The data of perception, however "immediate" they may be, are "contents" of awareness only in the sense that they are the *objects* of awareness. But the sense-datum theory fails to do justice to another important point, since it follows from the sense-datum theory that perceptual awareness always is an awareness of objects which *exist* in the ordinary sense of that word. The price to be paid for acknowledging the transcendent character of all awareness is thus a denial of the evident fact that we sometimes do perceive objects which fail to exist outside of any of our perceptions. This of course can only mean substituting for the non-existent objects which we sometimes perceive utterly different, though existing, ones. To do full justice to the phenomenon of intentionality, then, it is necessary to accommodate both of these important facts about awareness: first, all awareness is awareness of something which is in no sense contained in that awareness itself, or in the mind which has the awareness; second, at least some awarenesses are awarenesses of objects which do not exist apart from the mind. Neither of the classical theories which we have examined does justice to both of these facts.

2

Intentionality and Intentional Relations

Our occupation, in Chapter 1, with the problem of awareness centered primarily around the notion of an *object* of awareness. Brentano saw the necessity for avoiding two equally mistaken views about this notion: that objects of awareness enjoy, *qua* objects, a real extra-mental existence and that, if they do not, then they enjoy some sort of real *mental* existence. It is, however, the aim of this book to arrive at a more positive characterization of the phenomenon of awareness and hence of the notion of an "object" of awareness. Though our earlier discussions led to the rejection of any effort to characterize awareness of objects in the classical sense, in terms of the possession of "mental content," I shall try to develop a theory of awareness which rests upon a more adequate notion of mental content. Now, however, we must continue our examination of the notion of an *object* of awareness, concentrating more exclusively on the problem of awareness *of* such objects.

The specific issue which must of course be faced is posed by the fact that awareness of objects may or may not be awareness of anything that really exists. This fact has suggested to some philosophers that any adequate account of awareness must rest upon the introduction of a class of "intentional relations" or at least of irreducible relation-like properties, that is, a class of relations (or relation-like properties) which may relate one thing to something else that *may or may not really exist*. If this is so, then any adequate account of awareness will apparently reveal that mental phenomena exhibit a feature which is quite unlike any ordinary physical relation or property:

> When Brentano said that these attitudes "intentionally contain an object in themselves," he was referring to the fact that they can be said to "have objects" even though the objects which they can be said to have do not in fact exist. . . .
>
> But *physical*—or non-psychological—phenomena, according to Brentano's thesis, cannot thus "intentionally contain objects in themselves." In order for Diogenes to sit in his tub, for example, there must be a tub for him to sit in. . . .
>
> The statements used in these examples seem to have the form of relational statements. "Diogenes sits in his tub" is concerned with a relation between Diogenes and his tub. Syntactically, at least, "Diogenes looks for an honest man" is similar: Diogenes' quest seems to relate him in a certain way to honest men. But the rela-

tions described in this and in our other psychological statements, if they can properly be called "relations," are of a peculiar sort. They can hold even though one of their terms, if it can properly be called a "term," does not exist. It may seem, therefore, that one can be "intentionally related" to something which does not exist.[1]

There are at least three tasks before us: first, to see, at least in a general way, how seriously to take the appearance that awareness of objects involves some peculiar sort of relation (or relation-like property); second, to examine more closely the general idea of an "intentional relation," and in particular to inquire whether the countenancing of such relations must go hand in hand with the countenancing of some special ontological status for merely intentional *objects*; third, to see whether any particular *theory* which rests upon the notion of an "intentional relation" can be regarded as an adequate account of awareness. The third of these tasks I reserve for Chapter 3; the first two are taken up in this chapter.

The Ontological Significance of Intentionality

The suggestion that mental phenomena exhibit, at least with respect to their intentional aspects, some unique sort of property or relation may best be approached by considering some of the sorts of sentences that we use in talking about such phenomena. To do this, we may rely on Chisholm's criteria (individually sufficient) for "intentional sentences":

1. Following the verb is a substantival expression, and "neither the sentence nor its contradictory implies either that there is or that there isn't anything to which the substantival expression truly applies."

2. Following the verb is a phrase containing a subordinate verb, and "neither the sentence nor its contradictory implies either that the phrase following the principal verb is true or that it is false."

3. Following the verb is a name or description of something, and "replacement by a different name (or description) of that thing results in a sentence whose truth-value may differ from that of the original sentence."

4. Compound sentences containing one of the above as a component.

Chisholm claims that such sentences as these are unnecessary in any description of non-mental phenomena and avoidable in the ascription of intentional psychological states (e.g., perceiving, assuming, believing, knowing, wanting, hoping) to a person only with the aid of special "technical terms" specifically introduced to *avoid* such intentional language (e.g., 'cat-perceptive,' 'that-there-is-a-cat-assuming,' 'cat-wanting').[2]

It has recently been argued that Chisholm provides no adequate characterization of a merely "technical" term.[3] Particularly unsatisfactory appears to be his suggestion that any technical term which may succeed in replacing intentional language in the ascription of intentional states to a person must be a term which has been introduced for the explicit purpose of *avoiding* intentional language in psychological contexts. Nothing seems to stand in the way of supposing that some language contains a single term T, not in any way built up out of words, like 'cat' and 'perceptive,' which ordinarily designate by themselves certain sorts of objects and certain sorts of psychological states respectively, and where the term T nevertheless has the same meaning in that language as 'cat-perceptive' (or 'perceiving a cat') in our own. In that case, T will be a non-intentional term which may be used to ascribe an intentional psychological state to a person, even though there is no reason to suppose that it has been introduced for the explicit purpose of avoiding some alternative, intentional language in the ascription of such states.

While Chisholm does not explicitly consider such cases, it seems clear how he might naturally respond to them: though he might grant that some language contains non-intentional language for the ascription of intentional states to a person which is not merely an artificial device for avoiding intentional language, such language nevertheless could never provide an *analysis* of the intentional language in question, whereas the intentional language could always be regarded as an analysis of it. It seems clear, in other words, that Chisholm is not concerned with rejecting the claim that non-intentional synonyms can be found for the intentional language used in the ascription of intentional psychological states (whether those synonyms be artificially or naturally introduced into a language), but rather with rejecting the claim that non-intentional language can be used to provide an *analysis* of what we are saying about persons when we ascribe intentional states to them. While the notion of "analysis" is by no means a perfectly clear one, it thus seems to me that the best way to express Chisholm's thesis is to avoid the notion of a "technical term" entirely, and simply assert that while intentional language is not needed in the ascription of non-psychological states to things, it cannot be replaced, in the ascription of intentional psychological states (such as perceiving, assuming, believing, knowing, wanting, hoping) to persons, by any non-intentional language which can be regarded as providing an analysis of the meaning of the intentional language in question.

Chisholm's claim has been subject to repeated criticism and modification.[4] Nevertheless, what we are concerned with is not whether, as Chisholm proposes, the intentional features of mental phenomena provide some sort of criterion for isolating at least certain classes of mental phenomena, but simply whether the intentional features of mental phenomena provide any reason for regarding the phenomena which exhibit them as possessing any sort of ontologically special relation or relation-like property.[5]

Some of Chisholm's own formulations suggest that the problem of intentionality might turn out to have an important bearing on the problem of mind/body identity. They might have a bearing on the question whether psychological states which possess intentional features are themselves, or *could* be themselves, purely physical states of some organism—for example, certain states of the brain or central nervous system. As Chisholm expresses Brentano's thesis, which he then proceeds to defend, "But *physical*—or non-psychological—phenomena, according to Brentano's thesis, cannot thus 'intentionally contain objects in themselves.' " It might of course be argued that, despite the perhaps natural suggestion of Chisholm's formulation, it does not contain any claim incompatible with the view of mind/body identity. For the term 'physical,' as it occurs in Chisholm's claim, appears simply to function as a synonym for the term 'non-psychological.' Those who seriously debate, however, whether psychological states are physical in nature do not use the terms 'non-psychological' and 'physical' as synonyms. If they did, then they would simply be contradicting themselves by suggesting that psychological states which possess intentional features might be purely physical states of the brain or central nervous system; and their opponents, when they deny that psychological states are so describable, would merely be insisting upon a trivial truth. It is possible, of course, that Brentano and Chisholm are correct in maintaining that intentionality is an exclusive feature of psychological phenomena, without it being the case that the phenomena possessing this feature cannot be identified with states of the brain or central nervous system. In fact, as we have seen already, Brentano never made the latter claim at all. It is not necessary to suppose that Chisholm's efforts are any more ambitious than Brentano's in this respect, although Chisholm's thesis has often been *received* as such.[6]

The whole question of the bearing of the problem of intentionality upon the problem of mind/body identity is often complicated and confused primarily for two reasons. The first is that the claim that all mental states, including intentional ones, are identical with purely physiological states of the brain or central nervous system is compatible with the claim that the existence of intentional phenomena contradicts certain forms of the thesis of *physicalism*. According to Chisholm, his own claim that "the sentences we must use in describing psychological phenomena have certain logical properties that are not shared by any of the sentences we must use in describing non-psychological phenomena" is incompatible with "the basic thesis of physicalism and the unity of science"[7] There are of course various ways of formulating a physicalistic thesis, and it is not entirely clear which one Chisholm has in mind. However, it might resemble this:

> All phenomena are such that all the properties which those
> phenomena exhibit are either properties which might be
> exemplified by non-psychological phenomena or are *analyzable* in
> terms of properties all of which might be exemplified by non-
> psychological phenomena.[8]

It is clear that this formulation of the thesis of physicalism is indeed incompatible with Chisholm's claims about intentionality, since those claims imply that the property of being a psychological state which possesses intentional features (e.g., of being a belief about something, or a perception of something) either are *unanalyzable* properties, or are themselves analyzable only in terms of other psychological properties which involve intentionality. Hence the existence of at least certain psychological phenomena contradicts the ideal of the "unity of science."

But it is by no means clear that it follows from the fact that Chisholm's thesis is incompatible with certain versions of physicalism that it is also incompatible with the claim that psychological states are identical with states of the brain or central nervous system. If Chisholm's thesis is incompatible with physicalism, it is because that thesis insists upon the irreducibility of certain distinctively psychological *predicates* (hence, presumably, the properties which those predicates express). If Chisholm is correct, then at least certain psychological states are characterized by properties (perhaps relational ones) which might reasonably be said to be *nonphysical* properties. But it does not follow from the fact that something exemplifies certain non-physical properties that it does not also exemplify certain physical ones. Thus the fact that the intentional language which we use in describing psychological phenomena is irreducible to non-psychological and non-intentional language is compatible with the claim that the phenomena described by means of such language are also describable as being states of the brain or central nervous system.[9]

The possible bearing of the problem of intentionality upon the problem of mind/body identity may also be complicated by certain more general difficulties. These concern the general problem of individuating events. In effect, this issue has already been broached in my preceding remarks. Suppose we demand that in order for an event E_1 to be identical with an event E_2—say for the event of my imagining a unicorn in Central Park to be identical with some event in my central nervous system—the sentences describing these events must be analytically equivalent. Then it would follow from the fact that intentional language is needed in the description of my imagining a unicorn but not needed in a description of the relevant state of my nervous system, that my imagining a unicorn could not be identical with that psychological state. But that criterion for event-identity seems clearly to be too restrictive.

Though a definition of event-identity in terms of analytical equivalence may be too restrictive, it might be argued that any plausible definition of event-identity must at least require that E_1 and E_2 have the same *constituents* if they are really to be the same event. Thus if my imagining a unicorn in Central Park is identical with a certain event that occurs in my nervous system, then my imagining of this object must contain all the same constituents as are contained in that event in my nervous system. This condition might seem to show that Chisholm's thesis is incompatible with the thesis of mind/body identity. Suppose it was granted that the intentional language employed in the description of certain psychological phenomena has the features that Chisholm attributes to it. Then it apparently follows that such language requires, as a condition for its truth, the introduction of special psychological relations involving such merely imaginary objects as the imaginary Central Park unicorn. This, as we have already seen, is a suggestion about intentional phenomena which Chisholm makes—at least as a suggestion. But it seems to imply that intentional phenomena could not possibly be identified with states of the brain, since intentional phenomena, on this view, turn out to be events which involve certain intentional *objects* in an essential way, hence the psychological events in question contain such objects as constituents. But it is impossible to maintain that certain states of my brain or central nervous system contain as constituents such objects as the imaginary Central Park unicorn. Therefore it would be impossible to identify the event of my imagining a unicorn in Central Park with some event in my brain or central nervous system.

Even if this argument were successful against the thesis that all psychological events are identical with neurophysiological ones, there is still nothing in it to give any special comfort to the traditional mind/body *dualist*. It would still be possible to maintain that intentional phenomena simply involve certain unique sorts of relations between states of the central nervous system and intentional objects. The only irreducibly *mental* "entities," on such an account, are just the intentional relations which would then be in question. As the mind/body dualist's position is usually understood, however, it involves the claim that there are certain sorts of *particulars* (whether "minds" or mental states) which are irreducibly mental in nature. One might of course be tempted to describe the merely intentional objects which are on this view the objects of certain psychological states as irreducibly "mental" entities. But insofar as such objects would themselves be neither minds nor mental states, but merely the possible *objects* of minds or mental states, the "dualism" in question will still fall far short of any traditional mind/body dualism. It would in fact appear merely to amount to a distinction between the two domains of actual and merely possible being. The domain of the "mental," on such a view, would simply be the domain of the merely possible.

But it seems to me in any case that the argument in question rests upon the mistaken assumption that any event which involves a relation to some object must itself *contain* that object as a constituent. There seem to be all sorts of counterexamples to this assumption. One of the most obvious is found in the case of psychological states which relate a person, not to objects which may or may not happen to exist, but to objects which in fact *do* exist. Consider, for example, my thoughts about Gerald Ford, construed as thoughts about that particular individual who *is* Gerald Ford. Surely the event of my thinking about Gerald Ford on some occasion involves some sort of relation between myself and that individual: whatever we might eventually decide about the relational (or non-relational) nature of intentionality (understood as involving some reference to objects which may or may *not* really exist), that claim seems uncontroversial. Yet it seems equally certain that we would not say that Gerald Ford is therefore a constituent of the event which consists in my thinking about him. If the individual in question could be said to have some sort of existence "in my thoughts," this would seem at best a metaphorical expression for his being the *object* of such thoughts. Hence it seems that quite apart from the problems of intentionality and of mind/body identity, the principle that any event which involves a relation to some object must contain that object as a constituent is a mistaken principle.

Many other examples could also be found to discount this assumption. Consider an event which consists in my accidentally driving a car into the side of your house. This event involves a relation to you in some way, insofar as it is the event of my driving a car into *your* house. Yet it would not seem necessary to say that you are therefore a *part* of my driving the car on this occasion. Or consider, again, an event which consists in my bleeding on your priceless Persian carpet. This event surely involves a relation to your carpet, and yet we would hardly say that the carpet is a constituent of my bleeding on this occasion. In some cases, this point can be made with the help of certain terminological variations already current in English. Thus we might say, for example, that while some dog's howling at the moon is an event which involves the moon as a constituent, the dog's *howl* on that occasion does not itself involve the moon as a constituent; similarly, while my jumping in competition at the fair involves some actual fair as a constituent, my *jump* at the fair does not involve the fair as a constituent. Some psychological verbs seem to work in a similar way; thus while my *thinking* of unicorns in Central Park involves, one might claim, certain imaginary entities as constituents, my *thought* about those unicorns does not. (One does not need to use the term 'thought' merely to designate some *object* of thought in order to make this point.) Similarly, though my *dreaming* about you may involve you as a constituent, one would not conclude that you are therefore a literal constituent of my *dream*. But not all psychological verbs (e.g., 'imagining') transform in this way, and the point can in any case be made without reliance on such grammatical possibilities. We need simply observe that my driving a car *into your house* involves you as a constituent, even though my *driving* of the car on that occasion does not, by the same token the fact that my thinking *about unicorns* on some occasion is an event which involves imaginary unicorns as constituents is perfectly compatible with the fact that my *thinking* on that occasion does not involve any such constituents at all.

We can reasonably conclude, therefore, that the only bearing which an examination of the problem of intentionality might have on the so-called mind/body problem simply concerns the question whether the phenomenon of intentionality involves any irreducible properties (including relational properties) of an ontologically interesting sort.[10] This, after our brief digression, is a question to which we must now return. It is a question which can be asked quite independently of any concern whether psychological phenomena are merely states of the brain or the central nervous system, or whether they are rather somehow irreducibly "mental" in nature. By taking a closer look at the three sorts of cases that Chisholm calls to our attention, I shall argue that these cases, contrary to Chisholm's own suggestions, require more evidence in order to establish a point of ontological significance than the supposition that intentional sentences about psychological phenomena are not susceptible to an analysis into sentences of some different form.

Suppose that any relevant sentence of the form subject/psychological verb/substantival expression asserts that a certain relation obtains between the subject and some object or objects referred to by the expression following the psychological verb. Then the supposition that intentionality involves an ontologically special character of some kind presumably depends on this type of argument: to assert, for any non-psychological relation, that some object *A* stands in such a relation to another object *B*, where *A* is not a fictional entity, is to imply that there really is a *B*. While Hamlet, for example, might indeed stand in the relation of killing to Claudius, this is only because Hamlet and Claudius both are fictional characters. While it would be impossible, however, for a fictional character to stand in such a relation to a *non*-fictional one, a person may stand in all sorts of psychological relations to fictional entities. A person may believe, for example, in unicorns.

Therefore, the sort of relation that intentionality involves is not like any ordinary, non-psychological relation.

It might appear, however, that it is not at all difficult to find examples of non-psychological relations to purely fictional entities. Ulysses, for example, is stronger than I am, and his adventures followed his activity in the Trojan War. In order to consider this sort of counter-example, we ought to distinguish between two classes of non-psychological relations. With regard to one class we can show decisively that no relation belonging to that class could really connect fictional with non-fictional beings; the other class seems to present more difficulty. The first is the class of all relations which involve or imply such relations as *earlier-than* and *left-of*. Clearly a great number of non-psychological relations could not obtain between two entities unless those entities stood in such relations as these. However, we can show that no fictional entity or event might stand in such a relation to a non-fictional one. Consider, for example, the adventures of Ulysses following the Trojan War. Here we seem to find an actual event which precedes a series of purely fictional occurrences. (Whatever difficulties we might find in this suggestion, furthermore, it cannot be ruled out simply on the ground that it is nonsensical to speak in the first place of fictional entities or events as standing in relation to real ones, for then it would make no sense to speak of intentional relations either.) If, however, there really is a relation between two events A and B, then there must be some point in time which is such that, had B occurred either earlier or later than that point, it would *not* have stood in such a relation to A (and conversely). If it makes sense to suppose that A precedes B, then it must make sense to suppose that it might not have preceded B, possibly B having occurred earlier or A having occurred later than a certain point in time. But there is no point in time such that, had the Trojan War occurred after that point, we would retract our judgment that *fictionally* Ulysses' adventures follow the Trojan War. It follows, therefore, that the fictional events do not really stand in the relation *later-than* to any actual events, although they do perhaps stand in that relation to another series of *fictional* events which are similar to some actually occurring series of events.

The same point could be made about spatial relations. Consider the proposition that Sherlock Holmes was living in London in 1910. Since London is an actual city, the proposition appears to assert a relation between the fictional detective and an actual city. If the proposition did assert such a relation, however, then it would assert a relation which would *ipso facto* have failed to obtain had London not existed in the year 1910. But even if London had, for example, been destroyed before 1910, it might nevertheless remain a fact that fictionally Sherlock Holmes was living in London in 1910. Therefore, the proposition that Sherlock Holmes was living in London in 1910 does not assert a relation which obtains between a fictional detective and an actual city. If it asserts a relation between Sherlock Holmes and some city, then it could only be a relation in which Sherlock Holmes stands to some *fictional* city which happens to be similar to London.

The second class of non-psychological relations which ought to be considered is the class of what we may call relations of comparison. We must in fact appeal to such relations in order to account for the spatial and temporal relations which appear to hold between fictional and non-fictional entities or events. We say, for example, that the fictional city in which Sherlock Holmes resided was *similar* to the actual city of London. Or we say that the wanderings of Ulysses followed a series of fictional events which are *similar* to the actual Trojan War. Clearly, relations of comparison are relatively "weak" sorts of relations in contrast with any relations which are founded upon members of the first class that I considered. Particularly, any non-psychological relation which is constituted by the obviously physical *act* of one of the related entities necessarily involves a relation taken from the first class. I cannot, for example, hit a dog, unless there really is a dog to hit, since this involves standing in some actual spatial relation to it. We might therefore argue that while no ordinary physical act could possibly relate a fictional with a non-fictional entity, intentional acts can do this. The relation which psychological activity involves would then differ from the relations involved in any ordinary physical act. But this is a far weaker conclusion than the one Chisholm suggests, since he suggests that psychological relations are significantly different from any non-psychological relations, and not simply from those which involve obviously physical activity.[11]

The most reasonable approach to this difficulty would apparently be to inquire whether sentences which appear to express a comparative relation between fictional and non-fictional entities cannot be construed in an altogether different way. One suggestion is to take a comparative sentence such as 'Ulysses is stronger than Aquila' simply as shorthand for the sentence '(x) (If x is Ulysses, then x is stronger than Aquila),' where 'Ulysses' appears only as part of the predicate 'is Ulysses.' But even if this is no longer a relational proposition, nor contains a component which is, it would seem to be the case that we are still committed to an *instantiation* of this proposition from which we can derive a relational proposition, namely 'If Ulysses is Ulysses, then Ulysses is stronger than Aquila.' The only way to block this move is simply to deny altogether the possibility of instantiating variables by fictional terms. To deny this possibility, however, is also to deny the possibility of construing the proposition 'Jones *believes* in Ulysses' as a relational proposition, hence the possibility that it may express some very peculiar sort of relation. There remains, therefore, only one alternative which could account for the apparent fact that 'Jones believes in Ulysses' expresses a peculiar sort of relation, whereas 'Ulysses is stronger than Aquila' expresses no relation at all. We may suppose that the proposition 'Ulysses is stronger than Aquila' is simply shorthand for the proposition 'The *strength* which Ulysses has is greater than the strength which Aquila has.'

It appears, in other words, that no final decision of an ontological sort about the phenomenon of intentionality could be reached apart from a decision concerning the ontology of particulars and universals (e.g., "strength") generally, or at least that no such decision could be reached on the basis of the first sort of intentional context which Chisholm distinguishes. Thus merely to establish the *unavoidability*—unanalyzability—of intentional sentences about psychological phenomena would be insufficient for establishing that intentional states involve an ontologically unique sort of relation.

The second sort of context which allegedly suggests the existence of peculiar psychological relations is one that contains a psychological verb followed by a sub-ordinate clause. How do these contexts suggest the existence of such relations? Suppose that any sentence of this form expresses a relation between the subject and an entity which is the fact expressed by the subordinate clause in the sentence. Then we may consider the following argument. If I believe in the existence of unicorns, then I am in some *relation* to that fact. However, I may believe that unicorns exist whether or not it *is* a fact that unicorns exist, that is, whether or not the existence of unicorns is something actual. Therefore there is an important difference between intentional contexts of this sort and any non-psychological context.

It is important to realize, here as in our first case, that in order to arrive at any argument for an ontological thesis about intentionality, by way of an examination of intentional contexts which contain subordinate clauses, we need to go beyond the argument by which Chisholm attempts to show that such contexts are not analyz-able in terms of contexts of any other form. We also need to make an independent ontological assumption, since only if the subordinate clause which occurs in any intentional context of the second sort designates some *entity* which is a fact or state of affairs could we have some reason for supposing that such sentences sometimes express a relation between a believer and some non-existent thing. Suppose that the subordinate clause designates what some philosophers call a *proposition*. Then, since both true and false propositions would presumably exist in the same way, we would no longer have any reason at all for supposing that belief involves a relation one of whose terms is sometimes a non-existent entity. Even if belief does involve some sort of psychological relation, the relation in question might always be to terms which are something actual.

Some philosophers would of course argue that propositions, as the objects of belief, are a very peculiar *sort* of entity. They do not, for example, appear to enjoy an ordinary spatio-temporal existence. In this sense, then, belief might involve a relation to "non-existent" entities, hence a peculiar sort of relation. However, it is clear that Chisholm's own argument does not depend on the introduction of propo-sitions as a unique sort of entity, but simply on the consideration that what we believe in is sometimes something nonactual. Second, even if belief did involve a relation to nonspatial and nontemporal propositions, this would not be sufficient to establish that thinking beings possess a "funny characteristic" which no nonthinking being possesses. Many philosophers have contended that all particulars exemplify *properties*, and that properties are universals which do not have an ordinary spatio-temporal existence. Hence the relation involved in belief, as peculiar as it may be, would not involve a peculiarity which is unique to psychological phenomena. One might, of course, argue against the distinction between particulars and universals in the first place and against any talk about a relation of "exemplification" which would *connect* particulars with universals. As already argued, however, if we do not distinguish between particulars and universals, then we must either abandon talk about fictional entities altogether or else grant the existence of all sorts of *non-intentional* relations, of the comparative sort, which connect fictional with non-fictional entities.

It is essential, therefore, to any defense of an ontological thesis about intentionality, based on contexts of the second sort, that we make some ontological decision about the distinction not only between particulars and universals, but also between particulars and states of affairs. If we do not distinguish particulars from states of affairs, and states of affairs from what some philosophers have called propositions, then there is no reason why the sorts of linguistic consideration which Chisholm offers concerning "intentional contexts" should have any ontological bearing at all. If they have no ontological bearing, then they do nothing at all to show that living beings possess a "funny characteristic" which no non-living being possesses.

The third sort of context which Chisholm introduces is one in which some name or description follows the psychological verb and in which "replacement by a different name (or description) of that thing results in a sentence whose truth-value may differ from that of the original sentence." Suppose, for example, that I believe that the husband of Calpurnia was murdered. It does not follow from this that I believe that Caesar was murdered, even though Caesar is the husband of Calpurnia. How does this consideration have a bearing on the ontological thesis which we are considering? It can have a bearing only if we suppose that the proposition 'A believes that the husband of Calpurnia was murdered' expresses some relation between the believer A and some object which is designated by the expression 'the husband of Calpurnia.' In that case the relation would indeed be an exceedingly peculiar one, since it would be a relation which could sometimes obtain between A and the husband of Calpurnia, without at the same time obtaining between A and some object which is identical with the husband of Calpurnia. No non-psychological relation appears to admit this possibility. If I were, for example, to stab the husband of Calpurnia, then I would *ipso facto* stand in the "stabbing relation" to Caesar. It would seem to follow, therefore, that psychological relations are unique among relations.

Once again, the argument for this ontological conclusion could be reached only by going beyond the assertion that intentional contexts of the third sort cannot be successfully analyzed in terms of contexts of a different grammatical form. We also need to suppose that the portion governed by the psychological verb in these contexts contains expressions which are being used in their ordinary, designative way. We must assume, for example, that the expression 'the husband of Calpurnia' is being used in the same way in the sentence 'A believes that the husband of Calpurnia was murdered' as it is in the sentence 'The husband of Calpurnia was murdered.' Only if we make this assumption can any conclusion of an ontological sort follow. Furthermore, the assumption is an ontological one. It implies that belief is a relation to objects of a certain sort, although this may certainly be questioned. Even if the belief that the husband of Calpurnia was murdered does, for example, involve a relation between some believer and what is designated by the expression 'the husband of Calpurnia'—assuming that, in intentional contexts, anything at all is designated by that expression—it would still need to be established that what it designates is the ordinary object which is identical with Julius Caesar. It might be argued that the objects of psychological relations are not ordinary objects at all, but *intentional* objects. While Julius Caesar is then indeed identical with the husband of Calpurnia, the intentional object "Julius Caesar" might not be identical with the intentional object "the husband of Calpurnia." If this were so, of course, then while our argument might establish that intentional objects, if there are any such things at all, are very different sorts of things from ordinary objects, it is not clear how it could also establish that psychological relations are very different sorts of relations from any other. In any case, the assumption which we used to arrive at an ontological thesis about intentionality, by way of an examination of intentional contexts of the third sort, is one which cannot be justified merely by demonstrating that contexts of that sort cannot be successfully analyzed in terms of contexts of a different sort.

With respect to each of the three main types of intentional contexts, accordingly, it would by no means be a simple matter to establish, on the basis of an examination of those contexts, that psychological states exhibit an ontologically special sort of character or relation. In order to establish such a thesis, one needs to argue not only, as Chisholm has done, that the sentences in question are not analyzable in terms of sentences of some different form, but also to establish certain points of a properly ontological nature which are completely *independent* of the problem of intentionality.

It does not follow from this, of course, that no theory of intentionality which rests upon the introduction of peculiar intentional relations could be an acceptable theory, though it does follow that any proof of such a theory would face very considerable difficulties. In Chapter 3 we will consider the most prominent candidates for theories of this sort and argue that, with respect at least to the intentional character of *some* psychological verbs, such a theory might indeed be accepted. Before proceeding to these considerations, we need to clarify further the notion of an allegedly "intentional relation," and inquire whether countenancing such relations would commit us to granting some special ontological status to merely intentional objects.

Intentional Relations and Intentional Objects

It is at least clear from the discussion of the preceding section that any conclusion of ontological significance about the phenomenon of intentionality—that is, any conclusion which purports to show that living beings possess some ontologically distinctive feature—depends on the assumption that intentional contexts are genuinely relational in form, and do not merely appear to have the form of relational propositions. This raises an important point. If intentional contexts are relational in form, then there are intentional relations which do not require the real existence of their terms. Our assumption therefore appears to commit us to a metaphysical *distinction* between merely intentional "being" on the one hand and ordinary existence on the other. We have already seen that merely intentional being could not in any case be what some have called purely "mental existence." Hence if all genuine relations require the being of all their terms, then we are committed, by the admission of "intentional relations," to the view that merely intentional objects possess a genuine sort of being apart from the mind. It is possible, of course, to talk about intentional objects without making any such assumption. We might construe all talk about intentional objects simply as a certain way of talking about psychological phenomena themselves. However, if intentional sentences really are relational in form, then talk about intentional objects must involve something more than this.

Chisholm appears to feel that the question which he is raising about intentional contexts does not involve any question about some peculiar mode of being possessed by merely intentional objects:

> I wish to emphasize that my question does not concern "subsistence" or "the being of objects which don't exist." Philosophers may ask whether it is possible to think about unicorns if there are no unicorns for us to think about. They may also ask whether you and I can believe "the same thing" if there is no proposition or objective toward which each of our beliefs is directed. But I am not raising these questions.[12]

Brentano's disclaimer is even stronger:

> It might occur to someone to say that whenever a person related himself mentally to something as object, this object must always *be* just as properly as he himself, even though it need not always *exist* just as he does. . . .
> I confess that I am totally incapable of deriving any sense from this distinction between being and existence.[13]

Brentano denies that merely intentional objects possess some sort of merely intentional being. Hence there is no sense in which there "are" merely intentional objects, unless it is in the sense that there are thoughts or other psychological phenomena which *intend* such objects. Assessing the consistency of such claims requires determining the precise sense in which Brentano or Chisholm may be prepared to maintain that intentionality is or is not relational. Since the phenomenon of intentionality is an ontologically interesting one only if intentionality is at least relational in the sense of involving a multiplicity of "terms," we must also ask whether a phenomenon can be relational in this sense without requiring the ontological status of its terms, hence some distinction between modes of being.

Consider this passage from Brentano:

> If someone thinks something, that thinker must of course exist, but the object of his thinking need by no means exist. . . . Thus the thinker is the only thing which mental reference requires. The term of the so-called *Relation* need not be given at all in reality. On account of this, one might doubt that we are here really dealing with *etwas Relatives*, and not rather with *einem Relativen ähnlichen*, which one might accordingly call *etwas Relativliches*. The similarity consists in the fact that just as when one thinks about a relation in the proper sense, similarly when one thinks about a mental act, he must in a certain sense think two objects— one, so to speak, *in recto*, the other *in obliquo*. If I think about a

flower-lover, then the flower-lover is the object which I think *in recto*, the flowers are what I think *in obliquo*. But this is similar to the case where I think someone who is taller than Caius. The taller one is thought *in recto*, Caius *in obliquo*.[14]

Brentano here distinguishes between relational and merely relation-like properties, and he counts intentionality as a case of the latter. In what respect, then, is a merely relation-like property such as intentionality like and unlike an ordinary relation? There seem to be two features which are shared by any propositions that assert the existence either of a relation or of a merely relation-like property. First, any such proposition would appear, at least in some way, to contain a reference to more than a single *term*. Brentano seems to imply this when he says that in thinking about either sort of property, "one must in a certain sense think two objects." This, of course, would not be a sufficient condition for a proposition's being relational in any ordinary sense. 'John is tall and Harry is short,' for example, is a proposition in which I think two objects, though it is not a relational proposition. We must thus add as a second condition that any proposition which asserts the existence either of a *Relation* in Brentano's sense or of *etwas Relativliches* must be such that, in addition to containing a reference to more than a single term, it is not reducible to a truth-function of propositions each of which refers to only one of these terms to the exclusion of the others. It does seem to be this sort of condition which Brentano is introducing when he declares that both a proposition asserting a *Relation* and a proposition asserting *etwas Relativliches* are not only such that in these propositions one "must in a certain sense think two objects," but they are also such that one of the objects which is thought in the proposition is thought in a different *way* from the other. One object is thought *modo recto*, the other *modo obliquo*.

Consider, for example, the proposition 'John is taller than Harry.' There does seem to be a sense in which we can say that this proposition is *about* John in a way in which it is not about Harry, although there is also a sense in which the proposition is about Harry too. We can express this sense by saying that though the proposition is about both Harry and John, it is about John "directly" and Harry only "indirectly." We may also note that the same distinction is one which we cannot make in the case of the obviously non-relational proposition 'John is tall and Harry is short.' There is no sense in which a truth-function of propositions, some about one of two entities and some about the other, is more directly about one rather than the other of the two entities which the proposition is about. It is true, of course, that the proposition 'John is taller than Harry' is, in one important sense, *not* more directly about John than it is about Harry, and we indicate this when we construe the proposition simply as an instance of the general form '$R(x, y)$.' But while construing the proposition as of the general form '$R(x, y)$,' and hence not more directly as about one rather than the other of the two terms of the relation R, we can *also* construe the proposition as an instance of the general form '$F(x)$.' There is no purely grammatical, or even logical, consideration which prevents us from construing the proposition 'John is taller than Harry' as ascribing to John the property of being taller than Harry. Secondly, it is precisely in this way that we should expect any philosopher to construe the proposition who, like Brentano, has a basic prejudice in favor of the ordinary subject-predicate judgment.[15]

We may well surmise, then, that Brentano offers two conditions as specifying the class of propositions which assert the existence either of a *Relation* or of *etwas Relativliches*. Any such proposition must contain some sort of reference to more than a single entity and must not be construable as a truth-function of propositions none of which contains such a reference. These conditions seem to be what Brentano is suggesting when he asserts that any proposition in the class under consideration must be one in which we think (at least) two entities, one *in recto* and the other(s) only *in obliquo*.

It would not be entirely accurate to say that any propositions which satisfy these conditions do assert what we would ordinarily call a relation between two terms. Consider, for example, the proposition 'John's hat is brown.' This does appear to contain some sort of reference both to John and to John's hat, and it does not appear to be construable as a truth-function of propositions some of which are about John alone and others about his hat. Hence the proposition does appear to satisfy the two conditions which Brentano has suggested. However, we would not ordinarily say that the proposition asserts a relation between John and his hat. Hence Brentano's conditions will not quite do as delimiting a class of propositions which assert what we would ordinarily call relations. The reason, however, does not lie in any difficulties concerning the notion of a relation, but rather concerns the notion of an *assertion*. It seems clear that if the proposition 'John's hat is brown' does not *assert* that any relation obtains between some hat which is brown and John, the proposition does nevertheless *express*, in some sense, that such a relation obtains. In this sense we may say that the proposition does "deal with" a relation. In this sense the two conditions which appear to be suggested by Brentano establish a class of propositions all of which "express" or "deal with" what we ordinarily regard as relations.

The class of propositions, therefore, expressing what Brentano calls a *Relation* turns out simply to be a sub-division of the general class of relational propositions. Propositions which are, in Brentano's sense, Relational are just a special case of propositions which are in the ordinary sense relational. The former are simply those propositions whose truth requires the existence of all of the terms of the relation with which the proposition deals. Those propositions which deal, by contrast, merely with something which is *etwas Relativliches* are those propositions whose truth does not require the existence of all of the terms of the relation with which the proposition deals. On this interpretation, then, intentional propositions are "non-relational" propositions *only* in the sense that they do not require the existence of all their terms, and not in the stronger sense that they are propositions which do not involve a multiplicity of terms at all. Strictly speaking, though intentional propositions would not be Relational propositions, they would nevertheless be genuinely relational propositions.

Chisholm, as we saw in the passage quoted in the introduction to this chapter, is prepared to grant that intentional propositions may not assert the existence of "relations," insofar as their truth does not require the existence of all the entities with which those propositions deal. But he is nevertheless committed to construing intentional propositions as relational at least in the sense isolated here. Indeed, Chisholm claims simply to be following Brentano in denying that intentional propositions assert "descriptive relations."[16] Since his reference is presumably to Brentano's claim that intentional propositions are not Relational but merely express *etwas Relativliches* and since, on the present interpretation of that claim, propositions which merely express *etwas Relativliches* are at least genuinely relational propositions, Chisholm may not after all be denying that intentional propositions are relational propositions.

If we restrict ourselves simply to the characterization which I have offered of the class of relational propositions, then there appears to be no contradiction at all in the notion of a proposition which is relational yet non-Relational, that is, in the notion of a relational proposition which does not require the existence of all the terms with which the proposition deals. It does not follow from the fact that a true proposition contains a reference to, in the sense of being genuinely *about*, some entity, that this entity really exists. 'Santa Claus lives at the North Pole' does say something *about* a certain fictional entity, but that entity remains fictional nevertheless. If, however, a true proposition's containing a reference to some entity does not imply that this entity really exists, then there would seem to be no contradiction at all in the notion of a genuinely relational proposition which does not require the existence of all the terms with which that proposition deals. It is perhaps for this reason that Chisholm can feel that his views about intentional propositions may carry some point of ontological significance concerning psychological phenomena, without having to raise any question at all concerning the "being" of intentional objects. We ought to be perfectly free to consider the analysis of any proposition and, in particular, to conclude that some propositions are not susceptible to any sort of analysis at all, without ever having to raise a question concerning the real or fictional status of the entities with which the proposition deals. Since our classification of a given proposition as a relational proposition concerns only the question of the sort of *analysis* of which that proposition is susceptible, it does seem that our decision concerning the relational status of intentional propositions is one which we are able to make without raising any question about a realm of intentional being.

However, the matter is not this simple. While agreeing that it does not follow just from our characterization of a relational proposition that relational propositions require the existence of all their terms, it is not clear that we can accept that characterization as an adequate *definition* of a relational proposition. Moreover if we do accept that characterization as an adequate definition of a relational proposition, then we cannot infer anything of ontological significance concerning psychological phenomena from the fact that intentional propositions are relational in form. The point is that we need to draw a sharp distinction between those purely syntactic and semantical features by which we recognize a proposition as being relational in form, and those features of the *world* which relational propositions assert to exist or to obtain—relations. If we are to offer any definition at all of relational propositions, then it seems that we might define them simply as those propositions which assert or express the existence of relations. But whether we define relational propositions in this way or rather simply as those propositions which exhibit certain syntactic and semantical features, we do need to distinguish those features themselves from the sorts of states of affairs in the world which relational propositions, in virtue of possessing those features, assert to obtain.

What relational propositions presumably assert is the existence of relational states of affairs. Consider, for example, the proposition that A is to the left of B. What makes this proposition true is the existence of a certain state of affairs which contains both A and B. But there could be no such states of affairs in the first place if there were no A and B to be contained in it, since a relational state of affairs would appear to be nothing *but* two or more entities standing in a certain relation or connection with one another, and it is impossible that there should be such a connection as long as there is nothing to be connected by it in the first place.[17] As long as we fail to ask what relational propositions say *about* the terms to which they refer—that they are connected in a certain way—and simply notice that they are propositions which do refer in certain ways to certain terms, then we shall detect no contradiction in the notion of a relational proposition which does not require the existence of all its terms. But if we simply define relational propositions in terms of their syntactic and semantical features, without inquiring what those propositions say about the terms which they are about, then the fact that intentional propositions are relational propositions whose truth does not require the existence of their terms can no longer have any bearing at all on our concern with the peculiarities of psychological phenomena. In order that it have this bearing we must suppose that there is something peculiar which intentional propositions assert *about* psychological phenomena, and this requires that we be concerned after all not merely with what certain propositions are about, but also with what those propositions *say* about what they are about.

There is also a second disturbing consequence which will arise if we define relational propositions simply in terms of certain syntactic and semantical features which they possess, without a concern for the features of the world which those propositions assert to exist. The consequence is simply that we shall then be in no position to understand why *any* relation requires the existence of its terms. If it is alleged that, because of the sort of relation which it is, intentional relations may obtain without involving the existence of all their terms, then it is presumably also the case that, because of the sort of relation which *it* is, Being-to-the-left-of may *not* obtain without requiring the existence of its terms (given at least the existence of *one* of those terms). But if by the obtaining of the relation Being-to-the-left-of I simply *meant* the truth of a proposition of the form 'x is to the left of y,' then, since there is nothing in the form of such a proposition which requires the existence of *both* the terms which are referred to by expressions which we substitute for 'x' and 'y,' there would be nothing in the nature of Being-to-the-left-of which prevented the consequence which we wish to avoid. It is only if we mean by the obtaining of a relation such as Being-to-the-left-of not simply the truth of some proposition of the form 'x is to the left of y', but rather the existence of a certain sort of state of affairs which would *make* a proposition of that form true, that we could find any reason "in the nature of things" for denying that fictional entities could stand in spatial relations to really existing entities.

In general, if we are to understand that *any* relations by their very nature require the existence of all their terms (so long as any one of those terms exist), we cannot define the concept of a relation in terms of the concept of a relational *proposition*. We must rather define relational propositions as propositions which assert the obtaining of relations. But once we have done this then we must see that *no* relational proposition can fail to require the existence of all its terms (so long as the existence of any one term is given). It is perhaps no surprise, then, that some commentators have found in Brentano not only the explicit claim that intentional propositions are non-Relational, though presumably relational, propositions, but also at least the tendency to wonder whether *any* relational proposition is a Relational one.[18]

Our discussion has proceeded upon an interpretation of Brentano's distinction between propositions which express *etwas Relatives* and propositions which express only *etwas Relativliches*. This interpretation was required in order that the claim that intentional propositions assert *etwas Relativliches* be one that has some ontological significance concerning psychological phenomena. It implies, however, that there is no way to avoid a commitment to the existence of merely intentional objects. If unicorns and centaurs do not exist in any ordinary way, then they must at least exist, so long as they are thought of, in some special mode of merely intentional being. To say, furthermore, that they do exist in such a merely intentional way could not be merely another way of saying that such entities are or might be thought of or imagined. In that case there would be no ontological force at all to the introduction of intentional relations. To assert the existence of intentional relations would not be making any claim at all about some peculiar feature of the world. It would simply be saying that people do or might sometimes think about or imagine entities which do not exist. But this is a point which, in itself, is of no philosophical significance at all. Our philosophical interest does not lie in the commonsense fact that we sometimes imagine the non-existent; it lies rather in an analysis or *account* of that fact. We are not engaged merely in an enquiry concerning the truth of such claims about mental phenomena, but rather concerning the features of the world which make such propositions true. It is precisely this distinction between the truth of intentional propositions and the existence of certain states of affairs which make those propositions true which would be obliterated if merely intentional objects were alleged to exist, but then only in the sense that people sometimes think about or imagine non-existent objects.

Thus the only ontologically useful interpretation of Brentano's claim that intentional propositions assert *etwas Relativliches* requires a genuine commitment to some mode of merely intentional existence. But Brentano explicitly rejects any attempt to distinguish between ordinary and merely intentional existence. Therefore, either Brentano's position contains an implicit contradiction, or we have not succeeded in correctly interpreting his distinction between *etwas Relatives* and *etwas Relativliches*. The latter is the case; we may see this by returning to Brentano's distinction between thinking something *in recto* and thinking it *in obliquo*.

Irreducible Intentional Properties

Brentano claims that whoever asserts "John is dreaming about unicorns" is "thinking" John *in recto* and unicorns *in obliquo*. This might be taken simply to mean that the sentence 'John is dreaming about unicorns' is properly of the subject/predicate form 'John has the property of dreaming about unicorns,' in the same way that 'John is taller than Harry' may be taken as properly of the form 'John has the property of being taller than Harry.' If it is a proposition of this form, then it would indeed be a proposition about John in a way in which it is not a proposition about unicorns. But if this is all that the *recto/obliquo* distinction amounts to, then it would appear that whereas the proposition 'John is dreaming about unicorns' is about John alone *in recto* and about unicorns only *in obliquo*, it is nevertheless logically equivalent to a proposition which is about unicorns *in recto* and John only *in obliquo*. 'John has the property of dreaming about unicorns' would appear to be logically equivalent to 'Unicorns are dreamed of by John' in just the way that 'John is taller than Harry' is logically equivalent to 'Harry is shorter than John.' In this case the objects or sorts of objects about which John is dreaming would be the proper *subject* of a proposition describing John's dreams. Brentano maintains, however, that we cannot succeed in referring to objects of intention in this way. When we try to do so we still only succeed in referring to such objects merely in an "oblique" manner: "Thus for example someone who is said to think about a thing thought about is really thinking about someone who thinks about a thing."[19] Sometimes Brentano explains the same point in a somewhat different manner, in terms of what we "acknowledge" in our assertion of some proposition rather than in terms of what we "think" or refer to in that way: "It turned out that when something is acknowledged as thought about, it is acknowledged in an improper sense, though at the same time something is also acknowledged in the proper sense, namely the person thinking about it."[20]

It does not follow that Brentano is committed to denying that we ever do succeed in referring to merely intentional objects. He is not committed to denying, for example, that 'Unicorns have one horn' is a proposition which contains a reference to (i.e., in which we "think") a fictional entity or kind of entity. Some of the things which Brentano says may suggest that he is committed to denying this. He claims, for example, that "it is a characteristic of all our thinking that it has something real (*Reales*) for an object."[21] Such passages may lead some to conclude that, at least in the final development of his views, Brentano was prepared to reject the possibility of a genuine reference to non-existent objects. But by something "real" Brentano simply meant such entities as concrete particulars, as distinguished from such merely alleged sorts of entities as properties, objectives, propositions, or possibilities.[22] Thus Brentano is not denying the possibility of reference to merely intentional objects, but only the possibility of reference to them merely *as* intentional objects (whether to such objects merely as intentional objects or merely as *merely* intentional objects):

> Even when it is said that something is in our mind or heart, because we are occupied with it as thinking or loving, it is only a matter of Being in a quite improper sense, and accordingly some-

thing thought *qua* something thought or something loved *qua* something loved is no thing at all. However, it is also no object of our thinking, but rather the thinker and the lover, who as such belong to the Real, are here to be designated as object—as also it may be said of that to which they themselves are directed in thinking and loving (e.g., if one thinks of a house or feels love for his friend), that they belong to the Real.[23]

The question whether some thinker is referring to an object still remains independent of the question whether the object exists or not: "To say that the thinker exists is by no means also to say that what he is thinking about exists."[24] It is possible to refer to and think about merely intentional objects, hence such objects may be the proper subjects of a thought. It is simply that we are not referring to such objects *when* we are merely affirming some proposition about what some person is referring to.

It follows, then, that Brentano is denying that the word 'unicorn' is used in any sort of referential way when it is used in the proposition 'John is dreaming of unicorns,' though he is not denying that the word is used in a referential way when it is used in the proposition 'Unicorns have one horn.' But where does this leave us with respect to Brentano's claim that the former proposition expresses *etwas Relativliches*? A necessary condition of any proposition which expresses *etwas Relativliches* is that it be a proposition in which one "thinks" *two* objects, although only one of those objects must be something which is thought "directly." It is clear that we cannot continue to suppose that a proposition asserting *etwas Relativliches* is one in which we actually *refer* to two distinct objects. To say, then, that such a proposition is one in which we "think" two objects could only mean that it is a proposition which contains *expressions* which refer to two distinct objects. Thus to say that in such a proposition one of the objects is thought directly, but the other only indirectly, must merely signify that while, in that proposition, one of the expressions which refers to some object is actually being *used* to refer to that object, the other expression in the proposition is being used differently. Since there is no contradiction in the notion of an expression which is not being used to refer to something to which that expression does in fact refer, the class of propositions asserting *etwas Relativliches* does not seem to be a necessarily empty class, and we may consider the suggestion that intentional propositions are of this sort.

We may thus express Brentano's view by saying that intentional properties are not in any way reducible to intentional relations of some sort. Chisholm concedes that at least the *later* Brentano held this view,[25] but according to him it could not possibly be correct. If, however, the claim that intentional propositions, or at least those which describe psychological phenomena, express *etwas Relativliches* is *not* given the present interpretation, then the only alternative appears to be to return to our original interpretation. To do so would give us the advantage of having a thesis about psychological phenomena which is of clear ontological significance. But it is impossible to return to that view without committing ourselves to a realm of merely intentional being, and Chisholm, as we have seen, is no more inclined than Brentano was to raise this issue. Chisholm, in any case, rejects the view that the intentional properties which psychological phenomena possess do not involve any sort of intentional relations:

> That this suggestion will not do, however, is indicated by the fact that "John believes that there are unicorns" (or "John *believesthat-thereareunicorns*") and "All of John's beliefs are true" together imply "There are unicorns"—a mode of inference that would not be valid if "unicorn" functioned here as an equivocal middle term.[26]

Before this objection can be assessed, we must of course decide what sorts of entities involved in belief can strictly be said to be "true." For example, when saying that somebody's belief is true, I am not ascribing the property of truth to some particular mental act or acts. This is not because belief is merely dispositional and not an act at all. Even in cases where we *are* speaking of mental acts, what is said to be true is never an act itself. It is nonsensical to claim that my act of thinking that unicorns exist is true.

We can take it for granted, then, that the claim that some particular belief or thought is true must be taken as a claim about the *content* of some actual or possible act of believing or thinking. There may of course be disagreement about what sort of "thing" the content of an act might be, and this matter will be considered in Chapter 4. But apart from a detailed examination of this question, it is impossible to find any force in Chisholm's objection. For example, suppose that it turns out, as argued in Chapter 5, that a *sentence* may properly be regarded as the content of somebody's thought or belief. Then we may construct the following argument:

1. John believes that *p*, if and only if the sentence '*p*' is the content of John's belief. (Def.)
2. All of John's beliefs are true, if and only if all those sentences which are the contents of John's beliefs are true. (Def.)
3. John believes that there are unicorns.
4. All of John's beliefs are true.
5. Therefore, there are unicorns. (By 1, 2, 3, and 4)

Whether something like premise 1 is in fact acceptable is a matter which of course deserves closer attention; in any case, it will be argued in Chapter 5 when we consider Wilfrid Sellars' views about intentionality.

Though Chisholm's objection does not succeed in refuting the view that intentional properties such as "believing that there are unicorns" are irreducible to properties involving intentional *relations* of some sort, the objection does, nonetheless, refute the view that such properties as "believing that there are unicorns" are irreducible *altogether*. In our counter-argument, for example, the predicate 'believes that there are unicorns' could not have been taken to be a primitive predicate. For the argument works only if 'believes that there are unicorns' is logically equivalent to 'has the sentence "There are unicorns" as the content of belief.' In general it would be impossible to avoid the force of Chisholm's objection if intentional predicates were in fact primitive predicates. While Brentano did deny that such predicates involve any sorts of relations, it is not perfectly clear that he was prepared to maintain that such predicates are primitive. It does not seem unlikely, however, that it was Brentano's position that intentional predicates *are* primitive, and in that case Chisholm's argument does have some force against Brentano's view, even though it fails to refute, as he thought it did, the claim that expressions do not retain their ordinary referring function when they are used in intentional contexts.

Conclusion

In this chapter two distinct questions have been considered, both of which are posed by the fact that the language by which we describe certain psychological phenomena, at least with respect to the intentional features of such phenomena, exhibits an apparently relational form. The first question was whether, assuming that grammatical appearances are not, in this case, misleading—and assuming, with Chisholm, that the sentences in question are not analyzable in terms of sentences of any other form—the conclusion could be drawn that psychological phenomena exhibit a special sort of intentional relation which is unlike any relation exhibited by non-psychological phenomena. These assumptions would not, contrary to Chisholm's view, be sufficient for drawing the conclusion in question. At least some further ontological assumptions would have to be made, some of which will be discussed in Chapter 3.

The second question was whether the introduction of "intentional relations"— that is, relations the obtaining of which does not require the real existence of all their terms (given that at least one term does really exist)—requires granting a special ontological status to merely intentional objects. Answering this question affirmatively, we argued that any attempt to escape granting some special ontological status to merely intentional objects must result either, as with Chisholm, in a failure to satisfy a necessary condition for establishing anything of ontological significance about psychological phenomena, or, as with Brentano, in a commitment to an untenable doctrine of irreducible intentional (non-relational, yet relation-like) properties.

3

Relational Accounts
of Intentionality

This chapter will consider some theories of mental reference which rest upon an introduction of special psychological relations, and in particular on the introduction of "intentional relations." With respect to at least *some* psychological states and to *some* cases of mental reference to objects, it will be argued that the intentionality of mental states can be accounted for, in a reasonable way, by appeal to a special intentional relation. In other cases, mental reference to objects cannot be accounted for by appealing to such relations. In order to account for these situations, a distinction will be drawn in Chapter 4 between (what we may call) the "contents" and the objects of mental acts. The referential character of such acts must be accounted for in terms of the presence of special "mental contents" in those acts. (In Chapter 5 the notion of "mental content" will be elucidated by regarding mental contents as quasi-linguistic items of a certain sort.) The notion of "mental content," furthermore, will be required even in the case of those acts which *also* involve a properly intentional relation. Now, however, we will examine what appear to be the main candidates for theories of mind which appeal to special psychological relations of some sort.

Perceptions and Intentional Relations

If perception involves intentional relations, then perceptual states are intentional states. They involve awarenesses of or mental references to objects that may or may not really exist. But the converse of this proposition is clearly not a logical truth. The fact that perceptions involve awarenesses of objects that may or may not really exist does not imply that perceptual states involve intentional relations, nor even indeed that perceptual states involve any sort of uniquely perceptual relation at all. There are some who maintain that perception in fact involves neither intentional states *nor* intentional relations. On such a view, it would be nonsensical to say that a person sees, or hears, or is in any way perceptually aware of something that does not really exist or is aware that something is the case which is not really the case. This is a merely verbal point which may quickly be put aside; though there is certainly a sense in which one cannot see what isn't there, there is just as surely also a sense in which one can do this, and we need to direct our attention to this sense. (The case of seeing-*that* of course requires an appeal to *judgment*, and it will be considered separately.)

Some theories of perception will grant that perceptions are intentional phenomena, but only because they involve beliefs or judgments which are intentional phenomena. It would be fair to say that on such accounts of perception, though perceptions may be held to involve some sort of intentional relations, they would not involve any uniquely perceptual intentional relations. In Chapter 1, it was argued that the intentional features of perception *cannot* be completely accounted for in terms of the intentional features of mere beliefs or judgments which perceptual states may involve. We will therefore consider only those accounts of perception that involve an appeal to intentional relations that do not introduce such relations simply to account for the intentional features of the beliefs or judgments which perceptions may involve.

It is also important to note that not every account of perception which does appeal to uniquely perceptual relations involves an appeal to *intentional* relations. On the sense-datum account, for example, perceptions of ordinary physical objects involve the apprehension of entities which are "sense data." The apprehension of sense data presumably is a unique perceptual relation of some sort between perceivers and the entities which are sense data. It is not, however, an intentional relation since the fact that a perceiver is apprehending a sense-datum implies, on the sense-datum account, that there really is a sense datum which he is apprehending.

Any account of perception, therefore, which involves an appeal to a special intentional relation must construe the object terms of such a relation as objects that may or may not really exist while they are the objects of the relation in question. The objects in question may thus be regarded as (a) physical objects which may or may not really exist, (b) properties which may or may not really be instantiated by anything, or (c) states of affairs which may or may not actually obtain. The third possibility is relevant only in connection with seeing-*that*; it will be ignored until the problem of judgment is examined. This section, after briefly indicating the inadequacy of (a), will defend a theory of perception which involves an appeal to intentional relations, the objects of which are properties which may or may not really be instantiated by anything.

Consider a perceptual state (an hallucinatory one) which is the seeing of a pink elephant. On the sense-datum theory, the object of the properly perceptual relation which this state involves is a pink elephant sense datum or "appearance." But on the view that perceptual states involve intentional relations with possibly nonreal physical objects, the object in question is simply a non-existent or an hallucinated pink elephant. There is then no real *distinction* to be drawn between pink elephant appearances and pink elephants. (To be more precise, there would be no such distinction if there were such things as pink elephants.) Pink elephant appearances just *are* pink elephants, and the only point of calling them "appearances" is simply so that we may withhold our judgment as to whether the elephants which we see are really existing elephants. If there are in fact no real pink elephants, then what is seen is a non-existent elephant, but it is all the same an elephant.

This view has some important advantages over the sense-datum theory. Unlike the sense-datum theory, this view allows us to insist that no domain of objects of any sort intervenes in principle between perception and the really existing objects which we may happen to perceive. But this theory differs importantly from the more conservative view defended in Chapter 1. It is one thing to insist that a person's seeing objects which don't exist does not imply that this person is seeing something altogether *different* from those objects (e.g., sense data), whereas it is quite another matter to suggest that the seeing of a non-existent object ought to be construed as involving a relation one of whose terms *is* such an object. This account of hallucination would require us to say that there are pink elephants even when they do not really exist. That there are such entities, furthermore, must amount to more than the claim that people sometimes in fact hallucinate them. But this consequence does not follow from our previously defended view, since the mere admission that perception involves a distinctive intentional state does not imply that there is an *object* corresponding to each such state. Thus the conclusion that there are pink elephants does not follow just from the admission that people sometimes see them, nor does it follow from that admission even when it is conjoined with the assumption that the proposition 'X is seeing pink elephants' is an unanalyzable proposition. The conclusion will follow only if we assume in addition that the expression 'pink elephants' is being used in this proposition in a strict referential manner. In that case the conclusion will follow, furthermore, not simply because some true proposition then contains this reference, but rather because if the proposition in question contains such a reference then it expresses a *relation* one of whose terms is pink elephants. It is this relational approach which must now be considered.

It is unlikely that this sort of relational account of sensory awareness is acceptable. The crux of the theory lies in the claim that the proper objects of sensory awareness may be either really existent or non-existent objects. If they are really existent, then they are simply identical with the ordinary objects which inhabit our world. But the sort of object which the theory regards as the proper object of sensory awareness is one that Meinong called an "incomplete object."[1] That is, any such object will necessarily be incomplete or indeterminate in certain respects. But all of the ordinary physical objects in the world are complete objects, and it is nonsensical to suppose that an incomplete or indeterminate entity might be identical with a completely determined one.

Suppose, for example, that in my hallucinations I see a pink elephant in an office doorway, and the elephant stands the full height of that doorway. Then there is some sense in saying that I have hallucinated a six-foot elephant. But suppose I hallucinate another elephant which does not appear as standing in any relation to the surrounding objects. Then how will the size of *this* hallucinated elephant be specified? I might try to estimate the size of this hallucination by comparing its appearance with that of an ordinary object presented at a fixed distance. Application of this method might then show the hallucination to be of some determinate height in the same way that, say, the sun's appearance is ordinarily the size of a nickel. But if this is my criterion for assessing the size of apprehended appearances, then there will no longer be a sense in which appearances really *are* the objects of which they are said to be appearances. Since the sun itself is not the size of a nickel, the appearance of the sun could not be the sun itself. On the view we are considering, however, the only possible general difference between mere appearances and really existing physical objects is that the former may be, though physical objects, nevertheless non-existing ones.

Thus the proposed standard for assessing the size of hallucinated elephants must be rejected if one is to preserve the conception of sensory objects as intentional objects—as entities which may or may not be actually existing objects and not simply existences which may or may not happen to stand in some *relation* to actual objects. It seems then, that there is no general method by which we may assess the size of "appearances." If there *are* such objects whenever they are apprehended by sense, then those objects will be, in some respects at least, incomplete objects. They will be objects which defy the law of the "excluded middle." Some if not all such objects, for example, will be neither greater, nor exactly, nor less than six feet in height; they will remain completely unspecified with regard to height. It is nonsensical, however, to suppose that such an entity as this might *be* an existing physical object, even if there might be such an entity which stands in certain *relations* to physical objects.

This sort of objection can be avoided if we suppose that the proper objects of sensory awareness are not particulars at all, but rather universals. In considering this theory, it is important to see that if sensory awareness does involve a distinctive relation, then the assumption that the proper objects of sensory awareness are universals is compatible with construing the relation which sensory awareness involves as an intentional relation, in a way in which the assumption of sense data as the proper objects of sensory awareness was not. If sensory awareness involves an intentional relation, then someone's apprehending a particular object of sensory awareness will not imply either that such an object does or does not really exist. This condition is satisfied by the assumption that universals are the proper objects of sensory awareness. Suppose, for example, that the "real existence" of some universal F is just F's being exemplified or instantiated by something. Then since someone's apprehending a given universal (seeing Red, for example) does not imply that the universal in question is in fact instantiated by anything (either by anything which he perceives, or by anything at all), it follows that if sensory awareness involves a relation between a perceiver, or some state of a perceiver, and universals, sensory awareness will involve an intentional relation.

If the proper objects of sensory awareness are universals, furthermore, then we will be able to avoid our earlier objection to the claim that while any object of sensory awareness need not be a really existing one, that very same object *might* nevertheless be or become identical with some really existing object, and not simply be or become related in a certain way to it. That someone is apprehending the universal Red does not imply that Red is something which really exists, but it is nevertheless *possible* that the very same object which that person is apprehending is identical with something which really exists. It is possible that there is in fact something which instantiates the universal Red, and that Red, therefore, really exists. The problem, furthermore, about indeterminate or incomplete objects does not seem to arise in the case of possible universals as it did with possible particulars.

We are not, therefore, faced with the prospect of identifying some entity which is indeterminate with respect to certain universals with the same entity which is completely determined in that respect. The entities with which we are now concerned are the very universals that characterize or determine certain particulars, and not the particulars themselves which we characterize in this way.

There are a number of objections which must be considered before this theory of sensory awareness can be accepted. Two conditions must be placed upon any term of an "intentional relation." The first condition is that an object of an intentional relation need not really exist; the second condition is that an object of an intentional relation must nevertheless at least possess *some* sort of ontological status. Thus there must be uninstantiated universals in order that universals may be the objects of sensory awareness. There must, furthermore, be such universals in a sense which does not simply amount to the claim that there are or might be awarenesses *of* them. This second condition may be satisfied by the following definition of being for universals: there is said to "be" a certain universal if and only if it is logically possible for something to *instantiate* that universal. This definition would allow us to speak of there being uninstantiated universals in a sense which does not simply amount to the claim that there are or might be awarenesses of them.

It is not clear that this move will serve our needs. If it can be said that there is a certain universal *F* only in the sense that it is logically possible that something is *F*, then it is hardly clear in what sense a universal is in fact some sort of *entity* which might serve as the term of a relation. The same point can be made for any proposed criterion of being or existence for uninstantiated universals solely in terms of the instantiation or non-instantiation, or the possibility of such, of universals. An account of sensory awareness that involves intentional relations with universals must tolerate a sense of being for uninstantiated universals which amounts neither to some claim merely about actual or possible awarenesses of universals nor to some claim merely about their actual or possible instantiations or non-instantiations. Though not all philosophers would agree that there is such a sense of being for universals, certainly some have thought that there is, and the issue appears to remain a controversial one. Thus while the second condition which must be met by the term of any intentional relation does raise some serious doubt about the possibility of intentional relations involving universals, I do not believe that any decisive point can be made in this regard.

There are other difficulties which appear to confront any account of sensory awareness as involving relations whose object terms are universals rather than particulars. For example, what it could mean to speak of *seeing* universals apart from seeing particulars is not at all clear. It is possible to see the blue of the sky or the oval shape of an egg, but what does this amount to except that one can see that the sky is blue or that some egg is oval? One might see a universal *F*, it might be argued, but only in the sense that one might see some particular to *be F*. Universals are properly the objects of judgment or belief, and the most that one can ever see, strictly speaking, are particular instances of them. Hence the account of sensory awareness as the awareness of possibly uninstantiated universals is an incoherent account. However, no clear reason has been given for accepting the view that one can see some universal F only in the sense that one can see something to be F, or that one can see that something is F. It seems, after all, evident that one does in fact see shapes and colors, and shapes and colors are universals and not particulars. If it is claimed that these shapes and colors are nevertheless the shapes and colors *of* the particulars which instantiate them, then this challenge will either be simply mistaken or an evasion. Often one sees shapes and colors which are not in fact instantiated by any of the physical objects which one might see at the same time, and to assume that all these shapes and colors must in that case be instantiated by some peculiar non-physical objects, say, by sense data, is clearly to beg the question.

Nonetheless, the following argument offers the conclusion that the notion of seeing universals makes no sense apart from the seeing of particulars. Earlier it was argued that sensory awareness, in the only sense which is of interest to us here, is not independent of a person's conceptual abilities. Although, for example, Macbeth's seeing a dagger ought not to be construed merely as his believing or having a tendency to believe, as a result of some visual experience, that there really is a dagger before him, nevertheless his ability to see a hallucinated dagger could not be independent of his ability to recognize a dagger when one is really before him. Even if Macbeth did not, after all, think that there was a real dagger before him, he would still have *recognized* what he saw before him as a dagger and not, say, as a wine cup. In general, if a person does not recognize what he sees as being a specific object, then it would seem impossible to speak of his having seen such an object in the first place, at least in the case of objects which do not actually exist apart from the awareness of them. Thus sensory awareness, at least in the sense that concerns us, involves the recognition of something, hence the recognition of something *as* something. But such recognition, it may be argued, involves the subsumption of some given item under universals which truly characterize it. Since seeing involves recognition, then, and recognition presupposes the subsumption of something under universals, it seems to follow that it is nonsensical to speak of seeing universals, unless to see a universal is just to recognize something which I see as *exemplifying* that universal.

This conclusion does not follow. It makes as much sense to speak of recognizing universals as it does to speak of recognizing particulars. One's ability, for example, to recognize that some color is Red is not at all different in kind from one's ability to recognize that some particular object is a book. One recognizes some particular thing as a book in virtue of some universal features of it, for example, its shape, and one recognizes colors in the same way. One recognizes that some color is Red, for example, in virtue of its difference from Green and its relation to other colors generally. There seems to be no clear reason, then, why we ought not to speak of seeing universals, but only of seeing that certain things *instantiate* universals.

Granting, however, that we can be said to see universals in a proper sense, a difficulty may still remain in the suggestion that we see universals which may or may not be instantiated by any particulars. Suppose that I am seeing a round spot on the wall; then perhaps there is some proper sense in which I am seeing not only a spot on the wall, but also the universal Round. But even if I may see universals themselves and not simply particulars which instantiate them, the universal in this case *is* nevertheless instantiated by some particular. If our suggestion is correct, then it must be possible to perceive at least some universals which are not instantiated by any particulars at all, since precisely what would make sensory awareness intentional is the possibility that the objects of sensory awareness are not really existing entities, and the sense in which a universal would be a really existing entity is that it is instantiated by some particular.

Suppose that one apprehends a red spot which is merely a visual afterimage and not identical with any physical spot at all. On our suggestion the spot is a universal which is not instantiated by any particular that one is apprehending. But it might seem that we cannot consider the apprehended spot as a universal rather than a particular, since it is always possible to simultaneously apprehend two or more such spots, one beside the other. If more than one such spot may be apprehended, then this spot must be a particular. Otherwise, since all of the universals in my perception are identical, there would be no way to distinguish the spots as separate entities. For example, we could not distinguish the two afterimages simply by perceiving that some universal is simultaneously in two different places. We speak of a universal as being in some place, it might be argued, simply in the sense that it is instantiated by some particular which is in that place. It apparently follows, therefore, that the two afterimages cannot be merely uninstantiated universals, but must be either nothing at all, or else two different particulars which instantiate the same universals.

The admission, however, that spatial locations for universals are always derivative from the locations of particulars which instantiate them does not imply that afterimages are particulars and not universals. The problem of giving spatial location to afterimages does not in fact arise at all. Even if I do *perceive* one afterimage as to the left of another afterimage or as standing in some spatial relation to some actual physical object, it is clear that the afterimage does not have any actual spatial location; it merely *seems* to. Certainly the afterimage does not have a location in physical space, and it is uncertain what one could mean in this case by a purely "mental" space, if not simply the possibility of seeing afterimages which are not *identical* with any spots in physical space. Since there is no problem of granting a real spatial location to the afterimages which one perceives, there is no problem which needs to be solved by appealing to the instantiation of universals by particulars which do have a real location in space.

But how then does one distinguish two qualitatively identical afterimages? If both afterimages have (or *are*) exactly the same universals, then how can one distinguish between the case of seeing two or seeing only one afterimage? There is a reponse which might be acceptable. Consider again the case where one perceives a red, round afterimage to the left of and at some distance from another afterimage with the same internal qualities as the first. Then we may say that what is seen when one sees the first of these afterimages is not some particular which exemplifies the universals Round, Red, and Left-of-something-which-is-round-and-red, but simply the *complex* universal Round-red-and-left-of-something-which-is-round-and-red. Since seeing the property of being round and red and to the left of something which is round and red does not imply that there *is* something which I see that conforms to this description, there seems to be no contradiction in this sort of response. So long as we grant that there is such a thing as seeing the universals Round, Red, and Left-of-something-which-is-round-and-red, there ought to be such a thing as seeing the complex universal Round-red-and-to-the-left-of-something-which-is-round-and-red. Accordingly, it seems that we ought to be able to distinguish between seeing a single red and round afterimage and seeing a pair of red and round afterimages without having to introduce some particulars which actually instantiate the universals Round and Red. To make this claim, however, is not to deny the very distinction between particulars and universals, nor is it to attempt an analysis of particulars as simply identical with complexes of universals. In the first place it is not evident that a complex universal is the sort of entity which philosophers who have considered a reduction of particulars to universals have meant when they identified particulars as complexes or bundles *of* universals.[2] Moreover, our suggestion does not deny that when something is really red and round and to the left of something else which is red and round then there is, in addition to the complex universal Red-round-and-to-the-left-of-something-red-and-round, a particular which instantiates that universal. The argument simply is that if there is a certain sense in which there might be such a complex universal, even when no instance of it exists, and if there is a sense in which universals might be the proper objects of perception, then there ought to be such a thing as seeing that complex universal even when no instance of it exists.

This theory, then, will construe the red and round afterimages as complex universals which may or may not happen to be instantiated by anything (and in fact *are* uninstantiated by any particulars which I may be seeing on the occasion in question). If such a theory is correct, then all sensory awareness will involve intentional relations, that is, relations whose terms may or may not really exist. It will involve a further question as to which of those terms do in fact exist, or whether Brentano was correct in denying their actual existence altogether. However, the present theory will allow us to avoid the difficulties besetting Brentano. If such predicates as 'seeing *x*' did not involve any relations at all but only designated, as Brentano thought, irreducible intentional properties, then there could be no sense in which some of the observed *x*'s might or might not really exist apart from the seeing of them. We would not be able, without ambiguity, to use any expression which replaces '*x*', in the predicate 'seeing *x*', to *refer* to something which we are said to see whenever we are said to be "seeing *x*." Further, we encounter insuperable difficulties if we construe sensory awareness as involving some sort of relation, but continue to hold, with Brentano, that the proper objects of awareness are in every case particulars and not universals, but are nevertheless not merely "sense data." The present theory avoids both of these difficulties, and, if it is otherwise sound, allows us to pose the question whether some or all of the things which we perceive by the senses are in fact identical with things which exist apart from any perception of them. The question will simply be whether any of the *qualities* which one apprehends by sense are in fact instantiated by anything.

This theory has advantages over the sense-datum account of sensory awareness. On the sense-datum theory, as opposed to this one, sensory awareness will involve the apprehension not of certain entities which may or may not happen to be identical with some really existing objects of veridical perception, but only of certain entities which may or may not happen to stand in certain *relations* to the objects of veridical perception. But there are other important advantages to be considered. A common objection to the sense-datum theory is that the proper objects of sensory awareness are private on that view. That is, no two people could be said to perceive numerically the same sense datum, though they might of course perceive sense data which are qualitatively indistinguishable. If the present theory is correct, this distinction will not apply to the immediate objects of sensory awareness; there will no longer be any reason why the fact that *A* perceives some entity, say, an afterimage, which is not identical with any really existing physical object, should imply that *A* cannot be perceiving some entity which is numerically, and not just qualitatively, identical with some entity which *B* is perceiving, for *A* and *B* may be perceiving just the same universals.

It is also possible, on the present theory, to deal in a natural way with cases of perceptual illusion or perspectival variation. Consider, for example, the perception of a drawing consisting only of straight lines and angles which might be perceived alternately as a hollow cube facing in direction *A* or a hollow cube facing in direction *B*. On the sense-datum account, we are required to suppose that our perception in this case is alternately the apprehension of two different particulars altogether, that is, of two different cube "appearances," although this conflicts with our natural inclination to say that the only particular which is apprehended is the single drawing on paper and the only changes in my apprehension are changes in the *way that I apprehend* that particular. We must also assume, on the sense-datum account, that each *time* that one perceives the drawing on paper in any particular way, the object which one directly apprehends is not numerically identical with any object which was perceived on some earlier occasion. The only particular which will have remained in continuous existence throughout the alternation of perceptions will be the particular drawing on paper, and this is never identical with the appearances which one directly apprehends. On the view, however, that "appearances" are universals and not particulars, we do not need to distinguish between the particulars which one directly apprehends and the particular drawing on paper. We need only suppose that in one case one perceives, in addition to the drawing on paper, the property of being a cube facing in direction *A*, and on the other occasion the property of being a cube facing in direction *B*. (Of course, one does not have to suppose that the perceived drawing *is* a cube facing in either direction *A* or *B*. The drawing on paper is not such a cube, nor is anything else which one perceives.) Furthermore, there will be no problem in identifying what one perceives on any such occasion with what is seen on a later occasion, since one may later perceive, as a result of observing the drawing, precisely the same universals which one had earlier perceived in the same way.

It is clear, finally, that on the view that "appearances" are universals, there will be no general problem whether the proper objects of sensory awareness are two- or three-dimensional. In one sense these objects will be neither, since it is only particulars and not universals which can have these features. But in another sense the proper object of sensory awareness might be either two- or three-dimensional. Simply, one sometimes apprehends such properties as being a plane figure of a certain sort, and at other times such properties as being a solid figure of some sort. It is possible, for example, to look at some drawing and see only the property "plane figure drawn on paper." This is a property which happens to be instantiated by some particular which one perceives. It is also possible to look at the figure and apprehend the property "hollow cube facing in direction A." This is a property which does not happen to be instantiated by anything perceived.

It seems, then, that though there are some very serious objections to this account, there is not any decisive refutation of the view, and it does have a number of points in its favor. Possibly we have found a defensible view in which sensory awareness is not simply an intentional state, but also a state which involves an intentional relation. That is, if we suppose that universals are among the proper objects of sensory awareness, then it is perhaps not unreasonable to suppose that sensory awareness involves a relation to entities which may or may not "really exist." In considering the question whether the same sort of point might be made for *non*-sensory modes of awareness and of reference to objects, we must determine whether it is likewise possible to construe the proper objects of judgments, as distinct from mere perceivings, as not only being intentional objects, that is, objects of reference which may or may not really exist, but also as being the terms of relations of some special, mental sort. It does not seem possible to do this, although some philosophers have thought differently.

Judgments and Possible States of Affairs

If judging does involve a special judgmental relation which is intentional, then the most reasonable supposition is that it involves a relation with states of affairs, or "facts," which may or may not be actualized. This view has been vigorously defended in recent years by Gustav Bergmann and others, and it will be closely examined.

Two points require consideration; first, some reasonably clear distinction must be drawn between facts or states of affairs and *propositions*. If a discussion of possible states of affairs which may or may not be actual were just talk about propositions which may or may not be true, then, since false propositions just as certainly exist as true ones, a mental state's being related to states of affairs which may or may not be actual would not imply that it involves any intentional relation at all. Second, while a distinction must be drawn between the class of actual and possible states of affairs and the class of true and possibly true propositions, we must also tolerate a sense in which there *are* merely possible states of affairs. If these do not have some sort of being, then they simply cannot serve as one of the terms of any actual relation. For some philosophers, to say that a's being F is a merely possible fact is to say that while a is not in fact F, it is possible for it to be so.[3] But if our discussion of possible facts constitutes only this, then there is no sense in which possible facts are *entities*, hence no sense in which there could be relations involving them.

It seems to me that while the word 'fact' is commonly used simply as an equivalent for 'true proposition' (as when I ask you to state the "facts" in some given case), there is a distinction which needs to be drawn between facts in the former sense and facts in the latter. It always makes sense to ask what *makes* any given proposition a true one, and it is not always, perhaps never, possible to regard particulars and universals as the sorts of entity which make propositions true. Consider the judgment that some particular a is green. To say that some entity or entities makes this, or any other, judgment true is to say that the judgment will be a true one on the condition that such entities actually exist. Since the proposition that a is green will be true in case a particular green thing actually exists, it might then appear that what makes the proposition true is some particular of a certain sort. Hence we require a distinction only between the true or false proposition that a is green and some actual or merely possible particular of which the proposition affirms the existence. If, however, we do say that what makes the proposition that a is green a true one is only the particular green thing which exists in case that proposition is true, then we shall simply have to introduce a distinction between "a particular green thing" and a particular thing which happens to be green. Otherwise, the particular which in this case happens to be green might make all sorts of contrary propositions true. This very same particular, for example, might confirm the judgment that something is *not* green; it need simply change its color. Thus it is not the particular which makes the proposition a true one, but only the particular's *being of a certain color*. If we say, therefore, that it is "a particular green thing" which makes the judgment that a is green a true one, then we shall simply have to distinguish between "a particular green thing" and the particular, namely a, which happens to be green.

Sometimes, when we speak of the "fact" of some particular a being green, we are simply speaking of the circumstance that the proposition 'a is green' is a true one. But so long as it makes sense to speak of something *other* than a true proposition being a condition for the truth of that proposition, then we must distinguish another sense in which there is such a thing as "a being green," and this must not be identical with the particular a, which happens to be green. The term 'state of affairs' will be used to refer to this sort of entity.

Though the state of affairs of a being green is not identical with the particular a, there is an important sense in which it "involves" that particular. The sense in which a state of affairs involves a particular, however, must differ from that in which a proposition might be said to involve a particular. Propositions, at least on any ordinary understanding of the term, involve particulars only in the sense that they are propositions which are *about* particulars. The proposition that a is green, for example, is a proposition about the particular a. (It does not follow from this that propositions are linguistic entities, e.g., that they are either sentence tokens or even sentence types. Even if we take propositions to be the sorts of things which sentences *express* and which are the *meanings* of those sentences, there will nevertheless be a sense in which propositions are "about" something, since every meaningful sentence presumably expresses something *about* something.) It is nonsensical, however, to speak of a state of affairs as being "about" the entities which it involves. The state of affairs of *a* being green is not *about* *a* being green, for example, since it simply *consists in* *a* being green. In this sense we must say that states of affairs "contain" the entities which they involve.[4] The word 'fact,' then, may be used to designate things that stand in two very different relations to the entities which sentences are about, namely for states of affairs or for propositions. In the former case, we are dealing with something which actually *contains* the entities which sentences are about.[5]

Although states of affairs contain the entities which propositions are about, they are never simply *identical* with the collection of all such entities. The state of affairs which consists in *a* being green, for example, is never identical with the particular *a*. It might be thought that a distinction between the particular *a* and the universal Green would permit a sense in which a state of affairs *is* identical with the collection of all its constituents. Then we might say that the state of affairs which consists of *a* being green consists not simply of the particular *a* which is green, but rather of that particular *a* *together with* the Green which *a* exemplifies. But this will not work, since if by "*a* together with Green" we simply mean the collection whose members are *a* and Green, then *a* together with Green is something that might exist even if it is not the case that *a* is green. The members of that collection would also exist if *a* were red and something else were green. We must therefore suppose that a state of affairs is never identical with its constituents, but rather consists of those constituents in some sort of *connection*.

Even if we regarded the connection between the constituents of a state of affairs as itself being an additional constituent of that state of affairs, in the way that Bergmann does,[6] a state of affairs could still not be identified with the collection of its constituents, since that same collection might also exist so long as that very same connection were connecting some other entities altogether. The only way to avoid this conclusion would be to suppose that the connection·between the constituents of any state of affairs is individuated by that particular state of affairs. In that case, then, we would not speak merely of the collection whose members are *a*, Green, and exemplification, but rather of the collection whose members are *a*, *Green*, and the exemplification of Green by *a*. But then we would simply be using the expression 'connection between the constituents of a state of affairs' as the equivalent of 'constituents of a state of affairs being in a certain connection,' and there would no longer be any distinction at all between a state of affairs and the connection among its constituents. We must conclude, therefore, that the "relation" between a state of affairs and its constituents is not the same as that between a collection and its members, and that a state of affairs is not in any case identical with the collection of its constituents.[7]

It is important to see that the distinction between a state of affairs and the collection which consists of all of its constituents is not dependent upon our position with regard to the ontological status of universals. Suppose that we refuse to distinguish between the entity which is the particular *a* and the entity which is the Green which *a* exemplifies; then the problem of distinguishing particulars from states of affairs would still concern us in the case of *relational* facts. Even if we do refuse to distinguish between the particular *a* and the particular *b* which stand in a certain relation—for example, where a is larger than b—and the entity which is the Relation between them, we would still need to distinguish between the collection whose members are a and b and the state of affairs which consists of those particulars. So long as a and b both exist, the collection whose members are a and b will exist, but it does not follow that a will be larger than b. Even if we refuse to distinguish between the particulars which stand in a certain relation and the entity which is a Relation between them, a distinction is needed between the particulars which stand in any given relation and the state of affairs which consists of those particulars in relation; it is impossible to identify that state of affairs with the collection of its constituents. However, if we *did* distinguish between the particulars which are in a certain relational state of affairs and the Relation between those particulars, our problem would not be any easier. If there is such a distinction between particulars and Relations, then Relations are universals which might be the constituents of several different states of affairs. Hence the collection whose members are the particulars a and b and the Relation R could exist even if a and b were not related by R at all, that is, if some *other* entities were related in this way.

The problem of distinguishing relational states of affairs from their constituents, therefore, is no easier if we distinguish particulars from Relations than it is if we refuse to make such a distinction. In other words, contrary to the thinking of many, Relations (i.e., relational universals) cannot be introduced on the basis that we need something which will account for the "unity" of a relational state of affairs. Insofar as Relations are universals, hence the possible constituents of several states of affairs, they alone cannot account for the unity of any state of affairs, that is, for the distinction between a state of affairs and the mere collection of its constituents. If there is any basis for distinguishing between particulars and Relations, it must simply be that we require an account of what is *common* to several relational states of affairs. However, an important weakness in this argument is that by introducing Relations in this way, we are assuming that if two states of affairs have something "in common," then they must have a common constituent, whereas this assumption is contradicted by the very distinction between states of affairs and their constitutents. Thus, if a exemplifies Green and b exemplifies Red, then though a stands in just the *same* connection with Green as b stands with Red, it is impossible to suppose that the connection between them, namely exemplification, is a universal which could be a constituent of several different states of affairs. If exemplification were a universal, then the collection whose members are a, Green, and exemplification could exist even if a did not exemplify Green, namely if some other entity exemplified Green. Hence we would have to distinguish between the collection of a, Green, and exemplification and the state of affairs which consisted of some *connection* among them. However, other states of affairs might involve that very *same* connection—for example, the state of affairs which would consist in b exemplifying Red.

By distinguishing between particulars and states of affairs, we then need to grant not only the possibility of complexes which are not identical with the collections of their constituents, but we need to grant that the possibility of several states of affairs involving just the *same* connection among their constituents provides no basis at all for the introduction of relational universals. The problem of Relations is thus independent of the problem of distinguishing particulars from states of affairs. Furthermore, as already argued, the problem of distinguishing states of affairs from particulars arises as clearly in the case of non-relational states of affairs as it does in the case of relational states of affairs, and the introduction of non-relational universals no more helps to deal with that problem than the introduction of relational universals.

If we refuse to introduce non-relational universals at all, then the very distinction between relational and non-relational states of affairs may of course appear to break down, since the most natural attempt to account for the state of affairs which consists of a being green, apart from a connection between a and Green, would be to construe it as a relational one. That a is green might, for example, be construed as the state of affairs which consists of a resembling certain other particulars in certain respects. To preserve the distinction between relational and non-relational states of affairs, while refusing to distinguish between particulars and non-relational universals, we must apparently suppose that there are some states of affairs with only a single constituent. For example, the state of affairs which consists of a being green would just contain a as its single constituent. Since it is difficult to see how a state of affairs might both contain only a single constituent and also fail to be identical with the collection of its constituents, this suggestion may appear to be incoherent. However, it ought to be just as difficult to understand how a state of affairs might contain exactly *two* constituents and yet fail to be identical with the collection of those two constituents. Hence it is not clear that the distinction between particulars and states of affairs precludes the possibility of states of affairs with only one constituent. At least one philosopher has attempted to take the possibility seriously.[8]

There are some sorts of judgments about the world which we have not considered and which might appear to undermine an attempt to distinguish states of affairs from true propositions. We introduced states of affairs by arguing that we must distinguish propositions and what makes propositions true. But what makes *negative* propositions true? One possibility would be to modify our original conception of "making" some proposition true. Rather than saying that what makes any given proposition true is something that must exist in case that proposition is true, we might say that either what makes a certain proposition true is (if it is an affirmative proposition) what must exist in case it is a true proposition, *or* (if it is a negative proposition) the proposition is made true by the *non*-existence of what would exist just in case its negation were true. But this sort of alternative has the disadvantage of requiring a different conception of truth for affirmative and negative propositions. In any case, the introduction of a distinction between a state of affairs and its existence or non-existence simply raises our original problem in a different form. What could we mean by the "non-existence" of a certain state of affairs if not the *fact* that the state of affairs does not obtain? It is precisely the nature of negative facts which we wish to elucidate.

The only possibility for preserving the notion that something is needed in order to make any proposition true is the introduction of negative states of affairs. This may seem to present an insurmountable problem, since the state of affairs which consists in *a* being green would seem to contain just the same constituents as the state of affairs which consists in *a* not being green. One way to avoid this conclusion might be to suppose that "negation" is somehow an entity which can be the constituent of a state of affairs;[9] but this is undoubtedly too unintuitive a move to be acceptable to many philosophers. The difficulty might be avoided, however, if we simply recall that no state of affairs could be identical with the collection of its constituents, which is a conclusion independent of the problem of negative states of affairs. If, however, states of affairs are not identical with the collections of their constituents, then it is not clear why we ought to insist that two states of affairs must be identical if they contain precisely the same constituents. There might then be a difference between the state of affairs which consists in *a* being green and the state of affairs which consists in *a* not being green, even though these two states of affairs contain just the same constituents.

This sort of treatment could not be given to negative *existential* propositions. It is difficult to see how the proposition that there are no unicorns could be made true by a state of affairs which involves unicorns in the same way that the proposition that *a* is not green may be made true by a state of affairs involving *a*. But existential propositions may be taken merely to assert a connection, or lack of it, between certain *universals*. The negative state of affairs which corresponds to the judgment that there are no unicorns would then contain only the universals Being-a-unicorn and Being-exemplified-by-something. The admission that Being-exemplified-by-something is a universal which may or may not be exemplified by other universals does not of course imply that exemplification is a universal, that is, that the word 'exemplifies' in 'Being-a unicorn exemplifies Being-exemplified-by-something' designates a universal.

We have drawn a distinction between states of affairs on the one hand and particulars (and universals) and propositions on the other, since this is a distinction which needs to be drawn if judgment involves a distinctive intentional relation. However, Alexius Meinong defended a theory of judgment which involves the introduction of intentional relations with what may be called "possible states of affairs," even though his "states of affairs" seem to be radically different from the sorts of entities which we have introduced. Meinong will be considered more closely, partly for historical reasons but also in order to deepen our grasp of the ontological issues involved, before we proceed to an examination of Gustav Bergmann's views.

Meinong maintains that the proper objects of judgment are not ordinary "objects," but rather what Meinong calls "Objectives." Consider, for example, the judgment that some object *a* possesses a certain characteristic *F*. On the traditional view, according to Meinong, the only objects with which our judgment would be concerned in this case would also be the objects of, or at least contained in the object of, an expression which expresses no judgment at all, but merely expresses some "idea" (or "presentation"), namely the idea of "*a* with characteristic *F*":

> In addition it is possible to convert every sentence (*Satz*) into a
> word-complex which is no longer a sentence, but which yet con-

tains everything by way of an object which was, according to traditional interpretation, to be met in the sentence. If I say instead of "This metal is light" simply "this light metal," then everything objective seems to be retained, although the form of a sentence and with it the peculiar function of the sentence is given up.[10]

However, the traditional opinion is mistaken, since we need to distinguish with any judgment two radically different sorts of objects altogether:

We find besides an object *about* which something is judged, or which is *be*-judged (*beurteilt*), yet another which is *judged* (*geurteilt*). . . . Object (*Objekt*) coincides here with what is bejudged, Objective with what is judged. To this extent judgment has not a single object (*Gegenstand*), but rather two, of which each has a claim to be called "object of judgment". If one prefers however, what in fact recommends itself in many ways, to name as the object of judgment that which belongs to judgment in a way which is similar to that in which the object of presentation (*Vorstellungsgegenstand*) belongs to presentation, then exclusively the Objective can be understood by "object of judgment". . . .
    If I look at the snow-covered street and judge as a result "There is snow outside", then "snow" is the object of presentation, the Object (*Objekt*) of this knowledge; besides this, however, "that there is snow" its Objective.[11]

It has been argued, however, that Meinong's Objectives are distinct from the sorts of entities which some philosophers call "propositions":

. . . those philosophers who have discussed a theory of propositions have regarded them as entities which might correspond to or accord with facts, but never as entities which could be identical with facts. As some of Meinong's objectives simply *are* facts, it is clear that it is wrong to identify objectives and propositions.[12]

The word 'fact' is of course sometimes used merely as an equivalent of 'true proposition,' and in this sense there would be no point in claiming that some propositions might be identical with "facts." But Meinong's position goes beyond the claim that true or factual Objectives are identical with facts. He also holds that true or factual Objectives have a different *mode of being* from untrue or non-factual ones.[13] Since even if we did identify true propositions with the "facts," there would be no reason for supposing that untrue propositions were not as real as true ones, Findlay appears to be right in claiming that Meinong's Objectives are distinct both from Objects and from propositions. If that is so, then since judging for Meinong involves the affirmation of Objectives, judging would appear to involve an intentional relation. The Objective, one of the terms of the judging relation, is an entity which might or might not possess a certain mode of being.

If it is Meinong's view that judging involves an intentional relation, then Meinong is systematically committed to granting some sort of genuine ontological status to unfactual Objectives. However, Meinong does not appear willing to do this. He describes unfactual Objectives merely as "pseudo-existing,"[14] but saying that something merely "pseudo-exists" is just saying that there is some *mental act* directed toward it.[15] Meinong even avoids the use of the expression 'Aussersein' in connection with unfactual Objectives, although it is an expression which he freely uses in connection with non-existent (and non-subsistent) Objects.

The question whether, and in what sense, Meinong's view commits him to the admission that there *are* such things as unfactual Objectives naturally parallels the question, more frequently discussed, whether his views commit him to the admission that there are non-existent (and non-subsistent) *Objects*. Meinong explicitly denies that they do; indeed, the expression which he employs to designate the status of such objects ('Aussersein') reflects precisely "the effort to avoid the recourse to a new, third mode of being besides existence and subsistence, in the indication of that strange 'there is' ('es gibt') which it does not seem can be taken away from objects which are the most alien to being."[16] To say that "there are" such objects, then, does not appear to say that merely possible objects do have some kind of being. It would, apparently, be just another way of saying that there are references to or awarenesses *of* such objects: "our grasp . . . finds something given in the objects without concern for how the question of being or non-being is decided. *In this sense* 'there are' ('gibt es') also the objects which are not *(die nicht sind).*"[17] Meinong, however, grants that one might well have misgivings on this point and gives no conclusive argument for the claim that *Aussersein* is not a genuine mode of being.[18]

Meinong's desire to introduce the notion of *Aussersein* naturally arises out of certain views which he holds about *reference* to merely possible entities. Whether or not there really is a golden mountain, for example, reference can be made to such an object and in some sense such an object can be "given" in thought.[19] Whether, similarly, it is really the case that there is a golden mountain, reference can be made to the possibility, the Objective, *that there is a golden mountain*. It does not follow, however, from the circumstance that we can refer to a thing of a certain sort that anything of that sort has being. It does not follow, that is, unless by the "being" of a thing we merely *mean* the possibility of there being references to it. There is no contradiction in Meinong's claim, then, that while we can indeed refer to things which neither exist nor subsist, such things do not occupy any realm of being.

However, a further issue must be considered. Though there is no contradiction in the notion of an imaginary object of reference to which being is altogether lacking, a contradiction may exist in the conjunction of that notion with certain views, which Meinong may also have held, about the *nature* of such reference. Suppose, for example, that in addition to the circumstance that there are propositions containing references to mere possibilities, it is also the case that propositions of that sort are not *analyzable* in terms of propositions which contain no such reference. Then it might seem that we are committed to a realm of merely possible being. The only way to show that we are *not* committed may of course be to show that our reference to possible entities is not essential to our ability to express all of the facts which we express with the help of that reference. However, that we can demonstrate an ability to avoid a commitment to merely possible entities only by analyzing in a certain way propositions which refer to them does not imply that we are committed to possible entities so long as we cannot analyze the propositions which refer to them. It is in fact unclear how our inability to analyze away references to possible entities could have any bearing at all on the question of whether there are such entities, so long as it is granted in the first place that the mere *fact* of reference to possible entities does not by itself have any bearing on that question.[20] If this fact does not imply that we are committed to such entities, then neither could the fact that reference to possible entities is *unavoidable*, unless all that we *meant* by saying that there is some particular thing or sort of thing was that reference to that thing or sort of thing is unavoidable. This would seem to be circular, however, since by "unavoidable" we must mean in this case unavoidable if we are to state all the true propositions which there are, and true propositions can be understood only as those which express all of the facts or states of affairs *which there are*. In addition, if this were all that we meant by "being," then no one could ever object to the view that there are all sorts of possible entities on the ground that this view offends our "sense of reality." The concept of "being" would then be a purely semantical one, and the introduction of possible entities could offend at most some possibly innate "semantical sense."

While it is not clear how a commitment to possible entities is implied by our inability to avoid referring to them, it is clear, nevertheless, that the view that we cannot analyze propositions about possible entities does raise a serious difficulty. It leaves us with a completely unintelligible relation between what a given proposition asserts and the conditions for the *truth* of that proposition. Consider, for example, the proposition that Sherlock Holmes was epileptic. This is a proposition which refers to and says something about a purely fictional character. We have a reasonably clear idea of the sorts of conditions under which the proposition would be a true one. It would be true, for example, if Arthur Conan Doyle had very explicitly said certain things in certain contexts about Sherlock Holmes. But if the proposition that Sherlock Holmes is epileptic cannot be *analyzed as* the proposition that Doyle had said some relevant things, then it is not clear what connection there might be between our understanding of the proposition and of the conditions for its truth. Our understanding of the conditions for the truth of this proposition would be a presupposition of our *understanding* the proposition, though the claim that those conditions obtain is no part of what that proposition *asserts*. This would be similar to the claim, which some have made, that the assumption that there is a present King of France may be a presupposition of certain utterances of the proposition that the present King of France is bald though not a *part* of any such utterance. Whatever difficulty there might be, however, in the notion of a "presupposition," such difficulties would be compounded in this case. Here it is difficult to see what the proposition in question could possibly express *over and above* its own alleged presupposition.

There is, then, some serious difficulty in the claim that while propositions about possible entities are not analyzable in a certain way, yet they do not commit us to a realm of merely possible being. Nevertheless, these difficulties do not center, as is often thought, around some straightforward necessary connection between the concept of being and the concept of reference. Furthermore, Meinong does not make any explicit claims about the analysis of propositions which refer to entities lacking both existence and subsistence. He simply takes pains to insist that we genuinely think about and refer to such entities. Thus it is not clear whether Meinong is committed to denying that propositions about possible entities can be analyzed so as to avoid any reference to such entities.

Meinong's insistence upon our ability to think about and refer to mere possibles might appear to be trivial were he actually prepared to grant the possibility of analyzing away such a reference. But the claim would not be trivial; there have been philosophers who have thought that it followed from the fact that propositions allegedly about certain entities could be analyzed so as to avoid any terms which refer to those entities (as opposed to terms which *describe* them) that the original propositions were not about those entities at all.[21] Furthermore, the claim that 'Sherlock Holmes lives in London' is "about" Sherlock Holmes is at least significant in the sense that it tells us something about the way in which the expression 'Sherlock Holmes' is being used in the proposition in question, that is, in a referential way. This is not an insignificant claim since it contrasts the case with one in which, according to some philosophers, a referential expression is *not* being used in a referential way. It contrasts the case with one in which a referential expression merely occurs as part of some intentional predicate.

It follows that any judgment as to whether Meinong is committed to the admission of a special ontological status for unactualized possibles cannot simply rest on his claim for the status of expressions like 'the golden mountain' in such sentences as 'the golden mountain is golden.' Though Meinong's critics seem almost universally to fail to appreciate this fact, we must instead examine only those cases in which expressions which refer to mere possibles occur as *parts of intentional predicates*. Only if such contexts as these contain genuinely referential occurrences of referring expressions is Meinong clearly committed to the existence of merely possible entities. These contexts would involve that commitment because they would then express an actual *relation* between some thinker and such entities.

This conclusion now leads us to a difficult exegetical point, for Meinong rests his *own* case for the genuineness of our references to, and the "givenness" of, merely possible objects only on the existence of meaningful sentences containing references to unactualized possibles in the *subject* position in the sentence.

However, unlike Brentano, Meinong did not distinguish in any general way between the uses of expressions in intentional and nonintentional contexts. Thus he does not appear to draw any distinction between the roles which are played by *Objectives* in intentional and in nonintentional contexts. He does not appear to distinguish, for example, between the role of the Objective *that there is a golden mountain* in the sentence 'It is the case that there is a golden mountain' and in the sentence 'A judges (supposes, etc.) that there is a golden mountain.'[22] In the former sentence, though not in the latter, the Objective in question is the object of a judgment. In the latter sentence, it is only the Objective *that A judges (supposes, etc.) that there is a golden mountain* which is the object of a judgment. The Objective *that there is a golden mountain* seems, nevertheless, to be an object of some sort in this case as well. While it is not an object which is judged (*geurteilt*), it does seem to be an example, for Meinong, of an object which is judged *about* (*beurteilt*). It seems to be an object about which it is judged, namely, that A judges it.

If Meinong drew no distinction between the use of expressions in intentional and nonintentional contexts, then his view would indeed force an admission of some special ontological status for the objects referred to in such contexts, hence for "Objectives" as the objects of judgment. But if Meinong *is* committed, despite his own disclaimers, to a realm of merely possible being, then this is not as often assumed because of his admission that we really can *refer* to and in some sense be "given" merely possible entities in thought. The commitment rather results from Meinong's admission of certain *relational* contexts, namely intentional predicates, which contain such references. Moreover, the exegetical point can never be as clear in this case as commentators have tended to think, since Meinong's primary motivation for insisting on the possibility of being "given" merely possible entities in thought lies in certain convictions that he has about the possibility of references to such entities in the *subject* position of a proposition. Meinong's paradigm in this regard was, after all, the sentence 'the golden mountain is golden.' Let us take for granted, in any case, that Meinong is in fact committed to the admission of a genuine ontological status for merely possible entities. Then Meinong's theory of judgment requires the introduction of special intentional relations. The object terms of these relations are Meinong's "Objectives."

The fundamental difficulty in Meinong's theory emerges once we realize that, while his Objectives are distinct from what some philosophers have called "propositions," they are also quite unlike "states of affairs": though always "involving" Objects, they nevertheless cannot be regarded as complex entities containing those Objects as constituents.[23] But if Objectives do not "involve" Objects in the sense of literally containing them, that is, being constituted out of them, then, like mere "propositions," they could only be regarded as involving objects in the sense of "referring to" or being "about" them. Therefore, any question that may reasonably be asked concerning the *truth of propositions* about objects must also be reasonable to ask concerning the *factuality of Objectives* which involve those objects. Consider, for example, the judgment that *a* stands in relation *R* to *b*, which involves affirming the Objective *that a stands in relation R to b*.[24] If this Objective is a factual one, then it would seem that there must be some difference in the world *besides* the factuality of that Objective, in the same way that the truth of the proposition that *a* stands in relation *R* to *b* implies that there is in the world not simply that true proposition, but also a state of affairs which *makes* that proposition true. However, while Meinong does distinguish between the relational Objective *that a stands in relation R to b* and the relational *complex a*-in-relation-*R*-to-*b*,[25] Meinong's complex Objects are not the same as relational states of affairs, and he did not regard them as accounting for the factuality of Objectives.

If there is such an object as the complex *a*-in-relation-*R*-to-*b*, then there must of course be some way to distinguish it from the mere collection whose members are *a*, *R*, and *b*. The two are distinct, according to Meinong, in that the complex does not simply contain a certain number of constituents, but it contains those constituents *in a certain connection.* The R stands in a *different* "relation" to those entities in a mere collection. In the former case those entities are actually connected by R. This, however, begins an infinite regress, since we must now introduce an R' in order to speak of the connection between a and b, on the one hand, and R on the other, which allows us to distinguish between the complex and the mere collection.[26] Some philosophers have considered this infinite regress to be a vicious one.[27] As Findlay observes, however, the regress would be vicious only if the original relation did not succeed in relating its terms in the first place, that is, only if the generation of further relational complexes was not simply a *consequence* of the original relation, but rather a prior condition for its obtaining.[28]

Thus to say that a and b stand in relation R to one another is not to say that R *itself* is what accounts for the connection of those terms. If it were, then R's standing in a certain "relation" to a and b (the relation of "connecting" those entities) *would* be a prior condition for the existence of the original complex generated out of a and b, and the infinite regress would be a vicious one. A second alternative would be to suggest that a and b standing in relation R to one another is explained by the three entities a, b, and R forming a complex unity which is not identical with the collection of its constituents. This sort of unity would then presumably be a "state of affairs." On Meinong's view, however, while there is a complex which consists of a, b, and R in a certain connection, so long as a stands in relation R to b in the first place, this is merely one of those complexes which is a generated *consequence* of the original relation obtaining between a and b. The original complex contains a and b in a certain connection, namely standing in relation R, but R is not a constituent of that complex.[29]

The notion of a and b being related by the relation R, therefore, cannot be explicated in terms of the notion of a, b, and R forming a certain complex unity. Nor would it do to suggest that the notion of a and b being related by the relation R might be explicated in terms of the notion of a and b by *themselves* constituting a certain complex object which is not identical with the collection of its constituents. On this sort of account, the very being of such entities as R would be altogether irrelevant to the obtaining of relational facts, and there would be no reason at all for Meinong to have introduced them. Furthermore, if there are such entities as R, then we could not, as this alternative suggests, avoid referring to them in our statements about the obtaining of relations. In order not to say simply that a and b are constituents of a complex because of their connection in some way or other but more precisely because they are constituents of a complex in virtue of standing in relation R, R itself must be clearly referred to.

There is, however, a more important reason why neither of these two alternatives is workable for Meinong. On both of these alternatives, the notion of a and b standing in a certain relation to one another, that is, the notion of a certain relation actually *relating* those terms and not simply co-existing with them in some collection, is to be explicated in terms of the more basic notion of a and b being contained in a certain complex unity which is not identical with the collection of its constituents. But if the distinction between a complex and the collection of all its constituents is to be a basic one, that is, not to be accounted for by appealing to some *other* entity or sort of entity, then complexes would have to be regarded as *categorially different* from the collections of contained objects. Meinong does not regard them in this way.

A complex, in order to be something different from the mere set or collection of certain entities, could not simply be an *additional* entity which contains those others as constituents. In order to distinguish the complex from the collection, it would not even be sufficient to add that the complex is not an object which contains certain others as constituents, but that it is an object which contains certain others *in connection*. To speak of an object which contains certain others "in connection" is ambiguous. It might, for example, refer to a whole whose constituents are entities *which are connected* to one another, but this would not allow us to distinguish between a complex and a mere collection, since the collection whose members are *a* and *b* is just as much a "mere" collection whether *a* is connected with *b* or not. To speak of an entity which contains its constituents "in connection," however, might be not to speak simply of an object whose constituents are connected, but rather to speak precisely of *the connection* among those constituents—of those constituents *being connected*. A connection among objects may itself be an object of awareness, hence in this respect the complex would be an object in addition to its constituents. But it would be of a categorially different sort, since its very "mode of being" would differ from that of the objects which it contains; the *being* of a complex would be nothing but the *being connected* of its constituents. The only way to distinguish, therefore, between a complex and the mere collection of its constituents, in terms of its intrinsic nature, is to recognize that the two are categorially different sorts of entities.

This categorial difference is also reflected in other ways: there are some properties that mere collections have which cannot be ascribed to states of affairs. The collection whose members are *a* and Green, for example, is smaller than one whose members are *a*, *b*, and *To-the-left-of*. But the state of affairs of *a* being Green is not smaller than the state of affairs of *a* being to the left of *b*, nor does it make any sense to wonder whether the latter is smaller than the former. There are also descriptions of states of affairs which do not apply to collections. For example, some are lucky or unlucky accidents. But while the *existence* of a certain collection might be a lucky or unlucky accident, it is nonsensical to say this about the collection itself.

However, Meinong's complexes are not categorially distinct from collections. Since they are all complex *Objects*,[30] and not simply complex objects, they are categorially distinct from Objectives, but they are *not* categorially distinguished from the Objects which Objectives involve, hence from a mere *collection* of such Objects. The distinction, therefore, between the being of a Meinongian complex and the being of a mere collection of the constituents of that complex is not one which could be drawn because of the very "natures" of the entities which are involved, without appeal to any further ontological ground for the distinction. Accordingly, the existence of a certain complex which contains *a* and *b* as constituents could not be what accounts for *a* and *b* standing in a certain relation to one another.

Only one alternative appears to remain: the claim that *a* and *b* stand in relation *R* is not to be explicated in terms of the notion of a and b, or of a, b, and R, being contained in a certain complex which is not identical with the mere collection of its constituents. Rather, to say that a, b, and R are contained in some complex, and not in a mere collection, hence that a and b are really related by R, is just to say that the Objective *that a and b stand in relation R* is a *factual* Objective. The being of complex unities, in other words, is not a *basic* fact for Meinong, but rather something to be explicated in terms of the notion of factual Objectives of certain sorts.[31] It follows, however, that there is no sense in which we may ask what *makes* any such Objective a factual one, that is, what accounts for its factuality. If there were something which could make the Objective *that a stands in relation R to b* a factual one, it could only be a certain complex which contains a and b in a certain connection. But saying that such an entity exists is for Meinong only *another way* of saying that the Objective in question is factual.

This exposes the main difficulty in Meinong's theory of judgment. Despite the fact that Objectives, which are the proper objects of judgment for Meinong, are not the same thing as what some philosophers call "propositions," his view is tantamount to the claim that there is no sense in which the truth of a given proposition involves the coming into being of something *in addition to* that true proposition. If the Objective that *a and b stand in relation R* is a factual one, then of course there is a certain complex object which there would not otherwise have been, but to say that "there is" this object is to have added nothing at all to the original claim. This view may seem less objectionable than it actually is, for it is easy to confuse with the more modest claims which have been made on behalf of the so-called redundancy theory of truth. On that theory, to say that a's being to the left of b is something "true" or "factual" is simply *another way* of saying that a is to the left of b. There is no ultimate difference between judgments of the truth or factuality of relational statements and the assertion of those statements themselves. In this sense, judgments of truth or factuality would be "redundant." However, Meinong's view is not that judgments about truth or factuality are redundant because they do not add anything to the claim that certain objects exist. Rather, the claim that certain *objects* exist is redundant because it adds nothing to the claim that certain judgments are true, that is, the Objectives which are their objects are factual. It seems to me that this view is not a coherent one.

Although it is not always made clear by commentators, this view follows from Meinong's claims about the *Aussersein* of "pure objects." That the "pure object" is *ausserseiend* is sometimes taken simply to mean that an object may be considered purely as object of reference without the need for any stand at all concerning the being or non-being of that object: "The doctrine that the 'pure object' is 'indifferent to being' (*ausserseiend*) is best viewed as simply recognizing in a rather 'pretentious' way such things as that the subject term of a subject-predicate proposition may very well denote something that does not exist, e.g., Santa Claus."[32] On this interpretation, Meinong's claim that the "pure object" is *ausserseiend* is only about objects *qua* objects of reference. Thus it is not really a claim about objects at all, but rather a claim only about our *references* to objects. This interpretation may appear to be confirmed by the fact that Meinong generally uses the word '*Gegenstand*' when he talks about the *Aussersein* of "objects," which suggests the notion of an "object" not as any particular sort of entity, but as something which "stands over against" our awareness of it. His interest appears to be not in the objects themselves but in their being presented to awareness. On other occasions, however, Meinong formulates a doctrine of *Aussersein* which is explicitly limited to Objects, that is, *Objekte*, rather than to objects (*Gegenstände*) in general. The very contrast, according to Meinong, between the being and non-being of Objects is "in the first place the affair of the Objective and not of the Object."[33] In other words, to say that some Object exists or that it subsists is really to say something *about a certain Objective*. The claim that something is *ausserseiend*, or "indifferent to being," is thus not just a claim about the awareness of or reference to objects and the ontological implications of that awareness or reference. It rather requires a *contrast* between one sort of object of awareness or reference and a very different sort of object, a contrast between Objects and Objectives: the claim that "der reine Gegenstand stehe 'jenseits von Sein und Nichtsein'" could be more properly put, according to Meinong, "der Gegenstand ist von Natur ausserseiend, obwohl von seinen beiden Seinsobjektiven, seinen Sein und seinem Nichtsein, jedenfalls eines besteht."[34]

The claim that objects are *ausserseiend* may thus be taken in two different ways. In one way it is simply that objects may be objects of awareness or reference whether or not they have any being at all, and in this sense the claim is one which applies both to Objects and Objectives. Meinong speaks of an object "pseudo-existing" to designate something being an object of awareness, although he notes that the pseudo-existence of an object is really no sort of existence of an object at all and that one might therefore prefer some other term.[35] The word '*Aussersein*', suggesting not a third mode of being in addition to existence and subsistence, but simply some sort of "indifference" to being altogether, was chosen to serve this purpose, though even after the introduction of this term Meinong appeared to prefer to speak of a "pseudo-existing" rather than an *ausserseiendes* Objective.[36] The explanation would presumably be that the claim that objects are *ausserseiend* may also be taken in another way, in which that claim applies to Objects but not to Objectives at all. This is the claim that the affirmation of an Object's being or non-being is just the affirmation of the Objective *that this object is* or the Objective *that this object is not*. As Meinong recognized, if this claim were extended to include Objectives themselves, a vicious infinite regress would arise. Affirming the being of some Object would be affirming a certain Objective *O* which "involves" that Object, but affirming the Objective *O*, as opposed to merely assuming or supposing it, would in its turn be the affirming of a higher Objective *O'* which involves the Objective *O ad infinitum*. Hence while an Object is said to become an existing or a subsisting one in virtue of the factuality (i.e., subsistence) of some Objective which involves it, "no Objective *becomes* factual precisely through, or *is* factual in virtue of, Objectives of higher order; it must carry its factuality within itself."[37] In this sense, Objects but not Objectives are "indifferent to being."

It is important to see that this second sense in which an object may be *ausserseiend* differs from some more modest claims which may be confused with it. The claim that Objectives, but not Objects, may carry their being "in themselves" ought not to be confused with the claim that no Object exists or subsists of necessity, while some Objectives do subsist of necessity. The claim that Objects are *ausserseiend* applies to the being *and* the non-being of Objects, and Meinong does at least grant that some Objects necessarily fail to exist or subsist.[38] Second, this claim should not be confused with the claim that existence (or subsistence) is not a predicate. Although the former claim might have the latter as a consequence, the former is a much stronger claim. The denial that existence is a predicate requires us to distinguish between propositions such as 'Philosophers exist' and propositions such as 'Philosophers are wise.' If the latter may be construed as ascribing some predicate to some object or sort of object, the former may not. But it does not follow that either sort of judgment is the ascribing of factuality to some Objective, although this may be the case for the related propositions 'The existence of philosophers is factual' and 'The wisdom of philosophers is factual.' We might agree that existence is not a property which philosophers might have in the same way that they have wisdom, and yet adopt the position that existential judgments merely involve the "affirmation" or "positing" of particular objects or sorts of objects, rather than the affirmation of objectives. Kant, for example, appears to adopt something like this view:

> "Being" is obviously not a real predicate; that is, it is not a concept of something which could be added to the concept of a thing. It is merely the positing (*Position*) of a thing, or of certain determinations, as existing in themselves. . . . If, now we take the subject (God) with all its predicates (among which is omnipotence), and say "God is," or "There is a God," we attach no new predicate to the concept of God, but only posit (*setze ich*) the subject in itself with all its predicates.[39]

One might wonder what it *is* to "posit" some given object, but one need not adopt Brentano's view that positing or affirming some object is a primitive act. For example, we might simply construe the positing of some object or sort of object as asserting a connection between certain universals, say, a connection between the universal Being-God and the universal Being-instantiated. The state of affairs which is Being-God instantiating Being-instantiated, that is, the state of affairs of there being a God, would not then be the same sort of thing as Meinong's Objective *that Being-God instantiates Being-instantiated*, since the former involves certain universals as constituents, whereas the latter would involve them only in the sense of being "about" or "referring" to them.

Thus Meinong's claim that Objects are *ausserseiend*, or "indifferent" to their own being and non-being, seems not the same as the claim that existence is not a real predicate. Indeed, Meinong appeared to grant that existence *is* a genuine predicate. In order to avoid the force of Russell's objection that if the "existing round square" is a genuine object, then one is committed to contradictory objects which exist, Meinong did not reply that "existing" was not a property which could be treated just like others. Rather, he granted that the existing round square is existing, and simply denied that it exists![40] Existence may, in other words, be a predicate among the other predicates of an Object; it is simply that existential judgments do not involve the ascription of such predicates to Objects. Rather, they involve the affirmation of, that is, the ascription of factuality or subsistence to, Objectives.

An examination of Meinong's doctrine of *Aussersein*, then, confirms our judgment that, despite the difference in the ontological status of unfactual Objectives and untrue propositions, his view claims that the truth of the proposition that *a* is in relation *R* to *b*, does not involve the coming into being of anything besides that true proposition, and *in virtue of which* that proposition would be a true one. While he does distinguish between the Objective *that a is in relation R to b* and a complex which contains *a* and *b* in a certain connection and is there only if the Objective is a factual one, that complex is a complex Object, and hence it is "indifferent to being." But this simply means that the existence of such an Object is *nothing more than* the factuality of the Objective.

It is now possible to apply this point to our earlier discussion of intentional relations in Meinong. He appeared to regard the awareness of objects as involving a distinctive intentional relation with those objects. Yet since he also saw no compelling reason for granting a genuine ontological status to all of the objects of awareness, his view appears to involve a contradiction. It should now be possible to see why Meinong would not have recognized this. As argued earlier, the claim that all relational "facts" require the being of all the terms which are involved in those facts will be self-evident only if we *distinguish* between relational facts in the sense of true relational propositions and in the sense of relational states of affairs. However, Meinong was unable to do justice to this distinction.

Any workable account of judgment as involving a distinctive intentional relation must thus regard that relation's object term as the sort of entity known here as a "state of affairs." Such an entity differs from what philosophers sometimes call a "proposition" and is the sort of entity which we must regard as *accounting* for the truth or falsity of propositions in the first place. Since Meinong's theory of judgment takes judging to involve intentional relations with entities which are very different from states of affairs, it was necessary to subject his theory to a rather close examination. The result of the examination confirms our original conclusion regarding the need for a special category of "states of affairs."

The view that judgment involves an intentional relation with "states of affairs" is defended by Gustav Bergmann, though he calls such entities "facts." Bergmann believes that there must be some relation between every mental act and the fact which that act intends. If there were not such a relation, there would be no way of "keeping minds and their intentions from falling apart," and we would be on the road to idealism.[41] Bergmann clearly grants, however, what Meinong appeared to deny, that there can be no relation at all between a thought and the fact which that thought intends, so long as there *is* no such fact for that thought to be related to in the first place.[42] Hence every belief is related to a fact which exists: true beliefs are related to actual facts and false beliefs are related to merely possible ones.[43] But what *is* a merely possible fact, and what distinguishes it from an actual one? It can be shown that if facts are to be distinguished from propositions as well as from Meinongian Objectives, then it is not possible to distinguish between actual and merely possible facts in such a way as to allow for a conception of judgment as involving a relation with facts.

Consider the fact that a is F. If this fact is something distinct from the true proposition that a is F, then it could only be construed as a complex entity, call it a-being-F, of which two of the constituents are a and F standing in a certain connection.[44] Bergmann would call this sort of connection the "nexus of exemplification."[45] It is clear that there can *be* no such fact, whether actual or merely possible, as a-being-F, so long as there is no such connection tying a with F, although, apart from such a connection, it might of course still be *possible* for there to be such a fact. Hence the distinction between the actual and the merely possible facts in this case cannot be due to the presence or absence of a connection between a and F. Accordingly, there are two alternatives for distinguishing them:

1. The possible fact that a is F is one in which a is connected with F by exemplification in the mode of possibility (exemplification$_p$); the actual fact is one in which they are connected by exemplification in the mode of actuality (exemplification$_a$).

2. The two different modes of the fact that a is F are a feature of those very facts as a *whole* and not simply a function of two distinct modes of the tie which connects their constituents.

On the first alternative, we need to distinguish between the two modes of a-being-F: a-being$_a$-F and a-being$_p$-F. When a is not in fact F, only the latter of these two complexes could exist, and this one would in that case be the object of the judgment that a is F. However, this alternative is unacceptable, since believing that a is F is clearly not the same thing as believing that a is *possibly* F. It would seem that if there is any fact which is the object of my intention in this case, it must be the fact of a's being$_a$ F, and not the fact of a's being$_p$ F. If it were the latter which comprised the object of my judgment, then I would not be judging that a is F at all, but only that a is possibly F. Only the latter fact, however, could exist when a is not actually F, that is, when my judgment is a mistaken one. Therefore, when a is not actually F, my thought that a is F could not involve an intentional relation with the fact which is the object of my judgment.

It might be thought that this criticism of alternative 1 rests on too ungenerous an interpretation of that alternative. My argument has been that if merely possible facts are complexes tied by a merely possible nexus of exemplification, then since mistaken judgment often involves, if it involves the intending of facts at all, the intending of actual facts (i.e., of complexes tied by actual exemplification), the admission of merely possible facts would be irrelevant to such cases. They would be complexes whose constituents are connected in a manner distinguished from that intended in our judgments. But it might be objected that this conclusion rests on an assumption which is not implied by the admission that the two modes of facts, actuality and mere possibility, are a function of two distinct modes of the connection which ties things into facts, namely of actual and merely possible exemplification. It does not follow from this admission, it might be argued, that exemplification$_p$ is a different way of connecting the constituents of a complex from exemplification$_a$. The only difference is in their *ontological status*. Thus exemplification$_a$ and exemplification$_p$ are not two different ontological ties at all, but they are rather the very *same* tie in two different modes of existence.

This objection would be an intelligible one only on the assumption that the connection among the constituents of a fact is itself an entity in addition to the constituents which are to be connected in that fact. Unless the connection between *a* and *F* is itself a real entity, it is nonsensical to distinguish two different modes of that connection from two distinct modes of the *existence* of that connection. In Bergmann's world, this condition happens to be fulfilled: the fact that *a* is *F* contains three constituents and not just two, one of those constituents being the nexus of exemplification itself.[46]

We need to consider, then, the collection of entities (*a*, *F*, *n*), where the third of the entities in this collection is to be assigned the task of connecting the other two into a complex whole. Now either the very nature of *n* will be such that to speak of *n* will be to speak of *some* connection among the constituents of *some* complex; or else it will be such that to speak of *n* is to speak in *particular* of a connection between *a* and *F*. If the former is the case, then no problem about the connecting of entities into complexes could possibly have been solved by appealing to such an entity as *n*. Since *n* would be as indifferent in its nature to *a* and *F* as these are to one another, it would be no easier to generate a single entity out of the three of them than it was to generate *a*-being-*F* from the mere collection of *a* and *F* alone. Hence another entity *n'* will be needed, and we have begun a vicious infinite regress. In order to avoid this regress, Bergmann draws a categorial distinction between entities such as *a* and *F* and entities such as *n*. The latter have by their very nature a radical *dependence* upon other entities, whereas the former are independent of one another and of any other entities. This categorial difference between *n* and the entities which it connects is what allows *n* to connect them without the help of any further entities; the regress may thus be stopped at *n*.[47]

However, it can mean two very different things to appeal to a radical and categorial dependence on the part of such entities as *n*. It could simply mean that it is in the very nature of such entities as *n* to be a connection among other entities, and that to conceive of *n* is thus already to conceive of it in terms of entities different from itself. Or it could mean that it is in the very nature of *n* to exist only as a connection between *a* and *F* *in particular*. Only the latter alternative appears relevant to the problem of our infinite regress. If it is not in the very nature of *n* to connect *a* and *F*, then either it is impossible to see why *n* should need nothing further in order to bring it into "relation" with these entities, or else it is impossible to see why *n* itself was needed in order to bring *a* and *F* into "relation" with one another in the first place.

But if this is what the claim must come to that *n* is a radically "dependent" sort of entity, then it is not evident what difference there could be between referring to such an entity as *n* and referring to the complex *a*-being-*F* itself. The sort of dependence which is being attributed to the former seems to be precisely that which must be attributed to the latter of these entities: *a*-being-*F* by its very nature is dependent upon the entities which it combines into a whole. It will not help to point out that *n* must clearly be something different from the complex *a*-being-*F*, on the ground that n is by supposition a *constituent* of that complex. This is just the point at issue; the question is simply whether to refer to such an entity as a nexus and to refer to such an entity as a-being-F is in fact to refer to two different sorts of entities, one of them a constituent of the other, or whether it is not rather to refer in two different ways to one and the same entity—a fact—one merely emphasizing the "fact" that it is a fact and not a mere collection of entities, and the other emphasizing its radical dependence upon the members of a particular collection of entities. Some further argument is needed in order to establish that a nexus is a constituent of some fact rather than simply the fact itself conceived under the aspect of its radically dependent nature. Indeed, while the sort of dependence which is in question here seems to be the sort which attaches to complexes themselves, it is not at all clear how that very same dependence upon the constituents of a complex *could* also infect one of the constituents of that complex.

Since it appears to be the notion of dependence alone which legitimizes the introduction of nexus, one might simply conclude that no distinction can in fact be drawn between n and the complex a-being-F. It would not, for example, be helpful to insist that there can be no such thing in the first place as the fact that a and F are connected unless there is also such a thing as the *connection* between a and F. That amounts only to the claim that there must be something in the world beside the entities a and F if a is in fact to be F. That would appear to be a requirement which is met simply by the presence in the world of a-being-F itself. It might be argued, however, that even if we were only concerned with a, F, and a-being-F, we could still not avoid introducing some nexus in addition to these entities. When a is F there are also such facts as a-being-a-constituent-of-(a-being-F), and each of these facts will presumably have constituents of its own. Though the sort of infinite regress which would arise in this way may not be a vicious one, it might neverthe-less appear to show the impossibility of avoiding nexus as something contained within facts. If we do not admit a nexus of exemplification, we must at least admit the nexus *being-a-constituent-of*. However, while there may have been some temp-tation to construe exemplification as an entity contained in facts, there is hardly the same temptation to construe being a constituent of some fact as also a constituent of that fact.[48] In any case, even if there is a nexus *being-a-constituent-of*, this would not help us to solve the problem of the *modality* of facts, since it makes no sense to speak of a or F as sometimes actually, and at other times only potentially, being a constituent of a-being-F, so long as there is such a thing as a-being-F.

Furthermore, even if we could distinguish between the connection n among the constituents of a-being-F and the fact itself which contains the entity n, we would still be in no position to deal with the problem of intentionality, even if we could deal in a satisfactory way with the problem of the modality of facts. If there is such an entity as n, it must at least be granted that it is in the very *nature* of that entity that it connect a with F. If it were not, then n could conceivably fail to connect a and F and the appeal to n will have had no point. But this is to say that the entity n is *nothing but* a connecting of a with F, for if it were only one *part* of n to be connecting a with F, then we would simply have our original problem all over again in connecting the two parts of n with one another and with the other constituents of *a*-being-*F*. Consequently, there could be no distinction between the modes of being of such an entity as *n* and the modes of connection between such entities as *a* and *F*. If it makes any sense at all to distinguish the different ways in which *a* and *F* are connected from the different ways in which a connection between *a* and *F* might exist, then the ways in which they are connected must be something which is in itself indifferent to their actual connection and in that case the infinite regress has not been avoided.

Thus the first of our two alternatives for distinguishing actual from merely possible facts must be abandoned. On this alternative, the distinction involves differentiating two modes of the connection uniting entities into a fact, while on the second alternative the distinction involves a fact as a whole and not merely the nature of the connection among the entities in it. If, however, we cannot *distinguish* between the connection among the entities in a fact and the fact itself which consists in a connection among those entities, then the first alternative simply reduces to the second. But even if we can make this distinction, we still cannot distinguish between two different modes of connection among the constituents of a fact and two different modes of *being* of one and the same connection, and this is a distinction which is needed if the first alternative is to provide an account of merely possible facts which is also consistent with an account of judgment as involving a distinctive intentional relation with facts.

On our second alternative, the distinction between the actuality and the mere potentiality of facts is not to be accounted for in terms of two different modes of connection in facts at all. Thus whether *a*-being-*F* is an actual or a merely possible fact, *a* and *F* must be connected in it in precisely the same way. But while this alternative might be possible on the conception of facts which some philosophers have held, it cannot be adopted if facts are regarded as "states of affairs." The feature which distinguishes states of affairs from propositions or Meinongian Objectives is that states of affairs actually *contain* the entities which are "involved" in them. This, in turn, requires a distinction between a state of affairs and the mere *collection* of the entities which are its constituents, which finally brings with it a categorial distinction between any fact and the entities of which it is constituted. The latter are independent, while the former is radically *dependent* upon the latter. But what does this difference amount to which distinguishes a fact from the mere collection of the entities which are its constituents? It could only be that a fact consists precisely in a *connecting of those entities* into a complex whole. There are only two ways to distinguish between the mere collection of some entities and the fact that those entities are connected. Either the fact, unlike the collection, does not literally contain those entities at all, but at most corresponds with or refers to their connection. Or the fact, while literally containing those entities, also consists in a *connection* among them. Yet, how can we distinguish between an entity's "consisting in" a connection among others and an entity's *being* that very connection? If the fact that *a* and *F* is *not* a connecting of *a* with *F*, then it cannot both contain those entities as constituents and also be more than a mere collection of those entities. The conception of facts as complex wholes distinct from the mere collections of their constituents thus requires a categorial distinction between facts and the entities which they contain, such that while the latter are things to be connected, a fact just *is* a connecting of them in one particular way or another.

Therefore, there is no distinction which attaches to a state of affairs, as distinct from its constituents, which could not be reduced to a distinction between the ways in which entities are connected into a state of affairs, since the latter simply *is* a connecting of entities and nothing else. But I have already argued that while a theory of possible facts might be adopted which rests on a distinction between modes of connection within facts, no such theory could allow for an account of judgment as involving a distinctive intentional relation with facts. Thus the first of our two alternatives provides for an account of possible facts which is consistent with our conception of facts as states of affairs, but inconsistent with the conception of judgmental intending as a relation to facts. The second of our two alternatives presents an account of possible facts which does not even appear to be consistent with a conception of facts as states of affairs. We must conclude, then, that if facts are distinguished from propositions and from Meinongian Objectives, it is not possible to provide an account of judgment as involving a distinctive intentional relation with facts.

Russell's Theory of Judgment

This chapter has been considering some attempts to account for the intentional features of psychological states in terms of special psychological relations which are in themselves "intentional," that is, which are such that some of their terms may be merely possible entities while their other terms are actual. In the case of judgment, the most natural suggestion appears to involve the introduction of actual and merely possible "states of affairs" as the object terms of those relations. What makes this suggestion a natural one is that a judgment is always a judgment *that* something is the case. However, while this kind of suggestion regarding judgment has not proved to be a tenable one, it does not follow that the intentional features of judgments cannot be accounted for in terms of certain special judgmental relations. Some have suggested, for example, that judging involves a relation with certain entities called "propositions." On such an account judging would not involve any special *intentional* relation, but it would presumably involve some relation which is unique and peculiar to the case of judgment (which is not to say that only judgments may stand in relation to propositions). It has been argued in this chapter that states of affairs and the constituents they involve, and not propositions *about* those constituents, are the proper objects of judgment. Therefore, we will not discuss in this chapter the ontological issues raised by the notion of a "proposition." However, in Chapter 4, a distinction will be made between the "contents" and the objects of psychological states, and the thesis will be offered that at least some of the intentional features of psychological states are to be accounted for in terms of the presence of certain "mental contents" in those states, rather than in terms of certain relations involving their objects. In that connection we may consider the notion of a "proposition," which properly falls on the "content" side of this dichotomy. Our considerations are restricted in this chapter to attempts to account for the intentional features of psychological states by appealing to special psychological relations with the sorts of entities that are the proper *objects* of those states.

As the above comments indicate, insofar as states of affairs are among the proper objects of judgment, it follows that their *constituents* will also be among the proper objects of judgment. Judgments about states of affairs are judgments about the sorts of entities which are properly their constituents, namely particulars and their properties and relations. Thus it is reasonable to consider attempts to account for the intentional features of judgment by appeal to special psychological relations with the possible *constituents* of states of affairs. Our primary consideration will be directed toward the sort of theory that Bertrand Russell has defended.

Regarding the objects of distinctive judgmental relations not as states of affairs but rather as the possible constituents of states of affairs does not imply that judging involves any properly *intentional* relations. To speak of "possible constituents" of states of affairs may not be to speak of entities which might or might not happen to be actual. It may simply be to speak of actually existing entities which might or might not happen to constitute certain states of affairs. On such a view, for example, to talk about a "possible red object" would only be to talk about some object's possibly *being red*, hence to talk about a possible state of affairs involving some object. Though on Russell's theory, the notion of a "possible constituent" of a state of affairs may be construed in this way, there have been philosophers who have regarded the proper objects of judgment as "possible objects" in a more literal sense. Since I have already argued for the defensibility of the notion of an intentional relation involving properties or relations which may or may not be instantiated by anything, I find no difficulty in principle for the admission of intentional relations with such objects. However, while on Russell's view judging involves distinctive relations with universals, he does not regard these as truly *intentional* relations: uninstantiated universals are as fully "real" as instantiated ones for Russell.

Though Russell does not tolerate the notion of a "possible particular," there of course have been philosophers who have taken the notion seriously. Brentano, for example, regarded possible particulars as the proper objects of judgment, and rejected any attempt to consider such "non-entities" as states of affairs as among the proper objects of judgment. Others, such as Hintikka, at least argue for the importance of reference to merely possible particulars for the elucidation of the concept of belief.[49] However, Brentano did not take psychological states to involve a *relation* of any sort with possible particulars, and it is difficult to see what plausibility there could be in maintaining such a view of judgment.[50] We may therefore turn directly to a consideration of the Russellian view.

On Russell's theory, judgment always does involve a relation between some believer and the objects of his belief, but it involves a relation neither with possible particulars nor with possible facts. The judgment that *a* is *F*, for example, would not require a relation, on Russell's account, between some believer and a possible *a* which is F, nor would it require a relation between some believer and the possible fact of a's being F. Rather it requires a relation only with the *constituents* of that would-be fact:

> The relation involved in *judging* or *believing* must, if falsehood is to be duly allowed for, be taken to be a relation between several terms, not between two. When Othello believes that Desdemona loves Cassio, he must not have before his mind a single object, "Desdemona's love for Cassio," or "that Desdemona loves Cassio," for that would require that there should be objective falsehoods, which subsist independently of any minds. . . . Thus it is easier to account for falsehood if we take judgment to be a relation in which the mind and the various objects concerned all occur severally; that is to say, Desdemona and loving and Cassio must all be terms in the relation which subsists when Othello believes that Desdemona loves Cassio. This relation, therefore, is a relation of four terms, since Othello also is one of the terms of the relation.[51]

Though judging, for Russell, thus involves not a relation to some fact which is the object of a judgment, but rather a relation only to the entities which would be that fact's constituents, it does not involve a relation merely between a believer and the *collection* of those constituents. As Russell grants, every judgment aims at some sort of unity or "knitting together" of such constituents.[52] The judgment that a is F, for example, does not simply affirm the existence of the collection whose members are a and F, since that is a collection which might exist even if a were not F. What this judgment affirms is rather an actual *connection* between the two members of this collection. Hence the judgment is not of the form 'x affirms (y, z),' but rather of the form 'x affirms that y is z,' in other words, the judgment is in this case a three- rather than a two-term relation. The judgment, similarly, that a is to the left of b must be a four-term relation of the form 'w affirms that x is y with respect to z.'

The virtue of Russell's account is that it provides for the relation of judging a set of actually existing terms even when a judgment is a mistaken one. Hence it preserves a relational analysis of judging without requiring merely possible facts or states of affairs. When combined with Russell's theory of descriptions, his account of judging also avoids any commitment to merely possible particulars. Consider, for example, the judgment that the King of France is bald, which, as Meinong would insist, is clearly a judgment about some imaginary king. To judge that the King of France is bald would, on Russell's account, simply be to judge that there is one and only one x which is a king of France, and that this thing is bald. Hence the judgment involves a relation simply between some believer and the properties Being-a-king-of-France and Being-bald. That is, it involves a three-term relation of the form 'x believes y to be instantiated uniquely by an instance of z.'

It is worth noting that if Russell's theory is correct, then there are no intentional relations involved in judgment even though judging does involve a relation and even though it may continue to satisfy the criterion for being something intentional. It does not follow from the fact that someone affirms that a is F either that a is or is not F; hence affirming is intentional. But while affirming is also a relation for Russell, it is nevertheless no intentional relation, for none of its terms is an entity which might or might not exist and yet still remain as a term of that relation. This is important since it brings out the very great difficulty which is encountered whenever we attempt to draw conclusions of some ontological force merely from observations about language. There is no reason for Russell to grant that 'affirms that a is F' is a predicate which can somehow be entirely avoided in our descriptions of actual judgments. But whether this would commit us to some peculiar sort of relation depends not just upon whether that predicate is or is not reducible, but also upon what sort of *entities* we take that predicate to designate. Whether that predicate designates a two-term relation involving some possible fact or a three-term relation involving only the constituents of that fact is a question whose answer could not follow directly from the admission that the predicate is unavoidable in our descriptions of certain mental phenomena.

The primary difficulty in Russell's account of judgment is that while he rightly attempts to account for the fact that judgment involves some sort of "knitting together" of its objects, he simply does not succeed in this effort. As he grants, judging that Desdemona loves Cassio involves something more than a relation which a believer has to *each* of the terms in the judgment; it involves rather a relation "to *all* of them together."[53] Judging that Desdemona loves Cassio, after all, involves more than affirming (the existence of) Desdemona, loving, and Cassio, although it does involve this at least in part. But what the judgment appears to involve, in addition to this, is precisely the affirmation of some *connection* between these terms. Hence the unity or "knitting together" which every judgment involves is, contrary to Russell's view, a unity *within the object* of the affirmation which every (affirmative) judgment involves. If judging does involve a relation with any objects at all, then it is this feature which would distinguish the sort of unity which judgment involves from the unity which is involved in other sorts of relations.

Considering, for example, the three-term relation "x gives y to z," we must grant that any instance of this relation does involve a unity or a "knitting together" of all three terms and not simply a relation which one of those terms would bear either to each of the other two terms or to the pair of the other two terms considered as a single entity. However, this sort of unity is very different from the kind of unity which a judgment involves. The difference is reflected in our ability to express any ordinary relational judgments of more than two terms with the aid of various prepositions. Thus that a gives b to c, for example, may be put by saying that a is a giver *of b to c*. The case of a judgment is very different. For example, the proposition that a believes that b is F cannot be expressed simply by saying that a is an affirmer of b in some relation to F, where the relation is one which could be expressed merely with the help of a certain preposition. Precisely what needs to be said is that a is an affirmer of b's *being F*. This shows, however, that there are two very different conceptions of unity involved in our conception of an act of judging. There is whatever unity obtains between a believer and the individual terms which comprise the objects of his affirmation, but in addition there is the conception of a unity among those terms *themselves*. It is the affirmation of the latter which distinguishes a judgment from the mere affirmation of a collection of isolated terms, and it seems impossible to collapse these two different sorts of unity into a single relation involving a believer and the members of such a collection.[54]

The extent of this difficulty in Russell's account of judgment may also be seen by observing his attempts to define the notion of truth with respect to judgments. We ought, presumably, not to require a different notion of truth for each of the different possible logical forms of judgment; hence we could not define the truth of a judgment in the following way:

1. x's believing y to be z is true if, and only if, y is z.
2. x's believing w to be y with respect to z is true if, and only if, w is y with respect to z.

. . .

Russell therefore undertakes to generalize the notion of a true judgment. To do this, he points out that any relation places its terms in a certain "order"; thus in the relation of a's giving b to c we are given an order—say $G(a,b,c)$—such that the judgment that a gives b to c is a true one if and only if a, b, and c are not only related by G, but related in the correct order. Similarly, according to Russell, the relation of *judging* involves the relating of terms in a certain order. If, for example, I assert that a believes that b is F, then I assert not merely some relation of believing which involves a, b, and F as its terms, but also a relating of those terms in a certain definite order. The judgment that a judges that b is F will be true only if a judges b to be F, not if b judges a to be F. We may, then, define truth in the following manner:

> Judging or believing is a certain complex unity of which a mind is
> a constituent; if the remaining constituents, taken in *the order*
> *which they have in the belief,* form a complex unity then the belief
> is true; if not, it is false.[55]

Consider, for example, a's believing that b is to the left of c. Since the relation of judging or believing, like any other relation, places its terms in a certain order, we may express this order in a definite way, say, $B(a,b,L,c)$. Then we may say that the belief is true in case there actually exists a complex unity comprising b, L, and c—that is, all the remaining terms of the belief "after" the believer himself—ordered in the same way that they are ordered in the belief itself, that is, $L(b,c,)$ rather than $L(c,b)$.

But Russell has confused two very different problems concerning the ordering of terms "in the belief," for there are two very different senses in which a relation may be involved "in the belief." There is the sense in which believing *itself* may be a certain relation, but there is also the sense in which *what is believed* may involve a relation. Considering again the judgment that b is to the left of c, if Russell is correct, there is a definite order required by the believing relation, but there is also a definite order required by the relation Being-to-the-left-of.[56] As he observes, we do of course *include* this latter ordering in our conception of the former, hence we write '$B(a,b,L,c)$' to express that a believes b to be to the left of c, rather than c to be to the left of b. We could, however, include this order which Being-to-the-left-of might involve in our conception of the order which a certain believing relation might involve only because we already know that *what is believed* involves a state of affairs in which b is to the left of c rather than c to the left of b. Hence it is only because we *already know* that belief involves the affirmation of terms ordered in a certain way that we are able to construe believing as itself a relation involving one definite order rather than another. Therefore, while the truth of judgments may be defined in terms of the existence of complex unities connected in the order in which those terms occur "in the judgment," the notion of such an order among terms as actually connected by a relation of believing or judging should be clearly *derivative* from the notion of an intended connection among terms which *may or may not* actually be connected in the order which is intended.

While we may then deny that believing involves a relation between some believer and the unitary fact which is the object of his belief, and maintain that believing is rather a relation only to the constituents of that would-be fact, we cannot at the same time deny that such a unitary fact *is* a genuine object of belief. While Russell may thus be right in denying that Othello's belief that Desdemona loves Cassio involves a relation one of whose terms is "Desdemona's love for Cassio" or "that Desdemona loves Cassio," he cannot be correct in maintaining that "When Othello believes that Desdemona loves Cassio, he must not *have before his mind* a single object, 'Desdemona's love for Cassio,' or 'that Desdemona loves Cassio.'" Consequently, we cannot avoid granting that judging does involve the intending of objects, or the having of objects "before the mind," even though it may involve no relation at all with such objects. But once it is granted, as it certainly must be, that the intending of an object in judgment is not dependent upon an actual *relation* involving an intended object, then it is difficult to see why one ought to consider a judgment to involve *any* relation with objects at all. This last point, however, calls for an important distinction.

Russell took it for granted that the sentence 'Othello believes that Desdemona loves Cassio' is to be taken as ascribing to Othello what has been called a psychological attitude *"de re."*[57] What we are saying is that Othello believes *of* (the person who happens to be) Desdemona and *of* (the person who happens to be) Cassio that the one loves the other, and this involves asserting some relation among Othello, Desdemona, and Cassio. We are primarily concerned, however, with the case of ascribing psychological attitudes *"de dicto,"* and Russell would certainly grant that in that case Othello's believing that Desdemona loves Cassio would be compatible with Desdemona and Cassio merely being figments of Othello's imagination, and with Othello's having the belief in question involving no relation at all with some person who happens to be Desdemona or some person who happens to be Cassio.

But it is also clear that Russell's theory of descriptions is supposed to show the way to "reducing" *de dicto* ascriptions to *de re* ascriptions.[58] For suppose that the terms 'Desdemona' and 'Cassio' are in fact disguised descriptions, the contextual definition of which requires introduction of the singular terms 'a,' 'b,' 'c,' and the property terms 'F,' 'G,' 'H,' where the singular terms are no longer merely disguised descriptions. Then while on Russell's view Othello's believing that Desdemona loves Cassio will no longer involve a peculiarly judgmental relation with Desdemona and Cassio, it will involve such a relation with the entities designated by the *other* terms in question. Thus our original objection applies in this case as well: even if Othello's believing that Desdemona loves Cassio *does* involve a peculiarly judgmental relation with the entities in question, the appeal to such a relation could not account for our demand that *what* Othello judges is that a certain unitary *state of affairs* obtains involving those elements. This demand will be later shown as satisfied only by the introduction of a distinction between the (possibly unitary) *content* of a mental act and the (possibly multiple) *object* of the act.

Furthermore, Russell's account offers an untenable view of the role of properties or *universals* as constituents of objects of judgment. (Of course not *every* disguised description requires a contextual definition in which singular terms occur; property terms may be sufficient. In that case Othello's judgment merely involves a relation with the properties in question: he believes *of* those properties that they are related to one another in various ways.) Consider, for example, the simple case of the term 'loves' in the judgment that 'Othello believes that *a* loves *b*,' where the ascription of this psychological state to Othello is, with respect to *a* and *b*, *de re*. Then on Russell's view we are saying that Othello believes of the person who happens to be *a* and of the person who happens to be *b* that they stand in a relation to one another which happens to be the relation of loving. It is perfectly possible, however, for a person to believe that *a* stands to *b* in the relation which *happens* to be identical with the relation of loving, without that person believing that *a* loves *b*. Othello may, for example, mistake love for hate in a very peculiar way. He may, in this case, believe that *that relation* (which we call loving) connects *a* and *b*, even though he doesn't believe that *a* loves *b*. Or suppose, more specifically, the following situation. Othello is told, and he believes, that the same strong emotional tie that binds two other persons of his acquaintance, say Romeo and Juliet, also binds Desdemona and Cassio. Supposing that this emotional tie is in fact the relation of loving, then it seems that we might well say that Othello believes of the relation of loving that *it* binds Desdemona and Cassio. If, however, Othello happens mistakenly to think that the relation in question binding Romeo and Juliet is that of hatred, then it would be false to say that Othello believes that Desdemona loves Cassio, even though it would be true that he believes of the relation of loving that Desdemona stands in that relation to Cassio.

What is necessary is to extend the distinction between *de re* and *de dicto* intentions to the case of psychological states which are "directed toward" *properties* as well as particulars. We would distinguish, for example, between Othello's believing that *a* loves *b* and his merely believing that *a* stands in the relation to *b* which just *happens* to be the relation of loving. In the latter case a belief "about" the properties in question involves some relation with those properties. But there is no reason at all to think that it always does so in the former case. If judgments about universals required some actual *acquaintance* with them, then there would of course be some justification for supposing those judgments to involve, as perceptual states do, a relation of some sort with universals. (Some philosophers have in fact argued that universals are also "directly presented" in acts of special *non*-sensory "intuition."[59]) But it is not clear what reason there could be for supposing that a

mere non-intuitive judgment involves any actual present acquaintance with anything at all.

Thus there are two reasons for rejecting Russell's view of judging in terms of a
distinctive judgmental relation. First, it fails to account for a unity not only between
the judger and objects judged, but within the object of judgment itself. Second, it
fails to provide for a distinction between two different *ways* in which certain entities
may be regarded as objects of judgment in the first place.

Conclusion

We have been concerned in this chapter with the question whether it is plausible to
attempt an account of the intentional features of psychological states in terms of
special psychological relations involving the objects of those states. It was important, in this regard, to distinguish the case of direct perceptual awareness from the
case of mere judgment. In the former case, insofar as we appear to be directly
"acquainted" with something, it is natural to attempt some sort of relational account
of the psychological state in question. To this extent the sense-datum theory is
bound to have a certain appeal, although the difficulties which such a theory poses
easily seem to outweigh the intuitive advantage which it offers. However, we
argued for an alternative account which avoids many of these difficulties by introducing a relation of direct acquaintance with *universals* rather than particulars.
Such an account would, like the sense-datum theory, satisfy our demand that there
always *be* something with which we are presented in perception; unlike the sense-
datum theory, it would also allow us to grant the existence of special psychological
relations which are *intentional* relations.

In the case of mere *judgment* the need for a relational account is naturally less
apparent. Though Bergmann maintains that failure to accept such an account leads
inevitably to idealism, it is not at all clear why this is so. Surely though *some*
psychological sentences express relations with the objects of the psychological states
in question, there is no need to suppose that *all* do. (The former, presumably, are
just those which ascribe a psychological state *de re;* the latter, ascribing psychological states *de dicto*, are primarily the ones which concern us here.) In any case, the
most natural suggestion for a special judgmental relation, namely one involving
possible states of affairs, proves to be unworkable. This fact, furthermore, reflects
on any *other* attempt, say, Russell's, to account for a judgment in purely relational
terms. While judging cannot be regarded as a relation with possible states of affairs,
nevertheless possible states of affairs *are* among the proper objects of judgment.
This shows that the notion of an "object" of judgment, unlike that of an object of
perceptual acquaintance, does not require, for its explication, the notion of a special
judgmental *relation* with such objects. But then it remains questionable why *any*
account of mere judging (*de dicto*) needs to involve such relations.

Though the cases of perception and mere judgment have been sharply distinguished in this chapter, it cannot be denied that judgment often enters *into* cases of

perceptual awareness. As indicated earlier the relation between the judgmental and the intuitive aspects of sensory awareness has generally been misconstrued. It will be argued in Chapter 4 that the intentional features of judgment are accounted for by the presence of "mental content" in a mental act, not by the presence of distinctive judgmental relations with the *objects* of an act. However, while the judgmental aspects of *some* perceptions are then accounted for merely in terms of a relation between a properly intuitive act and another which is merely judgmental, the judgmental aspects of other perceptions (including at least all of what we may call "basic perceptions") are accounted for by the presence of the appropriate "mental content" *in the intuitive act itself.*

4

Mental Contents

Any adequate theory of mental acts requires a distinction between the "contents" and the objects of those acts. I shall argue, in Chapter 5, that the notion of "mental content" can be elucidated with the help of analogies with certain linguistic phenomena, although, contrary to the views of some defenders of linguistic accounts of intentionality, these analogies cannot provide a complete analysis of the intentional aspects of psychological states. In this chapter, however, we must remain on a somewhat more general level in order to understand the ontological issues which are involved. For the sake of historical depth, some of these issues will be considered against the background of certain views defended by Meinong, Husserl, and Frege. It will also prove necessary to devote some special consideration to the role of mental contents in the case of properly intuitive acts, since an adequate treatment of this problem requires a much more intimate connection than is generally acknowledged between the intuitive and the conceptual or judgmental element in experience.

Psychological Assertions and the Ascription of Mental Content

It will be useful first to formulate some of the issues with the aid of formal notation and some purely semantical considerations concerning intentional psychological sentences.

Consider the proposition

(1) Jones judges that a is F,

where (1) is not construed as expressing some actual relation between Jones and an object in the world designated by the term 'a.' Then of course the predicate ('judges that a is F') in (1) cannot contain a straightforwardly referential occurrence of the expression 'a,' and (1) will be resistant to quantification with respect to that term. Proposition (1), that is, will not imply that there actually *is* someone of whom Jones judges that that someone is F:

(2) (Ex) (Jones judges that x is F).

We may, however, introduce a notation that will allow us to do justice to the fact that, while there may not actually be someone whom Jones judges to be F, there is nevertheless, according to (1), someone *in Jones' thoughts* (in a non-literal sense yet to be specified) whom Jones judges to be F. In order to do this, we might formally rewrite (1) as

(3) Jones j's ⌐a is F⌐,

which, in its turn, might be rendered (in quasi-English) as

(3a) Jones "judges" (or "bejudges") the judgmental content ⌐a is F⌐.

This formulation may do some justice to our inclination to say that there is at least someone *in Jones' thoughts* whom Jones judges to be F, because this formulation will at least allow a certain *sort* of quantification with respect to the sorts of items that might enter into Jones' "judgmental content." While (3), like (1), will continue to resist quantification with respect to the term 'a,' hence will not imply that there actually is someone of whom Jones "bejudges" the content ⌐a is F⌐ (or even the content ⌐is F⌐), (3) may nevertheless be taken to imply

(4) (Eα) (Jones j's ⌐α is F⌐),

which might be rendered (in quasi-English) as

(4a) There is, *within a judgmental content* "judged" (or "bejudged") by Jones, an individual *content* of which Jones "judges" the content ⌐is F⌐ (or ⌐α is F⌐).

In (4), the variable 'α' does not range over actual individuals such as some particular person whom Jones might happen to judge to be F, but to say that it ranges over the "contents" (or "partial contents") of judgments can hardly be illuminating at this point, since that notion has not yet been explained. David Kaplan, who employs this formal notation, simply regards the variables in question as ranging over linguistic items such as *words*.[1] Thus, instead of speaking, as in (4a), of individual "contents" which enter into some total judgmental content judged by Jones, Kaplan simply speaks of individual expressions which enter into some *sentence* judged by Jones. We may continue to follow Kaplan's reading, so long as we are in a position to extend the notion of a linguistic item to cover certain sorts of items that may exist only *in our thoughts*, and not, for example, in some actually spoken or written form.

Once having introduced the notion of "mental content," it is important not to assume that the contents of mental acts, such as acts of judging, are necessarily to be regarded as the *objects* of those acts or of components of those acts. It might be objected, for example, that it is impossible to identify the content of Jones' judgment that a is F with some (possibly "inner") *sentence*, because it is perfectly possible to have the thought that a is F without in any way imagining words in one's mind. This objection rests precisely on the supposition that mental contents are certain sorts of objects grasped by the mind. This is not a supposition which one needs to make, and it is in order to avoid making this assumption that the verb 'judge' has been replaced in (1) and (2) with the dummy-verb 'j' in (3) and (4), and scare-quotes are employed in (3a) and (4a). This is in order to avoid the temptation to infer from the fact that Jones' judgment, which appears, according to (1), to be a judgment "about a" (whether or not there really is such a thing as a) is *really* a judgment about a certain mental content.[2]

However, while it would obviously be unsatisfactory to assert that the content of a judgment is what a judgment is *about* (in the ordinary sense of the expression 'what a judgment is about'), we ought not to assume without further consideration that a distinction between the contents and the objects of mental acts *rules out* the possibility that a mental content is in some way an "object" of the act whose content it is. On Frege's view, for example, while it is not a judgment's content or any part of it which a judgment is "about," the "objective content" of any judgment is always in some sense something which is *apprehended* by that judgment or at least by the mind in making the judgment. This chapter will present an argument against the view of mental contents as objects of psychological states of a certain sort. The question will then remain precisely how such sentences as 'Jones j's ⌜$\bar{a}$ is $\bar{F}$⌝' are to be understood, if they are *not* to be understood as asserting that Jones stands in some psychological relation with the object designated by the expression ⌜$\bar{a}$ is $\bar{F}$⌝. The only plausible view is that the expression ⌜$\bar{a}$ is $\bar{F}$⌝, within such predicates as 'j's ⌜$\bar{a}$ is $\bar{F}$⌝,' functions merely by designating a certain non-relational *property* of a possible mental state. This requires that certain properties of mental states may be regarded as certain sorts of linguistic items, that is, as sentences.

It is also important to notice that this approach to the notion of mental content can be extended so as to allow for a distinction not only between, say, an individual object such as a and a "as a content of thought," but also between some particular property such as F and that *property* "as a content of thought." That the content/ object distinction can be extended in this way to our thoughts about properties as well as individuals simply reflects the often-overlooked fact that at least some of the issues generally raised with respect to the status of singular terms within intentional predicates also arise in the case of *predicate* expressions in such contexts. It is possible that a person (say Jones) may judge that a is F without it being the case that he judges, of some actual individual who *is* the a in question (or of any actual individual at all), that *it* is F. It might seem natural to formalize the case in which Jones judges of some actual individual that it is F in the following way:

(5) (Ex) (Jones j*'s ⌜is $\bar{F}$⌝ of x.)

The special case in which the individual in question happens to be the individual a would then seem to come to

(6) Jones j*'s ⌜is $\bar{F}$⌝ of a.[3]

We of course need, in (5) and (6), to introduce a psychological verb distinct from, though related to, the verb 'j' in (3) and (4). Here the verb is clearly a relational one, relating Jones, via at least part of the content of his judgment, to the individual a. In (3) and (4), even if the verb were also a relational one, merely relating Jones to possible judgmental contents themselves, the number of "places" the relation involved would be one less than in the case of (5) and (6); furthermore, as has already been suggested, it may turn out to be more accurate to regard such predicates as 'j's ⌜a is F⌝' not as relational at all, but merely as predicates which ascribe certain quasi-linguistic non-relational properties to some thinker.

The same distinction one draws in distinguishing between the occurrence of a singular term purely *within* a term designating "mental content" [as in (3)] and an occurrence of that same term in a context where it is used to designate some presumedly actual *object* [as in (6)] can be drawn in the case of predicate expressions as well as in the case of singular terms. In my earlier discussion of Russell it was argued that there may be cases in which a person judges *of* a certain property F that it is a property of *a*, without judging, in a certain sense, *that a is F*. Jones, for example, may judge of the property that happens to be the property of loving Cassio that Desdemona exemplifies that property, even though Jones (perhaps *ignorant* that the property in question is the property of loving Cassio) does not judge, in the relevant sense, that Desdemona loves Cassio. In that case, we may say, without a proposition of the form of (3) being true, it is nonetheless true that

(7) Jones j**'s being-F of ⌜a⌝.

Here again a new verb has to be introduced, since (7), unlike (6), does not imply that Jones judges of the actual individual *a* that *it* is F: the individual *a* might exist only "in Jones' thought." Nor does (7) say, of course, that Jones judges of the content ⌜a⌝ that *it* is F. It is the (possibly non-existent) *object a* that Jones judges to be F. What (7) tells us is simply that *a* does at least "exist in Jones' thought" as being F, though this is only a metaphor whose literal sense has yet to be exposed. We cannot, as some philosophers do, accept it as a primitive notion.

There are, then, at least three distinct readings of proposition (1), in which terms within the psychological predicate that (1) contains are regarded as designating what might be called the "content," or at least part of the "content," of some particular psychological state. These are:

(3) Jones j's ⌜a is F⌝
(6) Jones j*'s ⌜is F⌝ of a
(7) Jones j**'s being-F of ⌜a⌝.

There is, unfortunately, no natural English paraphrase, completely free of technical jargon, which allows us to distinguish these three readings of (1). For (3), one might try 'Jones judges that the proposition *that a is F* is true,' though the notion of a "proposition" at least borders on being a piece of technical jargon. For (6), we might try 'Jones judges of the individual *a* that *it* is F,' but this reading turns out to be ambiguous in the light of the content/object distinction that can be drawn for property-words as well as for singular terms. The closest that we can come, it seems, utilizes the notion of a proposition once again: 'Jones judges, by means of the proposition *that it is F*, that *a* is F.' But a problem still remains: our paraphrase at least strongly suggests that what Jones judges is the proposition *that a is F*, whereas (6) does not imply this. It is compatible with (6) that Jones judges *a* to be F by means of the proposition *that b is F* (where '*b*' is a term, not synonymous with '*a*', which expresses some description "under which" Jones thinks a to be F). For (7), finally, the paraphrase 'Jones judges of the property being-F that a has that property' has the defect of leaving it unclear whether the term 'a' is functioning in the paraphrase as a term merely serving to pick out the actual individual a, or whether it is functioning merely by designating an actual component of some propositional "content" which Jones judges to be true. Of course 'Jones judges, by means of the proposition *that a is F*, that a has the property of being-F' will not do either, since (7) is compatible with Jones merely judging the proposition *that a is G* to be true, where 'is G' is a predicate, not synonymous with 'is F,' which expresses a "description" of the property being-F under which Jones thinks that a is F. (Jones, for example, may judge that a is the same color as the shirt b is wearing, not by judging that the proposition *that a is the same color as the shirt b is wearing* is true, but rather by judging that the proposition *that a is red* is true.)

The distinctions between these alternative readings of (1) can be made clearer, at least on the technical level, by extending a suggestion of Kaplan's for expressing the relation between contexts in which a term functions purely referentially (or "transparently") in order to designate some object about which somebody happens to think something and contexts in which that term functions ("opaquely") merely as designating some (mental) *expression* (or "content") by means of which somebody thinks something. On this approach, we take (3) as basic. (6) then becomes the equivalent of

(8) $(\text{E}\alpha)$ $(\text{R}(\alpha,a)$. Jones j's $\ulcorner\alpha$ is $F\urcorner)$,

while (7) is the equivalent of

(9) $(\text{E}\alpha)$ $(\text{R}(\alpha,\text{being-}F)$. Jones j's $\ulcorner a$ is $\alpha\urcorner)$.[4]

What (8) says, in effect, is that there is some partial content/expression which "represents" the individual a to Jones (though it may not be at all "synonymous" with the term 'a'), and *this* (unnamed) content/expression enters into a total content, judged by Jones, of the form $\ulcorner\alpha$ is $F\urcorner$. What (9) says is that there is some partial content/expression which "represents" the property being-F to Jones (though it may not be "synonymous" with the predicate 'is F'), and this (unnamed) content/expression enters into a total content, judged by Jones, of the form $\ulcorner a$ is $\alpha\urcorner$. Proposition (8) implies, while (9) and (3) do not, that there actually *is* some individual ("apart from Jones' thoughts") whom Jones judges to be F. A reading of (1), finally, in which *all* occurrences of terms within the psychological predicate function purely "transparently," would be equivalent to the following:

(10) $(\text{E}\alpha)$ $(\text{E}\beta)$ $(\text{R}(\alpha,a)$. $\text{R}(\beta,\text{being-}F)$. Jones j's $\ulcorner\alpha$ is $\beta\urcorner)$.

So far the only cases considered are those in which an expression occurring within a psychological predicate functions either ("transparently") merely by designating some actual thing about which somebody has some thought or ("opaquely") merely by designating some "content" *by means of which* somebody thinks about something (whether or not there actually happens to *be* such a thing). It is, however, a point that is not often enough appreciated that a given expression in a psychological context might in fact perform *both* of these functions at once.

The case of predicate expressions might be thought to be a case in which an expression within a psychological predicate typically performs both a properly referential and also a content-ascribing function. It might seem reasonable to maintain that a proposition like

(6) Jones j*'s ⌜is F⌝ of a

always implies that Jones judges of the property being-F and of the individual a that the individual in question exemplifies the property in question. It is clear that the inference does not work in the opposite direction. That Jones, for example, judges of the property being-the-color-of-b's-shirt, and of the object a, that a is the color of b's shirt does not imply that Jones' judgment in any way contains the content ⌜is the color of b's shirt⌝. Jones may be judging that a is the color of b's shirt simply by means of judging the content ⌜a is red⌝, where red happens to be the color of b's shirt. However, if Jones judges the content ⌜a is the color of b's shirt⌝, then it would seem to follow immediately that Jones judges of the property being-the-color-of-b's-shirt that a has that property. It might seem, in other words, that while properly referential occurrences of predicate expressions are not necessarily also content-ascribing occurrences, a content-ascribing occurrence is always also a properly referential one.

The problem of the occurrence of predicate expressions within psychological contexts raises some questions which cannot be pursued here. One such question concerns the conditions under which there can be said to *be* such a thing as a given property. Suppose, for example, Jones judges the content ⌜a is the same shade of red as b's shirt⌝, but b's shirt is not really red at all, or perhaps b has no shirt in fact, or perhaps, finally, there really is no such person as b in the first place. Then *is* there such a property as the property being-the-same-shade-of-red-as-b's-shirt? It is not evident just how to answer this question, but in the face of a negative answer we shall have found at least one sort of case in which a predicate expression ('is the same shade of red as b's shirt') within a psychological predicate ('judges that a is the same shade of red as b's shirt') might perform a content-ascribing function without performing any properly referential function. Similar cases might be found in the case of thoughts about self-contradictory properties, assuming that one is reluctant to grant that there *are* such properties (in addition to one's *thoughts* about them.)

It is still possible to maintain that at least in those cases where there *is* a property designated by a term occurring within a psychological predicate, then a content-ascribing use of that term always immediately *implies* a proposition containing a properly referential use as well, though the reverse does not hold. If that is so—and it is not obvious—then this would constitute an important difference between the use of property-designating expressions and that of singular terms. Even assuming that there *is* such a person as a, it does not follow from the fact that Jones judges the content ⌜a is F⌝ that he judges of the individual in question that *he* is F. In most cases, we would also require that Jones actually *know who a is* before the inference in question might be drawn.[5] However, even if we do treat property-designating expressions differently in this case, this still does not amount to recognizing a case in which a given expression plays both a content-ascribing and a properly referential role *in the same proposition*. It at most acknowledges that a proposition containing a content-ascribing occurrence of a term will imply, under suitable conditions, another proposition containing a referential use of that term. We will have a situation in which a term performs both functions at once only in case a statement of the conditions in question are actually *part* of the original proposition, but this is at least not always true. It is not always, for example, *asserted*, in saying that Jones judges that *a* is *F*, that the property which Jones thinks *a* to have is not a contradictory one. Nor need we assert, in saying that Jones judges that *a* is the same color as *b*'s shirt, that there really *is* a *b*, or that he really has a shirt.

Most discussions of the use of terms within psychological predicates focus only on the problem of *implication*-relations between propositions in which such a term performs a merely content-ascribing function and propositions in which it performs a properly referential one. However, there is an often overlooked possibility of propositions in which both of these functions are performed at once; in fact in the case of certain *perceptual* verbs, it is very natural for even singular terms to play this double role. Consider, for example, the following:

(11) Jones sees that a man in grey is standing on the corner.

This proposition might very naturally be taken as having two implications. First, there is a man in grey standing on the corner and Jones sees *him*. Second, Jones recognizes the man in question *as* a man in grey.[6] Of course, there may also be natural readings of (11) that lack one or other of these implications, but my only point is that at least one perfectly natural reading contains them. In this case, then, the expression 'a man in grey' performs both a referential and a content-ascribing function. It serves, in other words, both to point out some actual individual whom Jones sees and also to indicate *how* Jones sees him. The expression, that is, designates both the object and the content of Jones' perception. This double function will be captured in the following formalization:

(12) (Eα) (R(α, a man in grey). Jones s's $\overline{\alpha}$ is standing on the
corner⌉). Jones s's $\overline{\alpha}$ is a man in grey⌉).

What the formalization shows is that the expression 'a man in grey' occurs in two different ways: once in a purely referential occurrence, where it serves to indicate the actual *object* of Jones' perception (a man in grey), and once in a context where it serves merely to identify part of the *content* of Jones' perception (⌈a man in grey is standing on the corner⌉). Since (12) does succeed in formalizing one perfectly natural reading of (11), we may conclude that (11) contains a singular term, on that reading, which simultaneously performs both a content-ascribing and a properly referential function.

An examination of this case also leads to a further conclusion of some importance. What it shows is that while inability to "quantify into" a psychological context may be a sufficient condition for concluding that some term in that context is performing a content-ascribing function, it is by no means a necessary condition. In the present case, for example, we are entitled to quantify into (11) in order to derive

(11EG) (Ex) (Jones sees that x is standing on the corner),

even though the term 'a man in grey' was performing a content-ascribing function (though not *only* such a function) in (11). We should notice, however, that while resistance to quantification is not a necessary condition for the identification of a content-ascribing context, resistance to *substitution* is a necessary condition. In the present case, for example, suppose that the man whom Jones sees is barefoot:

(13) The man whom Jones sees standing on the corner = a man who is barefoot.

We cannot infer, from (11), construed as equivalent to (12), and (13) that

(14) Jones sees a barefoot man standing on the corner,

where (14) is construed in the same way as (11) originally was. Hence failure of substitution with respect to a given term, and not failure of quantification, is the necessary and sufficient condition for that term's performing a content-ascribing function in a psychological context.

It might seem that in the preceding argument I am simply mistaken in claiming that (11) does generalize into (11EG) *on the reading that I have given to it.* Generalizing (12), which is our formalization of (11), seems only to yield

(12EG) (Ex) (Eα) (R(α,x). Jones s's $\ulcorner α$ is standing on the corner$\urcorner$). Jones s's $\ulcorner α$ is a man in grey$\urcorner$).

But it would seem that (11EG) ought to be formalized, on the reading in question, as

(15) (Ex) (Eβ) (Eα) (R(α,x). Jones s's $\ulcorner α$ is standing on the corner$\urcorner$). Jones s's $\ulcorner α$ is $β\urcorner$).

Since (12) does not generalize into (15), it might be argued, I must be mistaken in claiming that (11) is open to quantification within the psychological predicate. But the difficulty with this argument simply is that generalizing (12) *does* yield (15)! Of course, it yields (15) only when generalized with respect *both* to the individual man in grey *and* with respect to the content/expression $\ulcorner$a man in grey$\urcorner$. But there is no reason at all to insist that because a generalization of (11) involves only a single case of generalizing, an equivalent generalization of its *formalization* cannot involve more than a single case of generalizing. Indeed, this is just what we would expect in view of the fact that a single expression in (11) is performing a double function which its formalization makes evident!

The conclusion, then, is that in cases where a term plays both a properly referential and also a content-ascribing function in a psychological context, it will be possible to "quantify into" that context but not automatically possible to substitute co-designative expressions. Such cases will be ones in which we "quantify into (substitutionally) opaque" contexts. The need for such cases has been vigorously defended in recent years by Jaakko Hintikka, but the account offered here of such cases is much less metaphysically daring than his. On Hintikka's account, all uses of terms within psychological predicates are ordinarily "referential," but the terms in question always refer to a multiplicity of objects *across possible worlds*. Quantification is possible so long as there is a set of principles allowing the subject of the psychological verb to trace the *same* object through this multiplicity. It is easy for Hintikka to show that this condition can be satisfied even when substitution may still not be permitted. In the latter case, though an expression '*a*' may designate the same object across all the possible worlds in question, and the expression '*b*' may designate the same object as '*a*' in the *actual* world, since the two expressions may not continue to designate the same object in all the *other* worlds in question, it follows that the terms may not freely be substituted.[7] On the account offered here, opacity to substitution may simply be due to the presence of a "content-ascribing" use of an expression, which is not incompatible with a properly referential use permitting quantification.[8]

There is one final case worth considering involving the distinction between ascription of content and reference to objects in psychological contexts. Consider the following case:

(16) Jones judges that the dragons I am imagining are dangerous.

This may appear to provide a difficulty, inasmuch as the term 'dragons' is apparently being used in (16) both to express a part of the content of Jones' thought and also to refer to some object of my own thought; and yet our approach does not appear to handle the case, since the "objects" here are not regarded as actual objects at all. But this case can be handled simply on the level of *contents*:

(17) $(E\alpha)$ $(E\beta)$ (I imagine $\ulcorner\alpha$'s are dragons of type $\beta\urcorner$. Jones j's $\ulcorner$dragons of type β are dangerous$\urcorner$).

The same content, in other words, that functions in my imagination is "bejudged" by Jones to be dangerous. But this, of course, is not to say that Jones judges (in the ordinary sense) that the *content* in question is dangerous. It is *dragons* of a certain sort that Jones judges to be dangerous; dragons, however, which might happen to "exist" (by way of a content of the form $\ulcorner$dragons of type $\beta\urcorner$) only in the minds of Jones and myself.

The Contents and the Objects of Mental Acts

Our discussion of the notion of mental content has, so far, remained on a primarily semantical level, while it is on a properly ontological level that we ultimately wish to pursue our investigations. In continuing our discussion in this direction, it will be necessary to consider more explicitly the sorts of *arguments* that are alleged to indicate the need for an introduction of such entities as mental contents. Clarity with regard to this matter will convince one of the need for that introduction, and also of the absence of any need for supposing that we are thereby committed to regarding a mental content as any sort of peculiar object of awareness.

The introduction of mental content is, according to Meinong, demanded by three distinct considerations. The first consideration which Meinong advances simply appeals to the fact that there may be awarenesses of non-existent objects, or at least of objects which might not exist at the moment that there are awarenesses of them:

> Something can, finally, indeed be real, and in addition have existed or exist in the future, not, however, in the present. All the same it is presented to awareness in the present (*gegenwärtig vorgestellt*). The presentation therefore exists: but who would assume, except perhaps for some previous theoretical prejudice, that the presentation indeed exists, but its content (*Inhalt*) does not?[9]

Since the act, with its compresent content, exists, while the object of the act does not, some distinction must be drawn between the contents and the objects of acts; this argument has been accepted by a number of philosophers. Thus A. O. Lovejoy argues that "When I remember, for example, not only is there a present awareness distinct from the past memory-object . . . but the present awareness manifestly has, and must have, a compresent content. But the past event which we say the memory is *of* cannot be this compresent content." Hence we must distinguish between the contents and the objects of memories.[10] Bertrand Russell also offers a similar argument for belief:

> What is believed, and the believing, must both consist of present occurrences in the believer, no matter what may be the objective of the belief. Suppose I believe, for example, "that Caesar crossed the Rubicon." The objective of my belief is an event which happened long ago. . . . This event itself is not in my mind when I believe that it happened. It is not correct to say that I am believing the actual event; what I am believing is something now in my mind . . . since the event is not occurring but the believing is. . . . What is believed . . . is not the actual fact that makes the belief true, but a present event related to the fact. This present event, which is what is believed, I shall call the "content" of the belief.[11]

Since, Russell seems to be arguing, a belief may be present while its object is not, a distinction is needed between the content and the object of a belief. If this argument is valid, furthermore, it ought to be possible to extend it to cases where the object of a mental act is in fact an actually existing one, for no change could be made in the "content" of an awareness by the mere fact of actual existence or non-existence of the object of that awareness. That is, in order to state this point without appealing to the notion of mental content itself, the truth of propositions describing a mental state is not dependent upon the actual existence or non-existence of the object (or, with Russell, the "objective") of that state. Hence it must be dependent upon the possession or nonpossession of a certain "content" by that state.

Although Russell does not make the point very clear, whatever validity this sort of argument might have must rest on the position we take with regard to the ontological status of merely intentional objects. If we were prepared to grant some ontological status to non-existent objects, then the argument from the non-existence of objects would *not* appear to require a distinction between the objects and the contents of acts.[12] Granting that the actual existence or non-existence of objects for mental acts is irrelevant to those acts having whatever "content" they might have, hence irrelevant to the truth of propositions which *describe* those acts, would not require an ontological distinction between the contents and the objects of acts. We would only need to distinguish between those acts which involve a relation to actually existing objects and those acts which involve a relation to merely intentional objects. The *object* would thus provide whatever "content" an act might have.

It has been argued that even if we did accept a relational account of mental acts, a distinction would still be required between the contents and the objects of acts. J. N. Findlay has argued, for example, that even if we accepted such an account of mental acts, "their objects would lie outside of them, and nothing *in our experience* would tell us to what they were directed."[13] This argument is clearly question-begging since it assumes that the awareness of the "contents" of my mental acts is not the awareness which I have of certain relations in which I stand to objects. It assumes that knowledge of the truth of propositions which describe my mental acts is not knowledge of some relation in which I stand to certain objects. But if my being aware of some particular object rather than another just *is* my standing in such a relation to that object rather than another one, then it is not clear why knowing that I am in some mental state could *not* be just knowing the fact that I am related in a certain way to that object.

Findlay offers a second argument to show that a relational account of mental acts does not obviate the need for distinguishing between the contents and the objects of such acts. If knowing that I am in a certain mental state were just knowing some relational fact about myself, or about some part of myself, then knowledge about my own mental states would not be infallible: "We do not look into our minds and perceive a certain naked idea, then look outwards and see a certain object, and then finally perceive that they are related in a certain way, such that the one is the idea of the other. If this were our procedure we might quite conceivably connect an idea with the wrong object."[14] However, it is not clear why, given that we do at least possess the relevant conceptual abilities, knowing that I am aware of some particular object should be any less certain when such knowledge is the knowledge of a relational fact than it is when it is knowledge of a different sort. Given, for example, that I know what Being-to-the-left-of is, there seems to be no more difficulty in principle in knowing that something is to the left of something else than there would be, given that I know what Red or Green is, in knowing that something is red or green. Therefore, assuming that I know what the relation Being-aware-of is, and that I know what Red or Green is, there would seem to be no more difficulty in principle in knowing that I am aware of Red or Green than there would be, assuming that I know what mental contents are, in knowing that some mental act of mine has a particular content. Findlay is right in maintaining that if the knowledge of relational states of affairs were an inference totally based upon observation of each of the *terms* of some relation, then such knowledge would be very weak. But it is clear that the awareness of a relational state of affairs is the awareness of something *more* than the terms of a certain relation. Furthermore, the difficulty in question, if there is a difficulty, would seem to arise even if we *do* distinguish between mental acts and their contents, since the awareness that there is an act with some particular content would then presumably require the awareness of an act as well as the awareness of some content.

Findlay's third argument to show that even if awareness involves an actual relation with the objects of awareness, a distinction would still be needed between the *contents* and the objects of awareness rests simply on the claim that there is an immediately recognizable difference between the awareness of one object and the awareness of another: "the reference to *A* is nevertheless a different experience from the reference to *B*; *es ist uns anders zu Mute*, as Meinong says."[15] The fact that there is such a difference shows, according to Findlay, that we need a distinction between the contents and the objects of mental acts. But if we accepted a relational account of awareness, then there would also be some difference between the awareness of one object and the awareness of a different one. Hence the argument appears either to be invalid, or else to beg the question by assuming precisely what needs to be proved, namely that the difference between two awarenesses of objects could not merely be a matter of the relations which those awarenesses involve.

I agree with Meinong and Findlay that we do need some distinction between the contents and the objects of mental acts. The reason, however, that we need a distinction between the contents and the objects of acts is precisely that thinking about objects does *not* involve a relation with the objects of thought. If thoughts about objects do not involve any relations with those objects, then the knowledge that one is thinking certain thoughts, that is, knowledge of the truth of propositions which describe the "content" of those thoughts, must be something other than the knowledge of a relation involving the objects of thought.

Besides the argument from non-existent objects, Meinong offers another argument to show that the contents and the objects of mental acts are distinct entities. This is that while the object of an act may be an object with physical properties, the content of an act is always something mental: "Without a doubt it is clear, furthermore, that not only something mental, but also something physical can be presented to awareness: the content, on the other hand, of something mental, and thus in the first instance of a presentation, can also for its part be only something mental."[16] This argument presupposes that there *are* such things as the contents of acts in the first place; but the argument from non-existent objects has shown at least this much already. It is not clear, however, why one ought to assume that the content of anything mental, even if it is distinct from the object of a mental act, is itself something mental. One might of course define the term 'mental' so as to apply not only to mental acts, but also to the non-relational *characters* of acts.[17] But while Meinong does regard an act's content as one of the very characters of that act (or, as he puts it, a *Moment* of such an act[18]), nothing in the argument from non-existent objects, or in the failure of any general relational account of mental acts, implies that the content of an act must *be* one of that act's characters. All that the argument establishes is that within such a context as 'X believes that *a* is *F*' the expression 'that *a* is *F*' is not being used to designate what that expression may be used in nonintentional contexts to designate.

As already shown, Meinong does not appear to recognize the precise force of this point; he appears to think that the expression 'that *a* is *F*' must be used to designate an Objective both in non-intentional and in intentional contexts. Nevertheless Meinong did distinguish between two different ways in which an expression might be said to "designate" something. There is, according to Meinong, the fact that an expression "expresses" certain mental acts or the contents of those acts, and there is also the fact that an expression can be used to refer to (*bedeuten*) some object.[19] To put our point in Meinong's own language, accordingly, he has given no reason for supposing that the content which an expression expresses, as distinct from the object which it refers to, is the sort of thing which could be regarded as a *property* or *character* of some mental act. Thus the admission that the expression 'that *a* is *F*,' as it occurs in intentional contexts, is not being used in order to designate what is ordinarily that expression's *reference*—some actual or possible state of affairs—does not imply whether that expression is being used to designate something which stands to a mental act in the relation of a property to an instance of that property, or whether it designates something standing to that act in some other relation altogether.

If the content of an act is not one of the properties of that act, then it must be some sort of *object* which is apprehended by that act. This may appear to contradict our conclusion that the content must in every case be distinct from the object of an act. But in arguing for some distinction between the content and "the" object of an act, I have only tried to distinguish between the content of an act and what is its *ordinary* object. One might, for example, distinguish between the "ultimate" object of an act, toward which one's *attention* is directed in that act, and some other object which may be involved in attending to objects of the former sort, but which is not, in such contexts, itself the object of attention. An example of the former might be an objective state of affairs; perhaps an example of the latter would be what some philosophers have called a "proposition." My argument has been that within the context 'X believes that *a* is *F*' the expression 'that *a* is *F*' is not being used in order to designate the actual or possible state of affairs which is the ordinary reference of that expression. It may therefore be said to designate some *proposition* instead. However, so far we have no basis for deciding whether to construe that "proposition" as a *property* of the belief in question, or whether to construe it as some sort of *object* of *X*'s belief. If the latter alternative is correct, then while any person who is entertaining the thought that *a* is *F* must in some sense also be apprehending the *proposition* that *a* is *F*, he must, nevertheless, be directing his *attention* to some actual or possible state of affairs, and not to a mere proposition. But that same proposition will then *become* an explicit object of his attention when he is entertaining not the thought that *a* is *F*, but rather the thought that someone is *thinking* that *a* is *F*.

If we do distinguish between the "ultimate" object of a mental act and another sort of object altogether, and identify the latter as the content rather than "the" object of an act, then we must be careful not to confuse the distinction between the content and the object of an act with the distinction which some philosophers have wished to draw between the "immanent" and the "transcendent" object of acts. Some philosophers have distinguished between the object of an act as that object exists apart from the mind, and the object of an act as it may exist "in" the mind or "in" a mere idea in the mind. Insofar as the latter sort of object is a "content" of the mind, in the sense of being *in* it, it would of course be something mental. Brentano at one time appeared to use the notion of "content" and "immanent object" interchangeably:

> Every mental phenomenon is characterized by what the scholastics of the Middle Ages called the intentional (and also mental) inexistence of an object, and what we could call, although in not entirely unambiguous terms, the reference to a content, a direction upon an object (by which we are not to understand a reality in this case), or an immanent objectivity.[20]

However, the notion of an "immanent object" was not intended by Brentano to suggest that some object is "in" the mind, but only to suggest that it is an *object* for the mind. Hence he drew no explicit distinction between the content and the object of an act.[21] Nevertheless, Brentano was at least *committed* to a distinction between the contents and the objects of acts, since mental acts involve for him the exemplification of certain non-relational *characters* which are designated by the predicates of intentional propositions about mental phenomena, but this distinction is not the same as that between an "immanent" and a "transcendent" object.

Meinong had also once used the term 'content' to refer to the "immanent" object of an act, but he later came to realize that talk about an "immanent" object is either misleading talk about some *transcendent* object, or else merely about the fact that there is some *awareness* of such an object.[22] Though all awarenesses do have contents, there is no sense for Meinong in which these are objects of the acts of which they are the contents. In only one case does the word 'content' designate something which is for Meinong an object of the act which has that content: Objectives might be regarded as the "contents" of judgments, in order to distinguish them from the Objects which they involve. It is in this sense that Brentano used the word when he rejected Meinong's distinction between the "contents" and the objects of acts.[23] But even an act which apprehends an Objective possesses, for Meinong, a content as something *in addition* to the Objective which it apprehends. Contents are, strictly speaking, the *properties* of acts for Meinong, and Objectives are never the properties of acts.

So far we have seen two arguments for the introduction of mental contents. Meinong also offers a third argument based on the observation that the same object may be presented to several very different acts.[24] The city of Salzburg, to use Findlay's example, is the object of some thought about "the birthplace of Mozart," as well as the object of some thought about "the city erected on the site of ancient

Juvavum." Since the objects of these thoughts are the same, yet the thoughts do differ in their descriptive nature, there must be some distinction between the contents and the objects of these thoughts. As Findlay observes, this argument does not seem compelling, for it is possible to construe these thoughts as involving some difference in object: "there is some difference even in the *objects* of the two ideas; if they do concern the same city, they certainly also introduce us to other objects and relations which would suffice to distinguish them. For Mozart and ancient Juvavum are as much objects as the modern city of Salzburg."[25]

It is not evident, however, how the difference between an awareness of the birthplace of Mozart and an awareness of the city erected on the site of ancient Juvavum could be a difference in the *objects* of these awarenesses, unless some *distinction* were being drawn between the objects of these awarenesses and such objects as the birthplace of Mozart and the city erected on the site of ancient Juvavum, since these latter are clearly identical. Thus one would need to distinguish, as Reinhardt Grossmann suggests in commenting on this argument, between "objects" and "ultimate objects" of these acts.[26] It might appear that this sort of distinction, though not precisely the same as Meinong's distinction between the contents and the objects of acts, nevertheless satisfies our general conception of a content/object distinction. We do not need, in order to distinguish the contents from the objects of acts, to suppose that the contents of acts are *properties* of those acts. It is compatible with our distinction between contents and objects of acts that the content of an act be itself in some sense an "object" apprehended in an act. Meinong's third argument, however, does not even satisfy this more general conception of the content of an act.

It is possible to distinguish the "object" from the "ultimate object" of a thought about the birthplace of Mozart simply by distinguishing particulars from *states of affairs*. The "ultimate object," we might say, of a thought about the birthplace of Mozart is just the city of Salzburg, which happens also to be the "ultimate object" of a thought about the city erected on the site of ancient Juvavum. The *immediate* "object" of that thought, however, is a certain state of affairs, namely the state of affairs of some city's *being* the birthplace of Mozart. This state of affairs is different from that of some city's being erected upon a certain ancient site. Hence the two thoughts may differ with respect to their *immediate* objects, while the ultimate object of each is the same.

Though this distinction between the "immediate" and the "ultimate" object of a thought does bear some analogy to our distinction between the contents and the objects of acts, it is nevertheless a different distinction, since states of affairs, which on this view would provide the "contents" of acts, are entities which we have recognized already as perfectly ordinary sorts of *objects* of acts. The fact, therefore, that the same particular can be presented to awareness in several different ways does not require a distinction between the contents and the objects of acts, for it is compatible with a distinction only between particulars and states of affairs.

If the fact that some object may be presented to awareness in several different ways requires a distinction between the contents and the objects of acts, then the sort of case with which we must deal is a case, if there is one, in which the very same *state of affairs* (and not just the same particular) may be presented in various ways. In that case we would have to distinguish between the states of affairs which are the objects of certain acts and the *propositions* by which those states of affairs are intended. Consider, for example, the thought that a is to the left of b and the thought that b is to the right of a. Though the question is a difficult one, it seems not unreasonable to suppose that these thoughts intend the very same state of affairs. If they do, then we may distinguish between the objects and the contents of these thoughts and use the term 'proposition' to designate the latter. It might appear obvious to some, however, that a's being to the left of b and b's being to the right of a are *not* the same state of affairs at all. If a criterion for the identity of states of affairs is containment in them of all the same constituents ordered in the same way,[27] then, it might be argued, a's being to the left of b would not be the same as b's being to the right of a, since the one contains the universal Being-to-the-left-of and the other contains the universal Being-to-the-right-of. But this reply would be question-begging, since what is at issue here is precisely whether the terms 'left' and 'right' *do* designate different universals. So long as predicate expressions are taken to designate anything at all, then it is not evident why two such expressions might not differ in sense and yet designate just the same entity. One reason for rejecting this possibility might be the following: if 'left' and 'right' do designate the same entity then there would be no way to distinguish between believing that a is to the left of b and believing that b is to the right of a. But this argument would rest on the mistaken assumption that believing simply consists in a relation to the state of affairs which is affirmed in a belief. Apart from such an assumption, I can see no reason to insist that the thought that a is to the left of b and the thought that b is to the right of a must be directed toward different objects. Since the thoughts nevertheless do differ, we may thus distinguish between the contents and the objects of these thoughts, hence between propositions and states of affairs.

Even if this argument fails, however, we would still need a distinction between propositions and states of affairs. This follows simply from the fact that two acts may intend different states of affairs, neither of which is *actual*. Since the difference between the acts in question cannot be accounted for simply by appealing to intentional relations with their non-existent objects, a distinction is required between propositions and states of affairs. This argument, however, does not require us to decide what sorts of *entities* the former might be. (The distinction, of course, between propositions and states of affairs is one which Meinong was unable to draw, since he failed to recognize states of affairs in the first place.)

Mental Contents and Perceptual Acts

By considering Meinong's three arguments, what becomes evident is that the main arguments for the introduction of an ontological distinction between the contents and the objects of mental acts must ultimately appeal to the failure of any relational account of judgment. To this extent, the need for a notion of mental content emerges directly from some of our critical discussions in the preceding chapters. As we have seen, such an introduction of the notion of mental content will be compatible with more than one way of regarding the contents of acts. Mental contents might, for example, be regarded as peculiar sorts of *objects* of ordinary psychological states (or of some psychological components of such states); or they might be regarded merely as certain special *properties* of psychological states. It is the contrast between these two approaches which will be pursued in the following section. However, because of certain issues which are peculiar to the case of acts which are not purely judgmental or conceptual, but which involve some "sensuous" or "intuitive" character as well, it will be useful first to devote some attention to the role of mental contents in this case. A proper assessment of the case will provide a more adequate account than is generally given of the *relation* between a properly "sensuous" and a properly conceptual or judgmental element in perception.[28]

Even though immediate perceptual awareness may involve genuine psychological relations with possibly uninstantiated universals, we still need to draw a distinction between the contents and the objects of perceptual states. The need for such a distinction would of course be obvious if *no* relational account were possible for perceptual acts. In that case, the truth or falsity of an intentional proposition asserting what a perception is a perception *of* could not be accounted for in terms of the obtaining or nonobtaining of some relation involving the object in question. It would therefore be necessary to account for it by appealing to some other features of the perceptual state in question, and the term 'content' could then be used to designate anything which we would need to introduce in order to account for such features. If, however, a perceptual state's having the object which it has could in fact be accounted for in properly relational terms, then some philosophers have felt that there would be no need to suppose that such a state possesses elements that a perceiver could be aware of in *addition* to its relation with some object of perception. As G. E. Moore claimed, for example, "When we try to introspect the sensation of blue, all we can see is the blue: the other element is as if it were diaphanous."[29]

The need, nevertheless, for a distinction between the contents and the objects of perceptual states is evident from a consideration of the fact that every properly perceptual state not only involves the immediate apprehension of an object, but also involves some element of *recognition* of the object in question. Every perception, that is, apprehends its object in some particular *way*. When I see the color red, for example, I may see it on one occasion as the color of my favorite shirt, and see it on another occasion as the color of blood. There must clearly be some difference in the perceptual states involved, in addition to the common relation which they bear to the color red. When, similarly, Macbeth saw a certain dagger-shape before him he may have (nonveridically) perceived it at one instant as actually instantiated by some object standing before him, and yet at the next instant merely perceived it as a shape resembling the shape of some actual dagger of his own. Again, there must be some difference in the perceptual states involved, in addition to their common relation to a certain dagger-shape. This requires a distinction between the contents and the objects of perceptual states.

It might be thought that these considerations do not so much require a distinction between the contents and the objects of perceptual states as they require a distinction between two different senses of perceptual verbs, and a corresponding distinction between two different sorts of perceptual *objects*. We do after all say that, in some sense at least, on the occasion on which I perceived the color red, I "saw" the color of my favorite shirt, while on the other occasion I "saw" the color of blood. We might also say that, in the same sense, at the one moment during which Macbeth perceived a certain dagger-shape, he "saw" an actual knife before him, while at the other moment all that he "saw" was the shape of some actual knife which was not before him at all. It seems, however, that we might grant that the cases in question do require some distinction between perceptual *objects* without denying that they also require the notion of a mental "content" for perceptual states. For example, the distinction between the color red, which was seen on two separate occasions, and the "color of my favorite shirt" and the "color of blood," which were "seen" separately on only one of these occasions, can simply be regarded as a distinction between a property which was apprehended on two separate occasions and two distinct *states of affairs* involving that property, each of which was apprehended on only one of those occasions. If, in general, perceptual apprehension involves the recognition of an object, then it always involves the recognition of an object *as* a constituent of some particular state of affairs. Accordingly, that state of affairs may always be regarded as a proper object of perception, in *addition* to whatever constituents of it happen to stand in the appropriate perceptual relations with a perceiver. (Not all of its constituents need do so.)

This distinction between two distinct sorts of objects for perceptual states, hence two distinct senses of perceptual verbs, far from obviating the need for a content/object distinction for perceptual states, precisely requires such a distinction. It is impossible, as argued in Chapter 3, to account for the intentional features of mental states whose objects are states of affairs by appealing to special psychological *relations* involving those states of affairs. Though every perceptual state apprehends its object *as* something or other and hence apprehends it as a constituent of some state of affairs, there is nothing which requires that the apprehension in question be a veridical one: an object may be apprehended as a constituent of some state of affairs which simply fails to obtain. In order to provide a properly relational account of such apprehension, it would be necessary to introduce special psychological relations involving merely possible states of affairs, but this is impossible. Thus the distinction between a perception's recognitional "content" and the fact that it has the immediate object which it has must be given some other ontological grounding, hence an ontological distinction is required between the "contents" and the objects of perceptual states as well as of purely judgmental states.[30]

The problem is to determine just *how* the conceptual content of a perception is related to that perception and to the properly "sensory" or "intuitive" elements which distinguish it from a mere thought or judgment. It is tempting to be satisfied with the observation that the fact that perceptual objects are invariably seen *as* something or other is simply a function of the fact that perception necessarily involves, in addition to whatever purely sensory elements it contains, the occurrence of judgments, thoughts, or beliefs. This observation may generate the impression that the role of conceptual or judgmental content in perception is simply whatever role it plays in relation to the thoughts or judgments which are in question. However, this suggestion threatens to return us to a view of perception already rejected in Chapter 1. This is the view that perceptions are really complex states, of which one component consists in the presence of mere sensations (whose presence at least accounts for the fact that the perception in question is a visual rather than an auditory one, or an auditory rather than an olfactory one), and of which the other component consists in the presence of certain thoughts or judgments which stand in some specific relation with the first component (presumably some sort of causal relation). It is convenient to call this the "causal" theory of perception, although it is also important not to confuse it with a similarly named view which attempts to account, by means of appeal to causal relations, for a perception's being a perception of some particular object that actually exists in the world. This latter issue concerns only the case of "transparent" rather than "opaque" perception, and it does not concern us here.

A rejection of the causal theory may seem to leave us in an untenable position with respect to the role of conceptual content in perception. Since rejection of that theory requires denying that the conceptual content of perception is merely a function of purely conceptual or judgmental acts which are causally *connected* with the sensations it involves, rejection of the theory would appear to require supposing that a perception's conceptual content is at least partly a function of the very sensations *themselves* which a perception involves. This may appear to be a contradiction, inasmuch as sensations are in themselves presumed to be purely non-conceptual states of a person.

This difficulty arises only on the assumption that mental contents are to be regarded, as some philosophers have regarded them, as the special objects of psychological acts of some sort. In the next section this view will be contrasted with one which regards mental contents merely as certain sorts of *properties* that are exemplified by psychological acts. It can now be shown, however, that, at least in the case of perceptual acts, only the latter of these two views can be satisfactory: we cannot suppose that a perception's conceptual content is a function of the sensations which it involves coming to possess a certain "conceptual content," so long as the latter performs its role in experience only insofar as it becomes the object of some mental apprehension. Since sensations are not in themselves intrinsically conceptual states of a person, it makes sense to speak of them as "apprehending" objects only to the extent that they have been *provided* with some properly conceptual significance in the first place. This implies, however, that conceptual contents, construed as certain sorts of *objects* of apprehension, cannot be what originally provides sensation with this conceptual significance, since the latter must *already have* this significance before they are in a position to generate any apprehension of the former in the first place. Thus so long as conceptual contents are regarded in this way, sensations themselves could be said to "apprehend" them only in the extended sense that they are apprehended by purely conceptual acts merely *connected* in some way with sensation, and this would return us to the theory which we are attempting to overcome.

The difficulty can be avoided by supposing that conceptual contents function, not insofar as they are objects of apprehension, but only insofar as they are *properties* exemplified by the mental states whose contents they are. Suppose, for example, that certain visual sensations are present in the mind, but (as sometimes is said) one is not really "attending" to them, and one is therefore not in fact apprehending any object *through* them. The difference between this case and a case in which the same sensations provide a vehicle for the genuine apprehension of some (possibly hallucinated) object can then be accounted for by appeal to "mental contents" without supposing that the latter function only by *also* becoming objects of apprehension. We simply suppose that in the second of these cases the very sensations which were originally present have come to exemplify a special sort of *property*, namely one which "constitutes" out of those sensations an awareness of the object in question. (We might then call this property the "concept" of that object.) There is no need to suppose, as on the causal account, that this awareness is constituted out of those original sensations only in virtue of some external connection between those sensations and a mere thought or judgment about that object. (A mere thought or judgment would *also*, on this view, be a mental state which exemplifies the concept of an object, but it would not also involve *sensations*.)[31]

This view of the role of content in perception allows us to do more justice than could otherwise be done to certain apparent phenomenological facts. Consider, for example, cases in which we are inclined to say that we perceive an object differently simply in virtue of the fact that we *recognize* the object in question. A room which one enters for the first time is somehow seen in a different way once it has become more familiar; an at first unfamiliar face sometimes actually appears to *change* once we recognize its owner. These phenomena can be explained by noting that the introduction of conceptual content into sensation, or the transformation of some content already present in sensation, will always be, on the view in question, a matter of those sensations undergoing some actual *alteration*; they will come to exemplify properties that they otherwise had not exemplified. We can offer this explanation, however, without supposing that the sensations in question thereby actually become *different sensations*. (Though our criteria for the identity of sensations may not be clear, there should at least be nothing in principle requiring us to say that whenever a sensation exemplifies properties that some previously existing sensation failed to exemplify, the two cannot be the *same* sensation.) Neither is it necessary to suppose, in order to offer this explanation, that the relevant experiential difference is therefore merely a difference in some purely intellectual *thoughts or judgments* which our sensations must be causing us to have. Sometimes the alteration appears to be more "immediate" and "intuitive" than this, and the present account can well accommodate that fact. (Other cases in which the same point can be made are cases in which some drawing is seen in different ways, for example, a line drawing seen first as a cube facing in one direction and then in another. Here again while the very same sensations are present on the two occasions, the recognitional difference is genuinely "felt" and not purely a matter of thoughts or judgments which one makes.)

This account of perception also provides for a more adequate foundation for the distinction between direct and *indirect* perception than would otherwise be possible. On the causal account, the distinction would appear to be this: directly perceiving a given object is being immediately caused (under the appropriate conditions) to form a certain thought about that object; merely indirectly perceiving the same object is being only *indirectly* caused to form some thought about it. But this way of drawing the distinction in question does not account for the fact that there seems to be some *experiential* difference which one tries to capture by distinguishing between direct and indirect perception. A mere difference in the causal conditions *underlying* my experience on an occasion has nothing at all to do with the nature of that experience itself. The alternative account, however, yields a natural distinction which does justice to this phenomenological objection. On that account, directly perceiving an object of some sort would presumably involve a case in which the "concept" of that object comes to be exemplified by certain sensations which I am experiencing; merely indirectly perceiving that object would then be a case in which sensations I am experiencing, and which exemplify some concept *other* than that of the object in question, merely cause me (under the appropriate conditions) to form a *thought* (of an appropriate sort) about that object. On this account, the difference between directly and indirectly perceiving something does involve a phenomenologically relevant difference in a perception. It is a difference which one might describe as between merely perceiving something *as* something or other and actually *perceiving* it as something or other. It is a difference between a case in which a conceptual identification (of a possibly non-existent object) is made merely via a thought or judgment *occasioned* by one's sensory experience on some occasion and a case in which that identification is made via that very experience *itself*.[32]

In at least the case of perceptual acts,[33] then, not only must mental contents play an essential role in determining the "direction" of mental states to their objects, but adequate justice can be done to certain phenomenological facts about perception only on the more particular supposition that those contents function not because they are *themselves* special sorts of objects of awareness, but merely because they are certain sorts of properties exemplified by awareness. A more abstract and merely semantical consideration of mental contents, as discussed in the first section of this chapter, would not have yielded this more particular conclusion. Many philosophers who draw a distinction between the contents and objects of acts do not, however, have the case of perceptual acts primarily in mind. Accordingly, both for the sake of systematic completeness and for the sake of historical depth, the present chapter will conclude with an examination of some of the views of two philosophers who, at least initially, approach these issues primarily out of a concern for the problem of linguistic meaning and the comprehension of words and sentences in judgment.

Contents and Objects in Frege and Husserl

Frege, unlike Husserl, does not draw a very clear or explicit distinction between the contents and the objects of mental acts. Indeed he fails to do justice to the very *existence* of mental acts. Yet Frege's notion, influential in semantical theory, of the "sense" (*Sinn*) as opposed to the "reference" of linguistic expressions, like Husserl's notion of linguistic meaning (*Bedeutung*), plays precisely the role which needs to be played by the notion of mental content. As we have already seen, Meinong had maintained that the content of any mental act is what a certain linguistic expression may always be said to "express," although that same expression might also be used, and generally is, in order to refer to some object. Frege, it is well known, maintains a position which is at least formally analogous to Meinong's: "A proper name (word, sign, sign combination, expression) *expresses* its sense (*Sinn*), *stands for or designates* (*bedeutet oder bezeichnet*) its reference. By means of a sign we express its sense and designate its reference."[34]

Like Meinong and unlike Frege, Husserl explicitly identifies linguistic Meanings with the contents of certain mental acts: "We distinguish, in a perceptual statement, as in every statement, between *content* and *object;* by the 'content' we understand the self-identical meaning that the hearer can grasp even if he is not a percipient."[35] Just as for Frege, similarly, the Sense of an expression is the "mode of presentation" (*Art des Gegebenseins*) of the object to which that expression refers,[36] so for Husserl a Meaning (*Bedeutung*) is that through which reference to an object is "constituted."[37] If an act, as we saw, had no content, then we could not understand how that act might refer to any object, since an actual *relation* with some object is irrelevant to any act's capacity for reference. There must therefore be some other dimension present in an act, besides its relation to an object, in virtue of which that act involves a reference to its object. Husserl describes this dimension as the Meaning which an act involves, and it then follows that it is in virtue of a Meaning that there is reference to an object. In the same way, for Frege, it is "in virtue of" a sense that some expression has a reference: though all expressions express some sense, it is not the case that every expression has a reference.[38] It is also by appeal to the sense of an expression that we account for the *difference* between two expressions which differ in meaning yet possess an identical reference, as it is by appeal to the content of an act that we account for the fact that two acts may differ qualitatively though they refer to the same object.

Though Husserl took it for granted that any concern with language as a carrier of meaning, and not as a merely physical phenomenon, leads ultimately to a concern with the contents and the objects of certain mental acts,[39] it may seem wrong to many philosophers to identify the meaning of some linguistic expression with the content of some mental act. Frege takes pains, after all, to distinguish questions about the meaning of expressions, which are something objective, from questions about merely subjective mental states.[40] But if we distinguish the content of some act from the act itself whose content it is, then the content of a mental act may also be something objective. If the content is distinct not only from the object, but also from the act which apprehends that object, then it is possible to suppose that numerically the same content might be the content of different acts in many different thinkers, and indeed that the content might continue to exist even when no particular act exists at all. Like Frege, therefore, Husserl also took pains to argue that since several acts might share the same content, a distinction is required between "content" in an objective and logical sense and "content" in a merely subjective and psychological sense. The former provides an objective unity as contrasted with a potential multiplicity of individual mental acts.[41] There is some justification for concluding, then, that despite the difference in emphasis between Husserl's phenomenological approach and Frege's more linguistic approach the two philosophers are not drawing fundamentally different distinctions.[42]

There is, however, an important difference between Husserl's *Bedeutung* and Frege's *Sinn*.[43] On Husserl's view, but not on Frege's, the self-identical Meaning which several acts may share stands to those acts, or at least to some component of those acts, in the relation of a universal to the particulars which instantiate that universal:

> Meaning is related to varied acts of meaning—Logical Presentation to presentative acts, Logical Judgment to acts of judging, Logical Syllogism to acts of syllogism—just as Redness *in specie* is to the slips of paper which lie here, and which all "have" the same redness. Each slip has, in addition to other constitutive aspects (extension, form, etc.), its own individual redness, i.e., its instance of this colour species.[44]

The content of an act of presentation (*Vorstellung*) is a universal instantiated by an act of presentation; the content of an act of judging something is, similarly, a universal instantiated by an act of judging. Thus Husserl's ontology of Meanings commits us to no more than mental acts (and their constituents) and their universal properties. The difference, accordingly, between two thoughts which refer to the same object yet which differ in content lies in the fact that each of them, or a part of each, instantiates a different Meaning—which is simply to say that the two thoughts are, at least in one respect, qualitatively different thoughts. What two thoughts which share the *same* content then have in common is simply the fact that they are, at least in one respect, qualitatively the same. Since we must in any case grant that mental acts do exemplify various sorts of properties, quite apart from any introduction of the *contents* of mental acts—mental acts have the property of occurring at a particular moment, for example—we may say that Husserl's ontology of Meaning is an economical one. It commits us to no more than mental acts and their properties, and this is something to which we are committed anyway.

Husserl's distinction between an act of presentation and a logical presentation, and between an act of judging and a logical judgment, is reminiscent of the distinction which Bolzano had already drawn between a *Vorstellung* and a *Vorstellung an sich*, and between an *Urteil* or a *Satz* and a *Satz an sich*. The former are merely subjective, the latter are objective and independent of the particular acts in which they might become involved.[45] But Bolzano's *Satz an sich*, or "proposition" in the objective sense, appears to be construed by Bolzano as some sort of object which is grasped by a particular mental act, rather than as a universal which is instantiated by some act. *Sätze* are, for Bolzano, the sorts of things which we think precisely in virtue of thinking *of* or *about* them.[46] Husserl's view is, however, similar to one which has been more recently defended by Gustav Bergmann. Every act, on Bergmann's view, exemplifies two universal characters. One is the character in virtue of which that act is either, for example, a doubting or affirming or perceiving, and this is called the "species" of the act. The other character is that in virtue of which some act is a doubting or affirming or perceiving *of* one particular state of affairs rather than another. This character Bergmann sometimes calls a proposition.[47] A proposition thus satisfies for him the two requirements for a mental content, since it is distinct from the proper intended object of an act (namely, some state of affairs), and yet at the same time something which is shareable by several different acts. But a proposition is not itself, under ordinary (non-reflective) circumstances, an object apprehended by a mental act.

On Frege's view too the Sense of an expression is something objective, and not a merely subjective content of somebody's thinking: Sense "may be the common property of many, and therefore is not a *part or mode (Teil oder Modus)* of the individual mind."[48] But the relation between a Sense and the awarenesses which refer to objects "through" that Sense is not merely that of a universal to particular instances of that universal. It is rather than of an *object* of particular awarenesses to awarenesses *of* that object. The *Gedanke*, or the Thought, for example, which is the Sense of a whole sentence, is some single thing which several thinkers apprehend in thinking a thought: "A particular mental capacity, the power of thought, must correspond to the apprehension of thought. In thinking we do not produce thoughts but we apprehend them."[49]

Now to say that we "apprehend a thought" is of course to say something ambiguous. While it might be only to say that we engage in some activity of thinking, it might also be to say something stronger, namely that through this thinking we are aware of some entity—a Thought—which is distinct from thinking. The only "relation" required in order to account for the former is just a relation that would obtain between certain mental acts and various properties *of* those acts. In order to account for the latter, we must suppose an additional relation to obtain between the thinking mind and the *Gedanken* which it "apprehends." That it is the latter which Frege intends is evident from his note to the passage just quoted:

> The expression 'apprehend' is as metaphorical as 'content of consciousness.' The nature of language does not permit anything else. What I hold in my hand can certainly be regarded as the content of my hand but is all the same the content of my hand in quite a different way from the bones and muscles of which it is made and their tensions, and is much more extraneous to it than they are.[50]

Thus two acts, for Frege, which refer to the same object and yet which differ in content—two acts which may be expressed by sentences which have identical references and different Senses—are more than two acts which happen to be qualitatively different. They are *also* two acts which apprehend different "objects," that is, different Senses. Similarly, two acts which share a common content—two acts which may be expressed by sentences identical in Sense—are not simply acts which happen to be qualitatively the same, since they are *also* two acts which apprehend a single sense. We may judge, accordingly, that Frege's ontology of Sense is a less economical one than Husserl's ontology of Meaning: though it grants, or is committed to granting, the existence of acts and their properties, it introduces, in addition, Senses as objects which are apprehended *by* such acts. As Husserl takes pains to argue, however, "In the act of meaning we are not conscious of meaning as an object."[51]

Frege appears to have held that Senses must be a certain sort of object apprehended through mental activity, on the grounds that any other view of them would fail to do justice to the objective nature of meaning. If the Thought which a sentence expresses were not some *object* of a special sort, then it would be a mere presentation (*Vorstellung*). It would, that is, be a presentation, as distinct from a thing which is *presented* in a presentation. Presentations, however, as contrasted with things presented, are individuated by the mind which is their "bearer" (*Träger*): "It is so much of the essence of each of my presentations to be the content of my consciousness that every presentation of another person is, just as such, distinct from mine."[52] Since the Sense which some sentence expresses is something which may be entertained by several thinkers, it follows that a Sense could not be a mere presentation, as distinct from some object of presentation: "If the thought I express in the Pythagorean theorem can be recognized by others just as much as by me then it does not belong to the content of my consciousness, I am not its bearer."[53] Senses, then, cannot be something objective unless they are *objects*. Otherwise they would be contained in the mind, not simply in the sense in which some object may be contained in my hand, but in the sense, rather, in which the very *structure* of my hand is contained in my hand, and in that case it would not be something which several minds might share.

Frege, however, has failed to distinguish two very different ways in which something might be "contained" in the mind, in addition to the clearly metaphorical sense in which some *object* is said to be contained in the mind so long as the mind apprehends it. He has failed to distinguish, that is, between the sense in which some particular "part or mode" of the mind is contained in the mind and the sense in which the mind contains all the properties which are exemplified *by* any of its parts or modes. As long as we do distinguish between particular states of affairs and the universals which they involve, it would not follow from the fact that a Sense is a presentation rather than some *object* of presentation that a Sense could only be a content of the mind in the first of these two senses. As long, however, as Senses are contents only in the second of these two senses, then we can satisfy the demand that linguistic meaning must be a function of something objective. The universal properties of mental acts are not dependent either in their nature or their existence upon any particular mental occurrences.

It might be thought that there is a second consideration to which Frege might appeal in order to show that the Sense of a sentence could not be construed as the property of some possible mental act. This is that if Senses are construed as possible properties to be exemplified by mental acts, then they must be "incomplete" or "unsaturated" entities; while, however, some of the *parts* of a *Gedanke*, or the sense of a sentence, may be incomplete entities, no *Gedanke* is itself an incomplete entity.[54]

Predicate expressions denote, for Frege, the universals under which particulars may fall as instances, and such entities may be designated by the mathematical expression for a function. Thus 'a is green' may be represented by the complete expression 'F(a).' The expression 'F( ),' taken just by itself, however, has no more a complete sense than does the predicate 'is green.' It makes no more sense to assert, for example, "F( ) is a function" than it does to assert "is green is a function." Similarly, it makes no more sense to assert "Frege admires the color F ( )" than it does to assert "Frege admires the color is green." The incomplete nature of predicate or function expressions simply reflects the fact that what these expressions denote is an entity which is essentially predicative in nature. Because of their essentially predicative nature, the expressions which denote universals can enter into meaningful discourse only *as* predicates.[55] However, the expressions which designate the Thought which some sentence expresses do *not* play a merely predicative role in discourse. I can, for example, say "Frege believes that *a* is green," and in such intentional contexts the expression 'that *a* is green' is in fact used to denote the very Thought which the sentence '*a* is green' expresses.[56] It would make no sense to say, however, "Frege believes is that *a* is green." If the Thought which a sentence expresses, furthermore, were a universal under which particular mental acts might fall as instances, then it should also make sense to say, of some particular mental act, that it is "that *a* is *F*," but this does not make any sense either. Hence we must conclude that the Sense of a sentence is not a universal.

This argument is question-begging. We may grant that the expression 'that *a* is green' is being used to designate the Sense of the sentence '*a* is green,' when it occurs in the context 'Frege believes that *a* is green.' It does not follow from this, however, that the expression is not being used predicatively. It is possible to suppose that it is being used simply as *part* of the non-relational predicate '*believes* that *a* is green.' Similarly, we may grant that it makes no sense to say of some particular mental act that it is "that *a* is green." But we might, nevertheless, introduce the predicate '*means* that *a* is green,' and then analyze 'Frege believes that *a* is green' simply as 'Frege is in some mental state S, such that S is a believing and S *means* that *a* is green.'

We must, therefore, distinguish two very different senses in which we might claim that the Sense of a sentence is a "complete" entity. First, there is the sense in which the sentence '*a* is *F*' expresses a complete *Sense*, whereas the expression 'is *F*' does not. But this is very different from the sense in which we might claim that the expression 'is *F*' denotes an incomplete *entity*, whereas the expression 'that *a* is *F*' does not. To make this latter claim assumes that the second of these two expressions is not being used in intentional contexts simply as part of some non-relational predicate. This, however, is precisely what needs to be proved.

Frege, then, could not have been, or at least *ought* not to have been, led to his conception of Senses as objects rather than as properties of possible mental acts simply on the ground that Senses are not merely predicative in nature. That this was not Frege's reason for rejecting the Husserlian theory of Meaning should in fact be evident from the argument that he explicitly offers for the objectivity of Senses. As already shown, he did not *argue* there that Senses could not be the properties of mental acts; he simply *failed to distinguish* mental acts from their properties. We may therefore shed some more light on Frege's motives by taking a closer look at the ontological status of properties in general in his ontology. Frege did not of course fail to distinguish in a general way between particulars and universals, since the former are, for him, the references of proper and common nouns while the latter are the references of predicate expressions. It can be argued, nevertheless, that the ontological status of universals in Frege's world is a very tenuous one.[57] This is because, though there are universals for Frege, there is no real "connection" in his world *between* universals and particulars (or at least whatever connection there is between universals and particulars must *itself* be accounted for by appealing to the very notion of Sense which is in question).

The claim that there is no real connection between Frege's particulars and universals will no doubt appear to be contradicted by some of his own statements: "I am concerned to show that the argument does not belong with the function, but goes together with the function to make up a *complete whole;* for the function by itself must be called incomplete, in need of supplementation, or 'unsaturated.'"[58] Frege certainly appears in this passage to insist that a universal does not simply stand side by side, as it were, with the particulars which are its instances, but rather *combines* with those particulars to form a complex whole. What combines these entities into such a whole is, we might say, the "relation" of "falling-under," or "being-an-instance-of." If this, however, is Frege's view, then how can we avoid the conclusion that a sentence such as '*a* is *F*' designates a complex entity one of whose constituents is *a* itself, in other words, that it designates a state of affairs consisting of a particular and a universal standing in the relation of "falling-under." According to Frege, however, when we demand a reference for some particular sentence, then we are "driven into accepting the *truth value* of a sentence as constituting its reference."[59] Truth values cannot be, like states of affairs, complexes which contain the particulars which certain sentences are about, since there are only two different truth values, whereas there must be at least as many different complexes as there are particulars for sentences to refer to. It is unclear, therefore, how "falling-under" *could* be a real connection between a universal and a particular after all.

It is interesting to note, furthermore, that while it is because of the need for a function and argument to combine into a "complete whole" that Frege insists upon the "unsaturated" nature of functions, the sort of combination for which the unsaturatedness of a function is called upon to account does not seem to be in the first instance a combination of a function with a particular such as *a* at all: "Not all parts of a thought can be complete; at least one must be 'unsaturated' or predicative; otherwise they would not hold together."[60] In this passage Frege refers only to the unsaturated part of a *Thought*, which is the Sense, not the reference, of a sentence. In general Frege's conviction that there must be some unsaturated entity (a function) which is the reference of a predicate term, and "under" which objects may fall, appears to derive primarily from his belief that the *Sense* of a predicate term must be some entity which is unsaturated or incomplete.[61] That predicate terms do have a reference is demanded, for Frege, by the fact that sentences are capable of expressing truths about concrete entities in the world, that is, about entities to which the subject term of a sentence refers.[62] However, that the reference of a predicate term is an *incomplete* entity seems never to be asserted by Frege on independent grounds, but always as a mere consequence of the fact that the Sense of a sentence, in order to hold together, must consist of both a saturated and an unsaturated component. The incompleteness of the universals which predicate expressions denote, in other words, is not demanded in order that a universal may combine with a particular in some complex whole. It is demanded only as a consequence of the fact that the *Sense* of a predicate expression must join together with the Sense of a subject expression in the Thought.

Frege does speak of a *"Verbindung"* between objects and the "concepts" which are the references of predicate expressions: objects are "subsumed" under concepts. However, "subsumption" is for Frege a purely "logical" relation between entities.[63] It is a "relation," that is, which is generated by a mere *thought:* "Die Verbindung, in die Gegenstand und Begriff durch den Satz gebracht werden, können wir nennen die *Subsumption* des Gegenstandes unter den Begriff."[64] A relation into which entities are "brought" by a mere thought or a sentence is, of course, really no relation between those entities at all. Thus all *real* combining of entities into complex wholes is involved for Frege in the Thought itself, and not in the world to which the Thought or its parts refer:

> One might also say that judgments are distinctions of parts within truth values. Such distinction occurs by a *return to the thought.* To every *sense* belonging to a truth value there would correspond its own manner of analysis. However, I have here used the word "part" in a special sense. I have in fact transferred the relation between the parts and the whole of the sentence to its reference.[65]

If this suggestion is to be taken seriously, then the judgment that *a* is *F* does not assert any real connection between the individual *a* and a concept; hence what it expresses is not such a connection. It does not of course follow from this that there is no real difference between *a*'s falling under a given concept and its merely being *thought* to fall under that concept. The particular *a* really falls under the concept *F*( ) if and only if the Thought which subsumes it under that concept refers to the True rather than to the False. However, *a*'s falling under the concept *F*( ) does not consist in any real connection between *a* and the concept *F*( ), and its being *thought* to fall under that concept does not consist in its being thought to stand in any such connection: the two are not thereby represented as combined into a complex whole distinct from the mere collection of its constituents. Thus "by combining subject and predicate, one reaches only a thought, never passes from sense to reference,"[66] and all real combination occurs only in the Thought, not in the world to which the Thought refers.

We need to distinguish, therefore, between two different notions of "subject" and "predicate" in a judgment. In one sense, the subject and the predicate are the constituents of some Thought, and these do come to form a genuine complex which *is* the Thought in question. In another sense, the subject and the predicate are the particular and the universal which are the *references* of the constituents of some Thought. The former of these entities may come to "fall under" the latter of these entities, but to say that this occurs is not to assert any real relation between a particular and a universal: it is not to claim that there is in the world any complex whole *in addition* to whatever Thought may be in question. Thus Frege's view turns out to be very much like Meinong's. Like Meinong, who does not distinguish between an Objective and a state of affairs containing the Objects which that Objective "involves," Frege fails to distinguish between a Thought and a state of affairs containing the entities which are the references of that Thought's constituents. Both philosophers are to be contrasted with Husserl, who distinguished not simply between objects and the contents of the judgments which we make about them ("Logical Judgments"), but also between objects and the states of affairs which contain them.[67]

If this appraisal of Frege's theory is sound, then we are finally able to understand why, unlike Husserl, he could not have appealed to the distinction between particular mental acts and the universals which they exemplify (or might exemplify) in order to account for a sentence's possessing a Sense. The reason is that such an account would necessarily be circular. The notion that some particular "falls under" a given universal is, for Frege, to be explicated in terms of a certain Thought being true. Therefore, distinguishing between a sentence and the Thought which that sentence expresses in terms of a distinction between a mental act and a universal which it might instantiate would be circular. To say, for example, that some particular act exemplifies the property "that *a* is *F*," or "*means* that *a* is *F*," would just be to say that the *Thought* of this particular act as exemplifying that property is true. We could not, then, proceed to explicate what we mean in the first place by the apprehension of a "Thought" by introducing the notion of some mental act's exemplifying certain properties.

Though Husserl's theory of Meaning differs fundamentally from Frege's, Husserl later abandoned it in favor of a more Fregean view. A number of commentators have compared the role of the "noema" in Husserl's later theory with that of Frege's Sense.[68] Noemata, for Husserl, are not universals in which individual acts (noeses), or parts of acts, participate; rather they are merely the "correlates" (*Korrelaten*) of acts, which provide the acts of which they are correlates with a particular "sense" (*Sinn*).[69] Like Frege's *Sinn* in addition, and the *Bedeutung* of the *Logische Untersuchungen*, we may say that reference to an object is constituted only *through* the noema which is correlated with a particular act: the intentionality of the latter "carries the former in itself as a correlate of consciousness, and its intentionality passes in a certain way through (*geht in gewisser Weise durch*) the noematic" intentionality.[70] Furthermore, while the relationship between acts of consciousness and the noemata which constitute reference to objects is not the same as that between consciousness and those very objects,[71] the noema is nevertheless in some sense an *object* of apprehension. This is evident from the sorts of examples which Husserl gives of noemata. He describes the series of noemata, for example, "through which" the same tree is perceived and recognized from several different perspectives as the "perceived tree as such": "The tree plain and simple (*der Baum schlechthin*), the thing in nature, is as different as it can be from this perceived tree as such (*dieses Baumwahrgenommene als solches*), which as perceptual meaning belongs to the perception, and that inseparably."[72] In this case the noema is the tree "as it is perceived," hence in some sense an *object* rather than a property of apprehension. In general, in the words of Aron Gurwitsch, "To each act there corresponds a noema, namely, an *object* such, exactly and only such, as the subject is aware of it and has it in view, when he is experiencing the act in question."[73]

What sort of entity an object "as the subject is aware of it" might be, in distinction from the object itself of which the subject is aware, is of course a difficult question. It is not unreasonable to attempt an answer by noting some of the similarities between Husserl's noema and Frege's *Sinn*. Frege also describes an expression's *Sinn* as the way in which an object is given (*Art des Gegebenseins*) to a possible act of apprehension; he also regards it as *itself* in some way apprehended as an "object" by the act through which the original object (its "reference") is thus given. There is therefore some justification for the judgment that Husserl's phenomenology ultimately makes sense only in the light of Frege's semantics:

> To see phenomenology as a theory of intentionality via intensions is, in the final analysis, just to make sense of phenomenology. And that is just to give Frege the credit for lending Sense to Husserl.[74]

But the justification for this claim is limited, since it applies only to Husserl's theory of the noema. That theory is very different from his earlier theory of Meaning, although the earlier theory, with its concern for the contents and the objects of mental acts, has as much of a claim as the latter to be regarded as a form of "phenomenology." Furthermore, Husserl's earlier theory is in fact superior to Frege's theory of Sense, since it is more economical and does not introduce any puzzling entities at all. It does not, that is, require a distinction between two radically different sorts of objects for mental acts.

It has been argued, however, that either Husserl's theory of Meaning in the *Logische Untersuchungen* does in fact require a distinction between two different sorts of objects for acts—"intentional" objects and real objects—or else that Husserl has no reason at all for distinguishing the objects from the "contents" of acts in the first place. One of the reasons, as we have seen, for distinguishing the content from the object of an act is that two acts may refer to the same object, yet differ in their internal nature. They might, that is, differ in such a way that anyone who experienced those acts could be aware of the difference even though he had no knowledge of the existence of an object outside of them. In Husserl's own example, the expressions 'the Victor of Jena' and 'the Vanquished of Waterloo' refer to the same object, though we do not *understand* just the same thing by these expressions.[75] Hence we must distinguish between the object of the acts expressible by means of these expressions and the contents of those acts. However, it might be argued that when we try to *specify* the contents of these acts—to specify what we understand in using the expressions which express them—we find that we are only specifying the *objects* of these acts. Despite any possible lack of knowledge concerning the existence of Napoleon, for example, a person

> would no doubt understand the two expressions, and he would recognize—in spite of his ignorance—that they differ in signifi-

cance. By the mere understanding of these expressions, this person would be "conscious" of different significations. . . . But what is he "actually conscious" of in understanding the two expressions? What is he referentially directed to? Obviously, such a person is unable to give different answers to these questions, i.e., he is unable to distinguish what he is conscious of (allegedly, the senses) from what is he (sic) referentially directed to (allegedly, the object).[76]

Thus I seem to know that the acts expressible by 'the Victor of Jena' and 'the Vanquished of Waterloo' are acts which differ in "content" only because I know that the *objects* of these acts are different. The object of the first is simply the intentional object *the Victor of Jena*, while the object of the second is the intentional object *the Vanquished of Waterloo*.[77] Neither of these intentional objects is identical with the man Napoleon, that is, with the person who was victorious at Jena and who was defeated at Waterloo. Each of these intentional objects is not Napoleon himself, but rather Napoleon *as he is (or may be) intended* by some act. In order, therefore, to distinguish between the contents and the objects of mental acts, we must suppose that "contents" are themselves a sort of object for an act, namely the *object as it is intended* rather than the object which is intended in an act.[78] If this is so, then Husserl's early distinction between the objects of acts and the Meanings which they embody must, if it is a legitimate one, be construed in the light of his own later theory of the noema.

However, this conclusion does not follow. Let us grant that a person who understands the expression 'the Victor of Jena' is immediately aware of its difference from his understanding of the expression 'the Vanquished of Waterloo'; let us also grant that the only difference which he is aware of in these two cases is that in understanding the former he thinks of someone victorious at Jena, while in understanding the latter he thinks of someone vanquished at Waterloo. It does not follow that the only difference which these two thoughts exhibit must be a difference in certain *objects* which that person apprehends. That would follow only if we assumed that the predicate 'thinks of someone victorious at Jena' and the predicate 'thinks of someone vanquished at Waterloo' were *relational* predicates. This is what we have no right to assume, since it is precisely the point at issue.

We may grant that if we *do* distinguish between real and intentional objects, or between objects and objects "as they are intended," then the distinction between the contents and the objects of acts is only a disguised distinction between two different sorts of objects for acts. However, no reason has been given why we should make such a distinction, or why, if we do, we should not take it merely as a distinction between real objects and the *way we intend* those objects, rather than as a distinction between real objects and some other sort of object altogether. Taking the distinction in the former way, we may describe the difference between our understanding of 'the Victor of Jena' and of 'the Vanquished of Waterloo' simply as a matter of two distinct *ways of being conscious* rather than of two distinct *objects* presented to consciousness. It might be argued that adopting this approach would then make it impossible to tell, merely on the basis of experiencing some act, whether that act in fact had any object *at all*, whereas Husserl insists that all acts do have objects. Again, however, this would follow only so long as "having an object" is a relational state of affairs involving some object—which is precisely the point at issue. In one sense, then, Husserl might grant that every thought necessarily has an object and that two qualitatively different thoughts necessarily have *different* objects. He might grant, for example, that 'the Victor of Jena' and 'the Vanquished of Waterloo' express thoughts about two different objects. However, this admission would not require an ontological distinction between the intentional object *the Victor of Jena* and the real person who was actually victorious at Jena, since it has not been shown that "thinking two different objects" is standing in two different relational states of affairs with objects.

There remains, then, an important difference between Husserl's conception, in the *Logische Untersuchungen*, of the distinction between the contents and the objects of mental acts and his later, more Fregean conception of that distinction. As earlier argued, furthermore, so long as our motivation for introducing such entities as Fregean "Senses" in the first place is to account for the objective meanings of expressions and sentences, then there is no good reason for preferring Frege's view to Husserl's earlier one. Frege was simply wrong in thinking that as long as "contents" of thought are not *objects* which are somehow apprehended in every thought, then they must be something merely individual and "subjective."

Some philosophers have attempted, however, to introduce such entities as Fregean Senses on a somewhat different basis from what we have so far considered. For example, there is the following argument. Any sentence "has the same meaning, whether it happens to express a truth or not. Consequently, if one is going to hold that such a belief *must have an object*, which will serve also as the meaning of the sentence that conveys the belief, some object must be found which is not necessarily a fact. And this request is met by the invention of propositions."[79] Propositions are not introduced in this argument simply in order that they may play the role of sentence *meanings*. They are also introduced in order that every belief and judgment, including a false one, might be said to have some *object*. Thus propositions might be defined either as the "meanings" of sentences (hence as the possible "contents" of any acts which those sentences might express) or simply as "the sort of thing which can be believed (or disbelieved)." Surely, it might be argued, there *is* something which everyone believes who believes the Pythagorean Theorem, and this is just the objective content of all their beliefs. However, it makes no sense to say that *what* several individuals believe, when believing the Pythagorean Theorem, is some property of a possible mental act. There is just no sense to saying, that is, "Frege believes the property *F*" as there is to saying that "Frege believes the Pythagorean Theorem." Therefore, even if there is a sense in which the properties which an individual act "bears" are something "objective" and shareable by several acts, they cannot be objective in the sense in which the content of a judgment or belief must be objective. Objectivity of the latter sort is secured only if the content of a belief is an actual *object* of apprehension in the belief whose content it is.

This argument for propositions as the objects of belief and judgment will simply not work. The argument begins from the premise that every judgment has some object, and it then infers that since there is often no fact or state of affairs to serve as the object of a judgment, propositions must be introduced in order to perform that function. This inference would be a valid one only if we could assume as a premise that for every act which is "directed toward" an object, or "refers to" an object, or "has" an object, there must *be* that object toward which that act is directed. This assumption is contradicted, however, by the very facts from which the argument began—the recognition that *not* every state of affairs which a judgment intends does in fact exist. Hence it is not the case that for every act which has an object there must be an object which that act has. The only way to avoid the force of this criticism is simply to deny that states of affairs are ever objects of judgment at all. However, so long as we grant that there *are* such entities as states of affairs, this reply must appear implausible. Only if we fail to distinguish, therefore, between propositions and the states of affairs which those propositions affirm will it be possible to accept this sort of argument for propositions.

Conclusion

A distinction between the "contents" and the objects of mental acts is unavoidable. Drawing the distinction, we simply acknowledge that the intentional features of thought, judgment, and the conceptual component of perception cannot be explained by psychological relations with the intentional *objects* of those states. Since awareness of an act's intentional character is not awareness of some actual relation with the object of that act's intention, it follows that it involves awareness of some other dimension present in the act, and the term 'content' may be introduced in order to designate this dimension.

Distinguishing contents from objects in this way, is neutral with regard to the question whether mental contents are objects distinct from the acts of which they are the contents. If they are distinct, then intentional acts "have" two very different sorts of objects—their intentional objects, which may or may not be real, and their "contents," which are as real as the acts themselves. In the terminology we employed earlier, this approach construes the predicate 'j's ⌜a is F⌝'—introduced to formalize one of three possible intentional readings of the predicate 'judges that a is F'—as a relational predicate involving an object designated by the term '⌜a is F⌝'. That object is distinct from the state of affairs "a-being-F," which is designated by the sentence 'a is F.' Similarly, this approach construes the predicates 'j*'s ⌜is F⌝ of a' and 'j**'s being-F of ⌜a⌝' as relational predicates involving the objects designated by '⌜a⌝' and '⌜being-F⌝.' Those objects are distinct from the individual a and the property being-F. Fregean Senses appear to provide an example of such objects.

The alternative to regarding mental contents as objects distinct from the acts of which they are the contents is to identify them with certain *properties* of those acts—properties whose presence in an act provides that act with a particular intentional character. On this alternative the predicate 'j's ⌜a is F⌝' does not express a relation between some possible thinker and an object distinct from his thoughts; it simply expresses the presence *in* some possible thinker's thoughts of the property designated by the term '⌜a is F⌝.' It has been argued in this chapter that this alternative is preferable to the first. An example of it can be found in Husserl's early theory of Meaning.

However, it is not possible to regard the introduction of predicates like 'j's $\bar{a}$ is $\bar{F}$' as the solution of any problems about the intentionality of the mental; it merely indicates a general direction of approach. To accept such predicates as primitive terms would leave us in the untenable position already exposed at the end of Chapter 2: it will be impossible to make any sense of the notion of a person's thoughts or judgments being true or correct ones. If someone judges correctly that a is F, then a is F. Intuitively, it seems that we might explain this inference in the following way: judging that a is F affirms a certain possible state of affairs—the judgment is correct when the state of affairs is actualized, otherwise it is incorrect. However, if judging is *not* explicated in terms of a relation between some judg-ment and a possible state of affairs affirmed by that judgment, but rather in terms of a person's being in a certain peculiar *state*, then there no longer is any apparent connection between the assessments we make concerning the correctness or incor-rectness of a person's judgment and the states of affairs which obtain in the world apart from that person's psychological states. Thus the distinction between correct-ness and incorrectness in judgment appears to be eliminated.

Husserl's early view appears to have been not only that the presence of a certain "content" in an act is what accounts for that act's intentional character, but also that the ability of this content to account for the character in question is an *indefinable feature* of that content. Certain properties in an act account for that act's intentional character, and nothing more needs to be said about the matter: intentional refer-ence (*Beziehung*) is

> understood in purely descriptive fashion as an inward peculiarity
> (*innere Eigentümlichkeit*) of certain experiences. . . .[80] Intentional
> experiences have the peculiarity of directing themselves in varying
> fashion to presented objects, but they do so in an *intentional*
> sense. An object is "referred to" or "aimed at" in them, and in
> presentative or judging or other fashion. This means no more than
> that certain experiences are present, intentional in character. . . .
> Only one thing is present, the intentional experience, whose es-
> sential descriptive character is the intention in question. . . . If this
> experience is present, then *eo ipso* and through its own essence
> (we must insist), the intentional "relation" to an object is achieved,
> and an object is "intentionally present."[81]

This view appears to differ from the interpretation of Brentano's position considered at the end of Chapter 2 only in virtue of Husserl's explicit distinction between a particular and the universal character or "essence" it exemplifies.

Rejecting the view that an act's intentional character is a "purely descriptive feature" of that act does not require rejecting the claim that the intentional charac-ter of an act is accounted for only by appeal to the presence of a certain "content" in the act. It only requires the admission that an act's intentional character is a charac-ter which it possesses in virtue of certain explicable facts *about* a particular content which is present in the act.[82] This point may be illuminated with the aid of a linguistic analogy. For example, it is not an immediate descriptive feature of a certain mark on paper that this mark is a word which possesses a particular semantical significance. However, it is only because the mark does *exhibit* certain descriptive features that one is aware of it in the first place as possessing the particular significance which it has. The following chapter will pursue this linguistic analogy, considering the plausibility of regarding "mental contents" as inner analogues of spoken or written words and sentences. At the very least, this suggestion appears to permit a straightforward response to our earlier considered problem of distinguishing correct from incorrect judgment once a relational account of judgment has been rejected: correct judgments are those whose "contents" are true sentences, incorrect judgments are those whose "contents" are false sentences.

5

Intentionality
and Language

At a number of points in the course of his writings, Wilfrid Sellars attacks the
assumption that intentionality is a real "characteristic" or "property" of some sort of
entity:

> 1. What persuades you that the "means" of
>   "..." means—
> must stand for a characteristic, even if a "funny" one? If, like Bren-
> tano, you conclude (rightly) that it is only ostensibly a relation,
> must it therefore be a characteristic of some other kind, perhaps a
> kind all its own?
>
> 2. The traditional puzzles about intentionality arise, in large
> measure, from the presupposition that because statements of the
> form "S means p" are often true, they must be capable of being
> gripped by such philosophical wrenches as "property," "relation,"
> "attribute," "describe," etc.
>
> 3. I doubt very much that the trouble lies in the area of
> "synonymy," "analysis" and such fashionable perplexities. Unless I
> am very much mistaken, it lies in the area of "fact," "property,"
> "describe," and their kindred. A discussion of "ought" would pro-
> vide a test case.[1]

According to Chisholm an examination of the "traditional puzzles about intentionality" leads to the conclusion that thinking beings possess a "funny kind of
characteristic" that is lacking in ordinary physical beings. Sellars' point thus seems
to be that once we are free of the mistaken assumption that intentionality is any sort
of characteristic at all, then the traditional puzzles could not possibly lead to
Chisholm's conclusion. This, of course, is not to say that the traditional puzzles lack
a philosophical point. They do at least show that the "logic" of 'means' differs in
some important ways from that of 'red' or 'to the left of.' Nonetheless this no more
shows, according to Sellars, that meaning or intending involves an importantly
different property from these sorts of properties or characters than the peculiar
logic of normative statements shows the need for recognizing unique value characters which particulars might exemplify in addition to all of their ordinary characters.[2] Statements about meaning are in fact, like prescriptive statements, not a kind
of "describing discourse" at all.[3]

It is important to distinguish two interpretations of the claim that statements about intentional meaning are not "descriptive" statements. If, as suggested in Chapter 4, the intentional character of a mental act is not due to the presence of some immediate "descriptive character" in an act, but rather to certain describable facts about an act's "content," then regarding the "content" of a mental act as a property rather than an *object* of that act implies that an act's intentional character is merely a "second-order" property or character of that act. Intentionality would be a feature of an act only in virtue of some character *of* a character of an act. This is one claim that might be intended in saying that intentional meaning is not really a "descriptive characteristic" or a "property" of mental acts. However, a second interpretation of this statement is more radical: regarding an act as possessing intentional features is simply a matter of having adopted a certain *attitude* toward that act (or toward some character of that act). On the first view there is an important sense in which intentionality may still be regarded as a property or character of an act; it is simply a *second-order* property of the act. The second view does not allow even this concession.

Many philosophers have regarded normative, or at least moral, discourse in the second of these ways: evaluating an event or state of affairs is merely expressing a certain attitude toward it or resolution concerning it—perhaps in addition urging or "prescribing" that others do so as well. There is no conception of objective conditions for the *truth or falsity* of the evaluation in question. However, normative statements are not ordinarily regarded in the first of the ways that I distinguished. It is of course generally recognized that normative judgments about particular events or states of affairs are judgments made because of the presence of certain *non*-normative, purely "descriptive" features in those events or states of affairs. For example, we regard a particular act of killing as wrong because it is a particular instance of a general *kind* of act that we regard as wrong. This, however, does not imply that normative statements merely involve the ascription of second-order characters to particular acts. It does not require maintaining that the description of an act of killing as "wrong" is to be explicated in terms of some *further* feature of the property of "killing." We are merely required to admit that particular acts are normatively describable only in relation to some previously determined non-normative classification of the acts in question.

It appears to be Sellars' view that intentional statements are "non-descriptive" in the more radical of these senses; the suggested analogy with certain views about normative discourse at least strongly indicates this. If this view of intentional discourse is correct, then to assert that a person is thinking some particular thought is not to make a judgment about that person for which there are objective conditions of truth or falsity, in the same way that, on a view of moral discourse as "non-descriptive," there are no objective conditions for the truth or falsity of the judgment that killing is wrong. However, it is possible to offer a more conservative interpretation of Sellars' claims about the non-descriptive character of intentional discourse. Instead of denying that intentional statements ascribe any real characteristic or property to acts at all, Sellars might simply be taken as denying that the intentional characteristics of mental acts are *first-order* characteristics of those acts.

I will not attempt to determine whether Sellars' view in fact involves the more radical or the more conservative of these approaches, but the more conservative account of intentionality considered in this chapter is at least sufficiently Sellarsian to warrant regarding it as an "interpretation" of his view.

The interpretation to be considered has the advantage of permitting retention of the commonsense assumption that there are objective conditions for the truth or falsity of assertions about a person's intentional states. However, it is important to observe that this is distinct from another assumption which has been called into question in recent years—the assumption that there is an objective *determinacy* in questions concerning the truth or falsity of intentional descriptions. On the Sellarsian view the intentional character of the mental is due to the presence in a mental act of a particular "content" which is "translatable" in a certain way: the content in question is regarded as an inner analogue of an overt linguistic item. It has recently been argued, however, that all translation is "indeterminate." According to Quine, there will always be more than one possible way of interpreting the meaning of an assertion in some language. Because of this, he concludes, it is nonsense to ask precisely what any given expression means; with equal legitimacy it might be said to mean a variety of different things, that is, be translatable in a number of distinct ways.[4] If this is correct, then the Sellarsian view would commit us to denying that there are objective conditions for the determinate truth of statements concerning the intentional character of mental acts—for example, concerning what a person happens to be thinking on some occasion. While it is beyond the scope of our investigation to consider Quine's argument, it is sufficient to observe that the denial of an objective "determinacy" in questions of meaning is not tantamount to denying the existence of objective conditions for the truth or falsity of answers to such questions. Denying that questions about meaning admit of perfectly *determinate* answers—answers which exclude all alternatives—is compatible with insisting that there are perfectly objective conditions for the admission of a range of *possible* answers. True assertions about what a person is thinking on some occasion might be regarded as those which fall within this range, mistaken assertions will fall outside it.

The Analogy Theory of Thinking

The Sellarsian account of the intentionality of the mental can best be approached by considering first the account which Sellars proposes for statements about the meaning of linguistic expressions. Consider the two propositions

    (1) 'dog' (in English) means *dog*

and

    (2) '*Hund*' (in German) means *dog*.

There is a temptation to regard such intentional propositions as asserting some relation between a linguistic item—the German or English word in question—and a non-linguistic item such as the class of dogs in general or the attribute Canininity. In fact, according to Sellars, it is more accurate to regard these propositions as assertions about linguistic items only. Thus the second sentence might simply be regarded as asserting that the word 'Hund' has the same use in German as the word 'dog' in English. However, as Sellars points out, this would do only as a first approximation. The sentence

(3) 'Hund' has the same use in German as 'dog' in English

is not equivalent to (2), since (3) asserts something which could be understood by someone who does not know what the word 'dog' means in English, whereas this is not so of (2).[4]

Sellars attempts to meet this difficulty by the introduction of a special quoting device, called "dot-quoting." We may introduce the expression '·dog·,' for example, as a common noun which applies to a linguistic item in any language which plays the role which is played in English by the word 'dog.' But we specify that such expressions may be introduced *only* in contexts where the item within the dot quotes may be taken for granted as understood. Presupposing this convention, then, Sellars is claiming that a sentence like (2) "has the sense of" a sentence like

(4) 'Hund' (in German) is a ·dog·.[6]

If this is so, then sentence (1) will have the sense of

(5) 'dog' (in English) is a ·dog·

Our talk about "meaning" in such contexts as (1) and (2), accordingly, does not simply serve to express the fact that a certain linguistic item plays the same role as a certain linguistic item [a different item in (2), but the same item in (1)]. Rather, it also serves "to remind us that in order for the statement to do its job correctly, the unique common-noun forming convention must be understood."[7] This, of course, means that (1) is analytic, which may be troublesome to philosophers who hold a relational theory of meaning. However, as Sellars points out, Bergmann, who does hold a relational account of sorts, also insists that statements of that form are always either analytic or self-contradictory.[8]

Some comments are in order before attempting to state how Sellars proposes to apply these notions to the problem of the intentionality of the *mental*. First, Sellars takes the above analysis to show that semantical discourse—for example, propositions about "meaning"—is a unique mode of discourse. We have seen that a semantical sentence such as (2) cannot be analyzed as a sentence such as (3), since the latter merely states that a certain word plays the same role as another word but does not tell us what this role might be. However, Sellars also denies that we could analyze (2) as something like

(6) 'Hund' (in German) plays the following role: . . .

where (6) is completed by an explicit statement of a parallel between habits of German speakers regarding that word in their language and habits of English speakers regarding the word 'dog.' It seems to follow, therefore, that the role of 'means' in (2) is, though a purely *linguistic* one, nevertheless a unique one. For example, Sellars concludes that someone asserting " '*und*' (in German) means *and*"

> is not metioning his habits, or the habits of English-speaking people generally, with respect to 'and.' He mentions the German vocable '*und*' but *uses* the English vocable 'and.' He uses the latter, however, in a peculiar way, a way which is characteristic of *semantical* discourse. He presents us with an instance of the word itself, not a name of it, and, making use of the fact that we belong to the same language community, indicates to us that we have only to rehearse our use of 'and' to appreciate the role of '*und*' on the other side of the Rhine.[9]

Sentences such as (2), then, do "convey" or "indicate" information about actual linguistic usage, but they do not *assert* such information. This appears to imply, however, that there is *no* "information" which semantical statements do assert; Sellars accordingly maintains that semantical discourse is, like prescriptive discourse, not a form of *descriptive* discourse at all.[10] This conclusion is a momentous one, since it is presumably in the light of it that Sellars offers his suggestion that meaning is not any sort of property or characteristic which entities might possess.

It is not clear, however, that this argument ought to be accepted. While it might be granted that statements about linguistic meaning do not "indicate" the role of certain linguistic items in virtue of making assertions about anybody's linguistic "habits," Sellars points out that the sorts of "facts" with which we are concerned in understanding linguistic "roles" in the first place are primarily facts about the *correctness or incorrectness* of certain linguistic moves, and this concern is very different from a concern with anybody's actual linguistic practices.[11] We might suggest, therefore, that if Sellars' general approach is a correct one, then we ought to be able to analyze (2) as

> (7) '*Hund*' (in German) plays a role which is defined by the following rules: . . .

where (7) is completed by an explicit statement of the rules which define the role of the word '*Hund*' in German, without any mention of the linguistic practices of English-speaking people. It may of course be possible that (7) is the correct analysis of (2), even though a person who can assert with understanding that '*Hund*' (in German) means *dog* may not be able to state very exactly the rules which pertain to the use of the word 'dog.' But it is possible to understand a proposition without knowing its complete analysis, and anyone, furthermore, who did understand sentence (2) in the first place would presumably at least *agree* with sentence (7), even if he would not himself have offered it as an analysis of the former sentence.

There is another difficulty which may also appear to show that (2) cannot be analyzed into (7). If (7) is the correct analysis of (2), then it is presumably also the correct analysis of

> (8) '*Hund*' (in German) means *chien*

where (8) is addressed to a person who understands the role of the French word in question. It may seem evident that (7) and (8) do not have the same sense, since sentence (8), after all, would not be understood by an English speaker who did not understand any French at all, although both (2) and (7) could still be understood by him. However, we must remember that if (8) is not understood simply because the word '*chien*' is not understood, then, on Sellars' view, (8) is simply not a well-formed sentence in English. So long as it is well-formed and so long as (2) is also well-formed, then anyone who understands (8) will also understand (2), and it is not evident why *under those circumstances*, both might not be analyzed along the lines of (7).

If this sort of move is acceptable, however, one might wonder why we should continue to resist the original proposal for an analysis of (2) into (3). We rejected that proposal on the gound that someone might understand (3) without understanding (2) at all; but if a condition for (2) being well-formed in the first place is that 'dog' be part of an understood vocabulary, this difficulty seems to disappear. Furthermore, if the role of the word 'dog' is understood, then (3) may be used to do the same job as (2)—to convey the role which is played by the word '*Hund*' in German, and not simply to convey the fact that there *is* such a role and that it is shared by a certain other word. However, even if the condition for (2) being well-formed does guarantee that (3) might be used to convey the same information that (2) itself conveys, the fact remains that an understanding of the word 'dog' is not directly a condition for (3) itself being well-formed. Hence while (3) *may* be used, given that (2) is well-formed, to do the job of (2), it is not the very *point* of a sentence like (3) to perform such a function. The only essential point of that sentence is to state an identity of roles played by two different expressions, not to convey *what* role this might be. A sentence of form (7), however, clearly does have the job of stating what the role of a certain expression is.

One might object to this whole proceeding in that it does seem odd to say that a certain expression might be ill-formed simply because one of its components is not understood by a particular person. What, after all, if some other person does understand the expression in question? Is the total expression ill-formed "for me" but well-formed "for him," as opposed to merely being not *understood* by me but understood by him? Whatever difficulties may be raised here, however, are also raised by Sellars' "dot-quoting," which, according to him, helps produce sentences which "have the sense of" ordinary sentences about "meaning." If Sellars is right, then we must, as he insists, simply grant that sentences about meaning do function in a unique way—that they involve the unique sort of formation convention which is reflected in our analysis by the introduction of dot-quotes. But it does not follow from this that such sentences do not ascribe a *property* to anything. If Sellars' view is correct, then sentence (2) ascribes to the word '*Hund*' the property of being governed by certain rules for its use. Our discussion has not urged that Sellars' view *is* correct, but only that one might grant its correctness without denying that intentionality is genuinely a property or characteristic of something.

In proceeding to a statement of Sellars' account of intentional sentences involving *mental* entities, we will require, according to him, an analogical *extension* of certain linguistic concepts, such as "word" or "sentence," to the domain of mental acts construed as inner, non-overt episodes. Thus we introduce the concept of a "mental word" or a "mental sentence," and contrast it with the concept of a word or a sentence as something actually uttered or inscribed:

> The concept of a proposition as expressed by mental and overt sentences is an analogical extension of the concept of a proposition as something expressed by overt sentences. Roughly, to be a that-p item in the more inclusive sense is to be an item of a kind which plays a role in *either* thinkings *or* overt speakings which is similar in relevant respects to that played in our overt speech by the design represented by "p."[12]

A mental sentence, then, is understood to be something which plays a certain role in thinking, where this role is one which could be specified by presenting an item which plays a parallel role in overt linguistic activity.

It is important to be clear where the *analogy* is supposed to lie in this account. The notions which involve an analogical use of certain concepts are those of a "mental word" and "mental sentence." Insofar, therefore, as mental episodes such as thoughts are construed as involving mental words or mental sentences, our concept of a mental episode is an analogical extension of certain purely linguistic concepts. However, every analogy between two things rests, presumably, on something which is actually regarded as common to the things in question, some actual similarity. In this case the point of similarity lies in the notion of something's "playing a role." Mental sentences, that is, are not to be construed as merely doing something which is *analogous* to playing a role, but are to be construed as literally playing certain roles in thinking. It is only *because* inner items might be construed as playing certain roles that it is possible to extend the concept of a "sentence" from the domain of the overt to the domain of the inner in the first place. If the concept of mental role-playing were itself only an analogical extension of some concept, then we would simply have no idea what the point of our original analogy was.

As Sellars points out, however, we cannot simply introduce a dot-quoted expression such as '·p·' with the understanding that it shall serve as a common noun applying to items which literally play the same role as the sign-design 'p.' The latter role involves, for example, the actual production of *inscriptions* in certain circumstances, and this is a notion which simply does not apply to inner episodes. Rather, we must suppose that there is something in *common* between overt and internal role-playing, and that dot-quoted expressions apply to anything which possesses this common feature.[13] With this understanding we might then construe the intentional sentence

(9) (The thought) T means p

as roughly (qualifications will be discussed presently) equivalent to

(10) T is a ·p·,

where (10) conveys information about a certain role in virtue of presenting a sign-design which plays that same role in overt discourse. If my previous argument has been correct, then (10) ought itself to be equivalent to something of the form

(11) T plays the following role: . . .

Peter Geach has also presented a version of the analogy theory of thinking. Consider Smith's episodic judgment that A is sharper than B. We must suppose, according to Geach, that Smith's judgment consists in a number of "Ideas" which stand in a certain relation to one another in Smith's thought. For this purpose, Geach introduces the relation §(sharper than), which is a dyadic relation obtaining between two Ideas in any judgment that one thing is sharper than another. (It may of course be a relation which is established between two Ideas in virtue of the interposition of a third, namely of the Idea of *sharper than* itself, but it need not be such a relation.[14]) We then construe

(12) Smith judges that A is sharper than B

as

(13) Smith's judgment consists of an Idea_A, which is the mental
     utterance of 'A,' and an Idea_B, which is the mental utterance
     of 'B,' in such a manner that his judgment as a whole is a
     mental utterance of 'C' . . .

where (13) is completed by a description of the structure of that sentence 'C' of which the judgment that A is sharper than B would be the "mental utterance," although Geach offers only the beginnings of such a description.[15] Geach's theory does not go far enough for us to assess its merits. The notion of a "mental utterance" is simply set out by Geach as the notion of someone's "saying-in-his-heart something to the same effect as . . . ,"[16] and it is not clear what this amounts to, since "saying in one's heart" is as metaphorical a notion as "mentally uttering." Sellars' account at least has the advantage of attempting to account for both in terms of the non-metaphorical notion of "playing a role." Therefore no special attention will be given to Geach's account.

There are a number of points about Sellars' account which need closer attention before it can be assessed. First of all, let us return to the sentence

(9) (The thought) T means p,

which we took to be equivalent to

(11) T plays the following role: . . . .

If T is a particular mental episode, then (11) would make no sense at all. It makes no sense to say of some particular thing that it plays a certain rule-governed role unless that thing is able to recur in many different circumstances, but a particular mental act is a momentary occurrence and hence does not recur. If (9) is equivalent to (10) or (11), therefore, we must construe T not as a particular inner episode, but as a particular *kind* of inner episode, in the same way that (2) is a statement not about some particular inscription, but about a particular *kind* of inscription. Thus (2) is a statement about any inscription with a certain specified *shape*, and what plays the particular role in German which is designated by the expression '·dog·' is this very shape itself. To say that *'Hund'* plays this role is to say that there are various contexts in which a certain shape may or may not (correctly) be exemplified *by* particular inscriptions. Sellars calls this the "empirical" or "factual character" which any role-player must possess:

> While a mental act which expresses the proposition that it is rain-
> ing is *ipso facto* an ·it is raining·, it must also belong to a specific
> variety of ·it is raining·, just as a token of the corresponding En-
> glish sentence is not only an ·it is raining· but has the specific
> empirical character by virtue of which it sounds (or reads) like
> *that.* [17]

If (9) is equivalent to (10) or (11), then T must be taken in these statements not as a particular mental act which is a thought that p, but rather a particular *kind* of act. T, that is, must be the empirical or factual *character* which stands to all particular thoughts that p in the same relation in which, for example, a certain shape stands to all particular instances of the word *'Hund'* in German.

As Sellars grants, we do not in fact *know* how to describe mental acts in this way. It follws that *'T'* cannot be taken, after all, as designating a particular *kind* of act, rather than a particular act, and we must accordingly find some replacement for (10). Therefore, (9) must, on Sellars' view, be equivalent to something like

(14) T is an instance of some kind K of mental states, such that K's are ·p·s,

where the second part of (14) would then be equivalent to

(15) K's play (in inner discourse) the following role: . . . [18]

This is to say that, as we discovered in Chapter 4, propositions about the intentional characters of mental acts (or at least about their *conceptual* characters) are propositions about those acts in virtue of being propositions about certain (non-intentional) characters of those acts. (Since the "empirical" or "factual character" of a mental episode thus serves the function of what I have called mental "contents," we might also formulate (14) as *'T* is a mental state of content C, and C's are ·p·s.') Sellars is committed to the view, then, that there is no kind of mental act, such that an act's being of that kind is *ipso facto* its having a certain intentional character, or that there is no "first-order" description of an act, such that an act of that description is *ipso facto* an act of a certain intentional description. This does, of course, distinguish intentionality from such properties as Red or Green, although it by no means implies that intentionality is no property of an act at all.

Some philosophers have taken the fact that we cannot describe a thought in any determinate way, except in terms of its intentional character, as a refutation of any attempt to construe intentionality in linguistic terms. W. J. Ginnane argues, for example, that "What we can *not* do is to describe our thoughts by describing, so to speak, their actual ingredients separately from what the thoughts were about. Here there is a huge gulf between thinking something and saying something. For if I say something, what I do can be described quite independently of what I am talking about." Hence, Ginnane concludes, "Thought is Pure Intentionality."[19] But the example which Ginnane uses of a candidate for the nonintentional "ingredient" of a thought is an example only of a specific sort of *object* for some thought. Thus he considers whether an *image* might be the actual ingredient of a thought, or whether it could only stand to some thought in the relation of a picture to some text which that picture merely illustrates.[20] It is not at all clear how a thought about one sort of object (e.g., a non-image) could ever stand in more than a merely external and accidental relation to an awareness of some *other* sort of object (e.g., an image), except insofar as the latter sort of object somehow might enter into the very constitution of the former sort. We have already decided, however, that we must construe the "content" of an act as a character rather than as an object of that act. Ginnane has offered no reason, then, why even though we may not be able to specify such a character, it ought not to enter into some thought as an actual "ingredient" of that thought. There is no evident reason, that is, why such a character could not stand in the same relation to thoughts as certain visible shapes stand to words, namely as *constituting* them, rather than merely standing to thoughts in the relation in which certain visible shapes completely *distinct* from certain words, such as pictures which illustrate a text, stand to those words.

A second preliminary point is that Sellars' account, if it is to be at all plausible, must presuppose the notion of a "mental state," and hence cannot be taken as an attempt to elucidate that notion. Certainly there is nothing distinctively mental about the sort of role-playing which Sellars takes to be definitive of the intentionality of the mental. This is proved simply by observing that while overt linguistic items such as certain sounds or marks on paper also play the sorts of roles which are allegedly definitive of intentionality, nevertheless no sounds or marks on paper are capable of conceiving and knowing the external world in the way that persons or minds are. Indeed, sounds or marks on paper are only relevant to such abilities in the first place insofar as they themselves *express* some human awareness or item of human cognition. Nor does the fact that it is *inner* episodes with which we are concerned, when we are concerned with the mental, make any essential difference to this problem. It is no easier to suppose that some internal, yet unconscious, state of an organism is an awareness or conception of some object simply in virtue of playing certain roles, than it is to suppose the same of overt linguistic activities. We must stipulate, then, as we have in (14), for example, precisely that it is a mental or a conscious state which we are conceiving, on Sellars' account, as playing a certain role in "inner discourse," and the notion of inner discourse cannot then be employed in order to elucidate the notion of a mental or a conscious state.

This point does not appear inconsistent with any view which Sellars holds. It does, however, present a serious difficulty for any attempt to define the notion of the "mental." Suppose, for example, that we defined the mental as an internal state of which I am non-observationally aware. Then unless we could define a notion of "non-observational awareness" independently of the introduction of any intentional terms (e.g., 'belief'), we could not without circularity hope to provide a general explication of the intentionality of the mental in terms of a Sellarsian account. This issue will not be pursued here, although it will later be argued on independent grounds not only that there are some mental states which cannot be given a Sellarsian account, but that there are also some *awarenesses of objects* which cannot be given such an account.

We have so far been considering Sellars' account with respect to the class of episodes of thinking, to the class of "thinkings," in a narrow sense. We have considered, for example, thinkings that p as opposed to wishings or imaginings that p, even though in a broader sense all three such episodes fall under the domain of "thought" as opposed to "experience," or immediate sensory awareness. Though Sellars himself does not make it clear how to extend his account to these other sorts of episodes, the account must of course apply to them as well, since wishing that p or imagining that p is every bit as intentional as thinking, that is, judging, that p.

A classical approach to this issue rests on distinguishing the "content" from the *species* or *mode* of a mental act.[21] Thus there is some character which is common to an act of judging or wishing or imagining that p, and also a character which serves to *distinguish* each of these acts from the others. On the view that the intentional character of an act is a first-order character of that act, the classical approach runs into immediate difficulty. This becomes evident when we consider what sort of property the content of an act, as distinguished from its mode, might be on such an account. It provides no help to say, for example, that what is common to an act of judging or wishing or imagining that p is just the *proposition* that p, since all talk about the propositional content of an act must be reducible to talk about the *sort* of act which it is, and it makes no sense to say that some act happens to be a "that p," in the way that it does make sense to say that the act happens to be a judging or a wishing or an imagining. Thus it would seem that if an act's "propositional content" is indeed a first-order character of that act, then it would have to be, not the character "that p," but a character which we might want to designate as the character of "*presenting* that p." While it makes no sense to say of an act that it happens to be a "that p," it does make sense to say that it happens to "present" that p, that is, that it presents a certain state of affairs. On this account, the content of an act, as distinguished from its mode, would thus be identified with a mere "presentation" (*Vorstellung*) of something. Judging, imagining, and wishing something would then involve some further character, in addition to the character of merely presenting something.

This account would be intelligible enough if all that it amounted to were the claim that judging, imagining, and wishing were just the three possible *ways* in which objects might be presented to thought, since that is compatible with construing the relation between "presenting" that p and judging, imagining, and wishing that p as the relation which obtains between a determinable quality and the determinate forms which are subsumed under it. Judging, imagining, and wishing that p would then stand to the quality of "presenting" that p in the same relation that green, yellow, and orange stand to the quality of color as such. However, this is a very different conception from the one which the classical account offers. On that account the relation between the mode and the content of an act would appear to be more like that between, for example, some particular color and some particular shape rather than that between some particular color and color as such. But, if the quality of presenting that p is *not* merely a determinable quality under which judging, imagining, and wishing that p can be ranged, then we· run the risk of simply being unable to distinguish presenting that p from *imagining* that p. "Presenting" that p seems to become nothing different from merely *entertaining the idea* that p. Since judging and wishing in that case become the only two "modes" of presenting that p, and since it is perfectly possible that there be an act which is a *mere* presenting that p, there would accordingly be at least one sort of act for which there could be no distinction at all between the content and the mode of the act. Thus the unity of the classical picture is destroyed.[22]

An analogy theory would appear to have at its disposal certain means for dealing with this problem. Consider the three sentences

(16) T is a judging that p
(17) T is an imagining that p
(18) T is a wishing that p.

On a Sellarsian account, we could presumably try to construe these as, respectively,

(19) T is a mental state of some kind K, such that K's are ·it is the case that p·s
(20) T is a mental state of some kind K, such that K's are ·suppose that p·s (or, perhaps, ·if p·s)
(21) T is a mental state of some kind K, such that K's are ·would that p·s.

In this way we might try to preserve the distinction between the mode and the content of any act. Thus the mode of an act of judging or imagining or wishing that p would be that quality Q of the act which is such that Q's are, respectively, ·it is the case that . . . ·s or ·suppose that . . . ·s or ·would that . . . ·s, and the identical "content" which is common to all of these acts would simply be that quality R which is such that R's are · . . . p·s—either ·it is the case that p·s or ·suppose that p·s or ·would that p·s.

This does not imply that any particular act—for example, a judging that p—must literally consist of two *parts*, in the way that the sentence 'it is the case that p' contains the two parts 'it is the case that . . .' and '. . . p.' The sentence 'it is raining,' after all, is an ·it is the case that it is raining·, even though it does not contain some sort of operator which prefixes the propositional content. Nevertheless, it would be wrong to say that if an act does not contain two parts which provide its content and its mode, then no such distinction could be drawn for the act. The distinction between the content and the mode of an act is a distinction drawn among its *qualities*, and there is necessarily some qualitative difference between judging and merely imagining that p, in the same way that there is a qualitative difference between an utterance of 'p' and an utterance of 'suppose that p.'

This account could not be accepted just as it stands. Suppose that someone is thinking (i.e., judging) that if q, then p. Then presumably part of that person's mental state will be an ·it is the case that p·. It would seem odd, however, to regard this particular state as an actual *judging* that p. One might, of course, abandon the attempt altogether to subject the mode of a mental act to a Sellarsian account, and simply reserve that sort of account for the content of an act. Like Brentano, for example, we might simply appeal to an unanalyzed notion of "affirmation" or "acceptance." Equipped with that notion, we might then maintain that an act of judging that p must, in addition to being an it is the case that p·, *also* be an act of affirmation or acceptance. It would seem possible, however, although at the expense of somewhat complicating matters, to attempt a modification of (19), simply adding that T does not occur merely as a part of some thought which is an ·if q, then p·. The same problem may also arise for imagining. If I am thinking that if p, then q, then there seems to be a sense in which part of my thought is a ·suppose that p·, although it might be odd to say that I am actually imagining or supposing that p. Again, one might take "imagining" as a primitive character of an act, without abandoning an analogy theory of thinking altogether, or one might simply add to (20) the qualification that T does not merely occur as part of an ·if p, then q·. It is difficult to say how far such qualifications would ultimately have to be carried, although there seems to be no objection in principle to undertaking the task of providing them.

There is also a more serious difficulty with the theory as formulated here. The fundamental notion which Sellars introduces in order to deal with intentionality is that of a role which is played by some item in inner or outer discourse. However, the sort of item which Sellars' own examples appear to favor is that of a *sentence* which plays a certain role, whereas it is not in fact clear what point there could be in talking about the "role" of a sentence.[23] We might try to say that the role of a sentence is determined by the sorts of things which people might legitimately *do* with a sentence. However, either we must grant that people might do anything whatsoever with any given sentence, or else we shall end up presupposing what we were trying to explain by introducing the role of a sentence in the first place. For example, consider the sentence 'Roses are red.' There are certainly all sorts of things that one might do with it. One might even use that sentence in order to state that violets are blue. (Suppose you and I have agreed to speak in code in order that no one could tell that we were talking about violets.) What, then, limits the "role" of any given sentence?

It might seem that this difficulty could easily be avoided if we limited ourselves to the sorts of moves which, in a given language, would be *correct or incorrect* moves, that is, permitted or forbidden. Then we might claim that using the sentence 'Roses are red' in order to state that violets are blue, while it might be a correct move in *some* language game (e.g., in some code game which you and I might play), is not a correct move in English. In the first place, however, it is not clear how the notion of "correctness" should *apply* to the use of a whole sentence, as opposed to a single word. There seems to be a considerable difference between the sense in which a person is said to do something incorrect when he points at a red rose and says "That's blue" and the sense in which a person might be said to do something incorrect when he says "Roses are red" in order to state that violets are blue. If there is in fact anything "incorrect" about the latter sort of behavior, then it could only be because speaking in code is itself an incorrect form of behavior, and it is not clear what it could mean to make a claim such as this. Furthermore, even if there is a sense in which saying "Roses are red" in order to state that violets are blue is an incorrect move in the English language game, all that we will have succeeded in showing is that the role of the sentence 'Roses are red' in this game is to state that roses are red. But since the notion of "stating that roses are red" is itself an intentional notion, we would then be prevented from using the notion of a linguistic role in order to elucidate that of intentionality, which is what we were attempting to do in the first place. To put the same point in a different way, I can see by looking at some person who is observing a red rose (and whose perceptual abilities are known by me to be standard) that he is making an incorrect move in English when he points at the rose and says "This is blue"; but I can never tell just by looking at some person that he is making an incorrect move, if he is, by saying "Roses are red." I could only tell that sort of thing if I knew something about his *intentions*.

It would seem, then, that an analogy theory of thinking must begin with the case of a "mental word," rather than that of a "mental sentence." Or if it does begin with sentences of any sort, then it must begin with sentences whose role is more like that of the sentences 'This is a rose' or 'This is red' than sentences such as 'Roses are red.' Thus the notion of something's being a ·roses are red· would seem to be derivative from that of something's being a ·roses· (or a ·this is a rose·) or a ·red· (or a ·this is red·). This is in fact the approach which Geach undertakes, since he defines the thought that roses are red as an Idea of roses being characterized by a certain property §(red).[24] As we have already noted, however, Geach was able to identify the various properties and relations of the form §( ) only by stipulating that they are the sorts of properties and relations which characterize a set of Ideas whenever the complete thoughts which contain those Ideas happen to be "mental utterances" of certain sentences, and it is precisely the notion of a "mental utterance" of a sentence which we are trying to elucidate.

It may be possible to deal with this difficulty simply by distinguishing, as Sellars does, between linguistic moves which bring us from a non-linguistic "position" into a linguistic one (e.g., the move from seeing something red to saying "This is red") and linguistic moves which bring us from one linguistic position to another one. The former are what Sellars calls "language entry transitions," the latter what he calls "moves" in a technical sense.[25] Thus we might regard someone's asserting "Roses are red" as a move which is permitted simply in virtue of the fact that any assertion of a ·this is a rose· legitimizes the assertion of a ·this is red·. To regard this assertion in this way, we might claim, is to pay attention to its *role*, and we are thus in a position after all to regard any sentence as playing a role which distinguishes it from other sentences. More complications would need to be introduced, of course, in order actually to carry out such a program. For example, the assertion of a ·this is a rose· legitimizes the assertion of any tautology, and this would have to be ruled out. However, there seems to be no objection in principle to the program, and one can therefore suppose that once a Sellarsian account is made good—if it *can* be made good—for certain predicates, or for certain sentences of the form 'This is . . . ,' then the application of that program to any sentence ought in principle to be possible. If it is not possible, then we would either have to abandon an attempt at an analogy theory altogether, or else accept the notion of a certain mental state's being the "mental utterance" of a certain sentence as an unanalyzed notion.

Critique of the Analogy Theory's Account of Intentionality

The most fundamental point at which the analogy theory of thinking could be attacked concerns the notion of a "role" which might be played either by some properly linguistic item or by a certain kind of mental state. The point of the theory is to claim that the intentional character of any mental state *is* its character, or at least the character of its "content," of playing a role of that sort. There are a number of difficulties which philosophers might find in this claim. It might be maintained, for example, that assertions about the roles of linguistic expressions, insofar as they have any bearing at all upon the question of linguistic meaning, are really only assertions about the *thoughts* or *ideas* which those expressions express. In that case we could not comprehend the notion of a mental episode which possesses the feature of intentionality by regarding it as an extension of a notion derived from certain facts about language.

This sort of objection raises a serious difficulty for any analogy theory of thinking. However, we do not need to consider it here, since in any case it would not be sufficient to refute the account of *intentionality* upon which the analogy theory is founded. Even if it is granted that the concept of linguistic meaning and reference presupposes the concept of *mental* meaning and reference, the question would remain how we are in fact to account for the latter concept. There is nothing in the fact, if it is one, of the conceptual priority of mental over linguistic meaning and reference which would imply that the intentionality of mental episodes is not to be analyzed in terms of the "roles" which such episodes play in thought. If, of course, we did analyze mental reference in these terms, then we would be compelled to grant that the concept of a mental episode's playing a certain role is one which arises *directly* from the awareness of our own mental states. This contradicts the claim of the analogy theory. According to that theory, the concept of a mental state as playing a certain role is to be regarded, originally at least, as a *theoretical* concept, although it is presumably to be regarded in this way not because the concept of something's "playing a role" is an originally theoretical concept, but only because the concept of something *mental* playing a role is an originally theoretical concept.[26] This only shows, however, that if the concept of linguistic meaning is to be analyzed as the objection maintains, then the analogy theory must be rejected, but it does not show that the account of intentionality which it offers must also be rejected. (This distinction could not be drawn, of course, if the analogy theory maintained that not only the concept of a thought, but also the concept of "playing a role" as *applied* to thoughts, was a merely analogical concept.)

The only way, then, to attack the Sellarsian theory of intentionality directly would be to show, not that the concept of linguistic meaning presupposes the concept of mental reference or intentionality, but rather that the more general concept of something's "playing a meaningful role" presupposes that concept. It might appear to be easy to show this if propositions about the role which some meaningful item plays were always to be construed as propositions about the actual *habits* of the persons for whom it plays that role. Roderick Chisholm grants, for example, that 'The German word *Riese* means giant' says something about the use to which speakers of German put certain marks and noises. But when we try to say what that use *is*, Chisholm claims, we find that we need to resort to concepts involving intentional mental states:

> Our sentence "The German word *Riese* means giant" does not mean merely that people in Germany—however we may qualify them with respect to their desires—would call a thing *ein Riese* if and only if the thing were gigantic. It means at least this much more—that they would call a thing by this name if and only if they *took* the thing to be gigantic or *believed* it to be gigantic or *knew* it to be gigantic. And, in general, when we use the intentional locution, "People use such and such a word to mean so-and-so," part of what we mean to say is that people use that word when they wish to express or convey something they *know* or *believe*—or *perceive* or *take*—with respect to so-and-so.
>
> I think we can say, then, that, even if we can describe a man's believing in terms of language, his actual use of language or his dispositions to use language in certain ways, we cannot describe his use of language, or his dispositions to use language in those ways, unless we refer to what he believes, or knows, or perceives.[27]

Thus if by the "role" of some meaningful item we meant something about its actual *use* by those for whom that item plays its role, then it would seem that the concept presupposes the very sorts of intentional concepts which we were attempting to elucidate by its means.

We might try to avoid this difficulty simply by observing that propositions about the role of some meaningful item may be propositions about that item's use without being propositions about its *actual* use, that is, about the actual dispositions of someone for whom that item is in fact meaningful. There is no contradiction in the fact, for example, that some word has a use in a certain language even though there do not exist any persons who know or use that language. Propositions about the use of words in a language which was at one time but is no longer spoken might be taken as an illustration of this point, although it might be objected that such propositions could simply be construed as statements in the *past* tense about the actual users of some language. Consider, however, some language which has never actually been used, a language, for example, which might have been designed for possible use at some future time. Surely some expression may have a use in that language, but we would not suppose that the fact that some expression does have a use in that language must in that case simply be a fact about the *inventor* of the language. Once that language had in fact come into general use we would not have any inclination at all to regard a claim about the use of an expression in it as a claim about some person in the distant past. If we did regard such claims in this way, then since many *other* languages presumably had no inventor at all, we would mean something very different when we talked about the "use" of an expression in this language from what we would mean in the case of many others. There is, then, a sense to talk about the "use" of some meaningful item which is not reducible to talk about the actual dispositions of persons who know or use that language. This, of course, is just the distinction between the "use" of an item in the sense of the *actual employment* of that item and the "use" of an item in the sense of the *rules for correct employment* of that item.

Even granting this distinction, however, between explication of an expression's "role" in terms of its actual employment, and explication of its role in terms of rules concerning the *correct and incorrect* employment of that expression, it might still be objected that we cannot use the notion of playing a role in order to elucidate that of intentionality. In order to assert that any move at all is a correct or an incorrect move, it is first necessary to determine what "game" that move is a part of. (The model of rules for a *game* is one that Sellars employs.)[28] The very same move might, after all, be permitted in one game and not in another. It might be observed, however, that what game a particular person is playing with a given item can be determined only by appealing to the *intentions* of that person. Hence our appeal to rules cannot without circularity be used to provide an account of intentionality.

This difficulty could be avoided simply by making the notion of a correct or an incorrect move relative to some possible *system* of moves from the start. Thus we may not be concerned to say whether some particular move is a correct or an incorrect move *simpliciter*, but only whether it is correct or incorrect *in S*. In this sense, one and the same move might be correct in S and incorrect in S', even though the intention of the speaker may only have been to make a move in S, and hence, from some other point of view, no incorrect move was made at all. If the Sellarsian account is correct, we ought to require only the notion of relative correctness and incorrectness. The sorts of contexts which we are trying to elucidate are always of the form 'T_1 is a thought that p,' where T_1 is, let us say, John Doe's thought at t_1 and 'p' is an expression in some specific language which must exist and be understood so long as the total context is well-formed. Accordingly, letting 'L' stand for this particular language, and 'S' stand for the system of John Doe's "inner language,"[29] Sellars is committed only to elucidating the original statement by regarding it as indicating rules for the correct or incorrect occurrence *in S* of items of T_1's "factual" description, in virtue of indicating that the rules in question parallel those for the correct or incorrect occurrence of expressions in L. The Sellarsian program will then fail only if we cannot succeed in formulating rules according to which a certain move *would* be a correct or an incorrect move in S or in L without appealing to intentional notions.

Now it may appear that the distinction between the "use" of an item understood in terms of its actual employment, and its use as understood in terms of rules concerning *correct* (and incorrect) employment, is a legitimate and useful one in the case of expressions in *public* languages, but that it has no application when we attempt to speak of a person's "inner language." We do have a conception of various systems of rules governing the production or manipulation of items of various sorts, and it is not in fact unreasonable to suppose that the names of languages are often used to refer, not to the actual (present or past) practices of certain peoples, but precisely to such systems of rules. When I speak of the German language, for example, I may not simply be referring to the linguistic practices of the German people, but to some particular system of rules. (That I almost always *help* myself refer to this system of rules by saying that it is, e.g., a system embodied in certain actual linguistic practices current at a certain time and place, need not detract from this point.) However, it does not seem as reasonable to make the same suggestion in the case of an alleged "inner language" of some person's mental life. What is possibly meant, one might ask, in speaking of some system of rules governing the occurrence of various *mental* states of a certain person? In the case of public languages or games I do in fact often distinguish between the actual practice of a person or group (which involves, presumably, the *intentions* of the persons in question) and certain *rules* which I might regard as manifested in that practice (and which might themselves be described without reference to intention). However, when I speak of Jones' "inner language" I have no conception, it might seem, of such a "separable" system of rules. Jones' "inner language," in other words, seems precisely to be *defined* by his actual mental activity, and it is not clear how one could succeed in referring to or describing it merely by referring to or describing some system of rules in abstraction from that activity.

Although Sellars endeavors to make it clear that the notion of some item's "playing a role" which determines its semantical significance can only be explicated by appeal to the notion of rules concerning correct (and incorrect) behaviors involving that item,[30] it is not always perfectly clear just how Sellars would have us proceed beyond this point; his position seems to be ambiguous. Sometimes he seems prepared to grant that any appeal to rules which "govern" a person's behavior in such a way as to permit description of that behavior as semantically meaningful must ultimately also involve some reference to a person's thoughts and intentions; he simply denies that it needs to involve a reference to *inner states* which are thoughts and intentions.[31] This admission is of course compatible with the view that the notion of an inner state which is a thought or an intention is merely an analogical extension of the notion of overt behavior which possesses semantical significance. However, it also implies that the notion of intentionality cannot ultimately be explicated by appeal to certain purely semantical notions, which appears to contradict a view that Sellars holds. Other times, however, Sellars clearly maintains that the relevant notion of some item's becoming involved in a system of rules which specify correct and incorrect patterns of occurrence for that item can in fact be given some content without appeal to the notions of thought or intention, whether these latter be regarded as thinkings and intendings "in one's mind" *or* merely thinkings and intendings "out loud." It is here that Sellars' notion of "pattern-governed behavior" must be considered.

Sellars attempts to distinguish "pattern-governed" behavior both from behavior which is to be explained in terms of intentions to *obey* certain rules of behavior and from behavior which happens merely to *conform* to certain rules which one might specify, though the system of rules cannot itself be regarded as in any way *explanatory* of the behavior.[32] The example he gives is of the bee's "dance" which signifies the direction of honey from the hive. The bee's movements do not, Sellars claims, merely *happen* to conform to certain patterns which one might specify in terms of rules (the rule, e.g., that the bee should wiggle in a certain way if the honey is in a certain direction from the hive); nor do we need to suppose that the movements are therefore instances of rule-obeying behavior. (It does not of course follow from this that the movements are *not* instances of rule-obeying behavior, but only that we don't need to suppose that they are such instances in order to regard them as "governed" by a certain rule-defined pattern.)

> What would it mean to say of a bee returning from a clover field that its turnings and wigglings occur *because* they are part of a complex dance? Would this commit us to the idea that the bee *envisages* the dance and acts as it does by virtue of intending to realize the dance? If we reject this idea, must we refuse to say that the dance pattern as a whole is involved in the occurrence of each wiggle and turn? Clearly not.[33]

Sellars goes on to suggest that an *evolutionary account* of the bee's "programming" (Sellars' metaphor: *wiring*) for the sort of behavior in question provides a middle road between the two alternatives. Once on this middle road, then, at least (presumably) in the cases where the behavior in question achieves a sufficient degree of sophistication, we are in a position to regard that behavior as properly *linguistic* behavior, without having anywhere appealed to the notion of "intention" to engage in such behavior.[34] The supposition, finally, that an organism's *internal* states (at least its conscious states) are "governed" by a similar pattern allows, on Sellars' view, for the introduction of the notion of a purely "inner language." (It may be worth noting that it doesn't follow from this that all human thinking is merely a matter of "pre-programmed" behavior. It only follows that *certain* thought-patterns will involve such prior programming, namely those patterns which are definitive of the very *language* of inner thoughts in the first place. Furthermore, even here it does not follow that it is completely impossible for behavior to *violate* the program in question, i.e., for "inner words" to be *misused*.)

I am not prepared to argue that Sellars' description of pattern-governed behavior does in fact yield a strong enough sense in which behavior is "governed" by systems of rules to allow for a notion of behavior as linguistically significant. However, it can hardly be taken for granted that the Sellarsian program is mistaken. It is worth taking note, in any case, of a point that Sellars himself perhaps does not sufficiently emphasize: There is a very direct connection between the kind of "programming" that Sellars has in mind and certain *normative* judgments that we make about behavior. In the case of the bee's dance, for example, there is a perfectly legitimate sense in which we might describe the behavior of any given bee returning from the clover field as *correct or incorrect behavior* in the circumstances in question, regardless of any supposition we might make about the bee's own intentions (if it has any). The ability to make such judgments, further, does seem to be essentially connected with the fact that it is *also* legitimate to describe certain bee-movements as "signifying" the presence of honey in a certain direction from the hive. Once, however, this is recognized in principle, we can go on to suggest that, on account of the conditioning of *human brains* (through evolution of the species as well as through more particular "evolutionary" patterns involved in various cases of socially conditioned learning), there are various sorts of "internal movements" of consciousness which can be described as correct or incorrect regardless of any conscious intentions one might have. Factual patterns of evolutionary development, in other words, might reasonably be regarded as providing the basis for *normative* judgments concerning standards of (internal or external) behavior. If it is, therefore, reasonable to maintain that the semantical significance of items in a language is definable in terms of certain rules concerning the correct and incorrect occurrence of those items in various circumstances, it would seem to follow that, at least as a general program, Sellars' proposal needs to be taken seriously.[35]

If the foregoing argument has force, then we ought to conclude that any fundamentally compelling objection to the Sellarsian account of intentionality must ultimately rest not on any difficulties which there might be in the very notion of something "playing a role" or being "subject to rules" independently of anybody's intentions, but rather on the difficulties which there might be in formulating, without any reference to intentionality or to semantical significance generally, the very *contents* of the rules which are allegedly in question. *Are* there indeed rules according to which certain moves are necessarily correct or incorrect in either our overtly linguistic or our mental life? If there are, is in fact the normative force of such rules quite independent of the fact that the moves on which they bear might already possess a certain intentional or semantical significance? An affirmative answer to both questions would seem to show the plausibility of the suggestion that semantical significance can be regarded as determined by rules of the sort which are also capable of accounting for the intentionality of mental states.

There are of course correctnesses and incorrectnesses concerning linguistic moves which do rest precisely on the fact that the items which are involved in those moves already have certain specific semantical characters. Thus I may tell you that you are always permitted to make a transition from saying "This is a glass of water" to "This is a collection of H_2O molecules," or that you are not, under ordinary circumstances at least, to make a transition from the former to saying "This is a quantity of one of the four primitive elements in nature." My *justification* for offering these rules bearing on the correctness and incorrectness of certain linguistic transitions presumably rests on the fact that the predicates of the sentences in question designate certain characters, and that I believe these characters to be connected in various ways. In this case the existence of the rules could hardly be said to be even partially constitutive of the meaning of the expressions in question, since they are rules which one originally formulates only with an eye to those very meanings.

Other sorts of moves seem to involve a different kind of correctness or incorrectness. Suppose, for example, that somebody rolls a "seven" in Monopoly and then proceeds to move his piece eight spaces. The only "justification" for ruling his action incorrect is that there is a certain rule; all we can say is "In Monopoly, that's not the way the pieces are used." Here we have a rule which has not been formulated "with an eye to" the significance of a certain piece, since the significance of the piece is itself a consequence of there being that very rule (and others), that is, a certain pattern of correctnesses and incorrectnesses. Moves of this sort will be called moves which are *"ipso facto"* correct and incorrect. It is important to see that moves which are *ipso facto* correct or incorrect are so regardless of the *intentions* of the mover, and regardless of whether, with respect to the mover's intentions, those moves might be regarded as *mistakes*. A person might move his piece eight spaces in Monopoly for the explicit purpose of cheating, and in that case his move would hardly be called a mistake. It might, nevertheless, be "against the rules." Conversely, a person who says "This is a glass of water; so it contains one of the four primary elements in nature" is certainly, under ordinary circumstances (e.g., if he intends to state fact), doing something mistaken. But it is not clear that the person is violating any rules for the very *use* of the pieces which he has used. So his move is not *ipso facto* incorrect.

The success of the Sellarsian program, so far as it concerns language directly, rests on our ability to envision a system of *ipso facto* correctnesses and incorrectnesses involving the use of the sounds and marks which constitute the factual character of any given language. In order to extend this program to the domain of psychological phenomena, it is therefore necessary to suppose that there is also such a system within the life of the mind itself. It is necessary to suppose that there are certain mental states which, for a given individual in a given set of circumstances, it is *ipso facto* correct or incorrect to be in. It may seem easy to find some examples in the case of linguistic moves. Thus the move from saying "The sun is shining" and "The wind is cool" to saying "The sun is shining and the wind is cool" would seem to be a move which is sanctioned just by the very rules for the use in English of the expression 'and'; hence the move is *ipso facto* correct. It is a purely intra-linguistic move, however, and if Sellars' account is correct these cannot be the only examples of *ipso facto* correctnesses and incorrectnesses. The meaning of *any* expression, on that account, is determined by rules, and certainly not every expression could have its meaning determined solely by reference to other expressions. Thus we must look for *ipso facto* correctnesses and incorrectnesses in the case of what Sellars calls "language entry" transitions.

The sorts of examples which Sellars gives of language entry transitions involve "responses" to various sensory stimuli. They also involve indexical expressions such as 'this,'[36] the presence of which presumably serves to show that the responses are indeed responses *to* some specific item or other. It will be argued that it is precisely the need for such an indication in any clear example of an *ipso facto* language entry correctness or incorrectness that ultimately shows the inadequacy of Sellars' account of intentionality. We might, however, attempt to avoid the sort of case which Sellars seems to take as paradigmatic. Instead of a sentence like 'This is red,' for example, we might take a sentence such as 'There is something red in the vicinity.'

It might be argued that there are a number of *ipso facto* correctnesses and incorrectnesses which involve the uttering of strings of words of this sort, and that it is in virtue of these that the words have the meaning which they do have. It is, for example, *ipso facto* correct to utter this sentence when, under standard conditions, I have a sensation of a red spot, and it is in virtue, we might claim, of this connection between the sentence and certain sensations under standard conditions that the word 'red' has the meaning which it does. If this were so, it would not of course follow that the word 'red' simply designates sensations of a certain sort. There are also, we might claim, other correctnesses of an intra-linguistic sort which must be mentioned—for example, the correctness of the move from saying "This is red" to saying "In standard circumstances, this would look red." Sentences containing the word 'red', then, are embedded in a total system of correctnesses in virtue of which they play their proper linguistic role.[37]

It is important to note, however, that to say that some move is *ipso facto* correct is not merely to say that it does not violate any rules, for the positive role of a piece in some game could never be determined solely by the fact that certain moves are not forbidden to that piece. What is needed, by way of positive correctness in some move, is the fact that certain moves are explicitly "called for" in some situation, in the way that certain other moves are presumably explicitly "ruled out." It is not immediately clear that there are any such things as *ipso facto* linguistic correctnesses in this sense. For example, while it would of course not be *ipso facto* incorrect to produce an instance of the sentence 'This is red' or 'There is something red in the vicinity,' when I am having a sensation of red, it is not at all clear in what sense an uttering of that particular sentence is actually "called for" in that situation. We might say that the sentence is called for in the sense that the existence of the sensation renders the *truth* of the sentence highly probable. However, this would not help us in the present case, since it makes the correctness of a certain move secondary to the significance of the piece which is involved in that move, hence not allowing us to regard its significance as a product of that very sort of correctness.

It would seem, then, that what we must look for are not *ipso facto* correctnesses involving such sentences as 'This is red' or 'There is something red in the vicinity,' but rather *ipso facto* incorrectnesses. Suppose, for example, that I am having a sensation of a green spot under conditions which are standard for the observation of colors in objects, and that I am having no other color sensations. Then, we might claim, it would be *ipso facto* incorrect to assert "There is something red in the vicinity," although it would not be *ipso facto* incorrect to assert "There is something green in the vicinity." To say, however, that some move is *ipso facto* incorrect in certain circumstances is to say that we could justify ruling it out, or correcting it, simply by observing "This is not the way we *use* that piece in this game." This would not in fact seem an appropriate response to the alleged incorrectness in our example. What, after all, *is* the way in which a certain word or sentence is here being used? The word 'red' is being used, in our example, simply in order to form an instance of the sentence 'There is something red in the vicinity,' which in turn is uttered upon the occasion of a sensation of green under conditions which are standard in certain respects. Since nothing is provided in the example, however, to indicate that the sentence was formulated precisely *as a response* to the sensation of green in those circumstances, it is difficult to see how any move has been made which is *ipso facto* incorrect, although it is clear enough that a move has been made for which there has been no epistemological warrant. The only way to find a move in this case which is *ipso facto* incorrect would apparently be to consider not simply someone's asserting "There is something red in the vicinity," on the occasion of a certain sensation under standard circumstances, but rather the more complicated assertion "I am having a sensation of green under circumstances which are standard for observing the colors of objects; *so* there is something red in the vicinity." The sort of move which this more complicated case involves does seem to be an instance of an *ipso facto* incorrectness. We might reasonably respond, in this case, "But that just isn't the way we use those words." Unfortunately, however, this sort of move is purely an intra-linguistic one, and we have been looking for a case of a language *entry* correctness or incorrectness.

We might try to take a different sort of case. For example, asserting "The red object on the table is heavy" may appear to be *ipso facto* incorrect when it is done in the presence of a table on which there is no red object at all. The "rules of the game" forbid, that is, the employment of that particular sentence in that particular sort of context. However, this sort of example will not take us any farther than we have already gone. In order to find any incorrectness in this case we would have to suppose that the assertion "The red object on the table is heavy" is performed not simply in the presence of a table upon which there is no red object, but that it is performed precisely "with a view to" that particular table. It is not clear how this is to be done without introducing some notion of the speaker's *intentions*. In order to avoid this difficulty, it would seem, we should once again have to resort to some more complicated assertion such as "There is no red object on the table, and that object is heavy," which clearly does involve some sort of *ipso facto* incorrectness. However, this is, again, not an example of a language entry incorrectness.

We ought to see, therefore, if we can have better luck with the sort of example which Sellars appears to take as paradigmatic, the case of a transition from a given sensation in certain circumstances to an assertion of a sentence like 'This is red.' Is it ever *ipso facto* incorrect, we may ask, to assert "This is red" when receiving, for example, sensations of green produced by some object under conditions which are standard for observing the colors of objects? In the first place of course we need to deal with the possibility that the sentence in question is not being *used* to refer to that particular object at all. We might try to do this simply by adding to our example the stipulation that there is no *other* object in the vicinity besides the one which is producing the sensations of green. However, it is also permissible to use a sentence of the form 'This is . . .' in order to refer to something which is merely *imagined* on a given occasion, so it is not *ipso facto* incorrect to assert "This is red" when there is nothing in the immediate vicinity which is red. (I might, for example, be trying to think of all the things which I know to be red, and each time I think of one I assert "This is red.")

The primary difficulty is to expand our original description of this sort of case so as to assure some connection between an assertion of the sentence '*This* is red' and a particular object which happens to be in one's vicinity on the occasion of that assertion, without presupposing the concept of some sentence being used to *refer* to some particular object. We might try to do this by considering a situation in which I do not merely assert "This is red" in the presence of some object which is producing certain sensations in me, but rather in which I also perform some indicative act such as *pointing* at the object in question. One might of course always point at some object without the intention of securing reference to it. However, it does not follow from this that we need to add to our description of the case some reference to my actual intentions in pointing in order to arrive at a case of *ipso facto* correctness or incorrectness. So long as there are *rules* which govern the activity of pointing at objects, or the combination of that activity with assertions of various sorts, a certain case of pointing-*cum*-asserting might well be a case of *ipso facto* linguistic incorrectness, despite the intentions of the pointer, that is, regardless of whether any sort of actual *mistake* has occurred. It is possible, then, that we have finally arrived at a case of language entry incorrectness of the sort which we have been seeking. This will exist, for example, so long as it is *ipso facto* incorrect to point at some object which is producing sensations of green under conditions which are standard for observing the colors of objects and to assert, in so doing, "This is red," that is, so long as it would be proper to respond "But that just isn't the way we *use* pointing and 'This is red.'"

There is no doubt a good deal more that needs to be done before even this much of a program for applying the concept of *ipso facto* correctness or incorrectness to linguistic moves can be made plausible. However, we have come far enough to see that the program cannot, without significant modification, be extended to the case of mental states. A condition for the success of the program lay in our ability to specify various sorts of linguistic moves which are *ipso facto* correct or incorrect moves, without appealing to the notion of reference or intention. If the program can be extended to the domain of the mental, then we must also suppose that, for any given mental state, there are specific circumstances under which it would be *ipso facto* correct or incorrect to come to be in that state, and that these are specifiable without introducing the notion of that state's having the particular object which it has. However, we saw that it is impossible to specify *ipso facto* linguistic incorrectnesses (at least of the "entry" sort) without appealing to the fact that linguistic acts proper are subject to rules only when they occur in situations involving publicly observable indicators (e.g., pointing) which are *also* subject to rules. Apart from the existence of the latter, it would appear that no linguistic entry transition is ever *ipso facto* incorrect. It is precisely the latter, however, which will be lacking when we consider the correctness or incorrectness of moves within the domain of purely mental phenomena.

Consider, for example, the sort of mental state which I am in when I recognize that some object is red. On the theory we are examining, the "content" of this mental state is a mental sentence of a particular sort; let us call it the mental sentence S. Under what circumstances, then, would it be *ipso facto* incorrect to come to be in a state whose content is S, that is, in a state whose content plays a role which is the inner counterpart of the role of 'This is red'? As a first approach, we might say that states of this sort are mental states which it is *ipso facto* incorrect to be in when one is experiencing a sensation of green, and no other sensation, but not *ipso facto* incorrect to be in when one is experiencing a sensation of red. To be in a state of thinking that something is red, then, is just to be in the sort of state which is subject to such correctnesses and incorrectnesses as these. As we have already seen, however, there is no description of a person's sensations at some moment which is such that it would be *ipso facto* incorrect for him to assert "This is red" at that moment. By the same token, therefore, there is presumably no description of a person's sensations which is such that it would be *ipso facto* incorrect for him to think a thought, while he is experiencing those sensations, which is the inner *counterpart* of an assertion of the sentence 'This is red.' Now we tried to avoid this difficulty, in the case of overt linguistic acts, by adding to our description of a person's sensations a description of certain of that person's overt acts which function, according to the rules of a certain "game," as indicators in linguistic contexts. The example of pointing was used for this purpose. What we require, then, is an inner *analogue* of pointing at some object. However, this is precisely what, on a Sellarsian account of intentionality, we *cannot* be required to presuppose, since the inner analogue of pointing, that is, mentally "pointing at" or intending some object, is what we are trying to explain in the first place by reference to certain correctnesses and incorrectnesses involving mental states. For this reason, the notion of rule-governed correctness or incorrectness cannot be used to explicate what it is for some mental state to be "directed toward" the particular object or sort of object toward which it is in fact directed. The semantical significance of "mental content" can only be defined by rules which specify a range of permissible occurrences of that content *in mental states directed toward particular qualities*—for example, a range of permissible occurrences in a mental state whose object is the (possibly uninstantiated) color red. Thus the notion of "mental reference" to a possibly unactualized object must be presupposed in any attempt to define the intentionality of mental content in terms of the notion of a system of "rules" which regulate that content.

6

Conclusion

If the argument of the preceding chapter is sound, then an explication of the notion of a mental state's "content," construed as a semantically significant feature of possible mental states (which might be regarded as "synonymous" with certain expressions in overt language), must presuppose the notion of at least certain sorts of mental states being directed toward certain sorts of *objects*. The semantical significance of mental content can only lie in the involvement of that content in some system of rule-governed correctnesses and incorrectnesses concerning its possible (i.e., permissible) presence in mental states *already regarded* as apprehending certain qualities. It follows that there must be at least some phenomenal qualities which are such that the semantical significance of mental contents ultimately lies (either directly or indirectly, through systems of correct or incorrect co-instantiation with *other* contents) in systems of correctness and incorrectness relating to the possible presence of those contents in awarenesses of precisely those qualities. We might call the qualities in question "primitive phenomenal qualities."

Now it has also been maintained, in our discussion of perceptual awareness, that immediate sensory awareness of qualities should be regarded as a case in which sensations come to exhibit mental content. The presence, that is, of a semantically significant element in sensation (which might otherwise have lacked it) is what converts that sensation into a genuine awareness *of* some object in the first place. This suggestion may now appear to be incompatible with any regulistic account of mental content. The latter account presupposes the notion of an immediate awareness of phenomenal qualities, yet the immediate awareness of phenomenal qualities is made possible only through the introduction of mental contents.

This difficulty is, however, only an apparent one. There is no circularity in maintaining both that the notion of mental contents which might be regarded as "synonymous" with overtly linguistic expressions presupposes the notion of mental states which immediately apprehend certain qualities and also that the latter sorts of mental states are themselves made possible only in virtue of the presence of semantically significant content in those states. The circularity would only exist if we attempted to *define* the notion of "immediate apprehension" in terms of the notion of mental content, but it is neither necessary nor possible to do this. To do it, in fact, would be to return to a view which we have already rejected, namely the view that regards predicates like 'is an apprehension of red' as primitive, non-relational predicates. To identify being an apprehension of the color red simply with being a mental state which possesses a given "content" would seem to come to precisely this sort of view. There is no need, however, to return to this view, for it is perfectly possible to grant that all apprehension of objects is necessarily apprehension of objects in particular *ways*, hence by means of particular *contents*, without attempting to explicate the notion of "apprehension of an object" solely in terms of the notion of mental content. Mental contents will, on this view, be defined as features of possible mental states which are governed by systems of rules which ultimately bear on the possible presence of such features in the apprehensions of certain qualities, and apprehensions of qualities will necessarily involve features which are governed by such rules. There is no more problem here than in the fact that *hue*, for example, is defined as being a certain property of colors, while color necessarily always possesses some hue or other. (Which is not, to be sure, to say that there is no problem here at all; but it is a problem which is not peculiarly a problem of intentionality.)

Allowing ourselves, then, as a primitive notion, the notion of an intuitive awareness being directed to some particular quality as an object, we might succeed after all in spelling out a regulistic theory of mental contents. On such an account, we would no longer encounter, in attempting to specify the sorts of *rules* which would be constitutive of the semantical significance of contents, a problem which is analogous to the one we earlier encountered concerning the determination of reference for overt sentences of the form 'This is. . . .' There is no problem, that is, of establishing a rule-bound connection between the mere presence of a certain content in experience and the object to which this content is being (intentionally or not) *referred*, in the way that there is a problem of connecting an utterance of 'This is . . .' with some particular object in the environment. The content, we may say, simply refers (or is referred) to that object which is the object of the act whose total content it *is*. To be aware of *this* color as the color red, for example (or as the color, for example, which is the same as my shirt's color), is to experience an intuitive act whose content is (i.e., which instantiates as a property) the counterpart of some particular expression (e.g., 'red' or 'the color of my shirt' in English) and whose *object* is this particular color. Exactly *which* possible property of mental states is the counterpart of which particular overt expressions may then be regarded as determined by rules regarding the permissible instantiation or noninstantiation of certain properties by the apprehensions of certain objects. The content which is "synonymous" with the English word 'red' might, for example, be regarded as a content which it would be *ipso facto* incorrect to instantiate as the total content of an act whose *object* is something other than the color red. This sort of rule-governed incorrectness, together with others, might be seen as constituting a system which confers a conceptual significance on the mental content in question.

If this general sort of approach is feasible, then we might proceed to move beyond the case of sensory intuition, with respect to which the notion of mental content is initially to be explicated, and distinguish several different *sorts* of acts of which the same "mental expression" might be the content. The content which corresponds to the word 'red,' for example, might be the content either of an act of sensible intuition (seeing the color red) or of an act of merely imagining some color, or it might be the content of an act of merely "thinking of" some color. The content of an act of "thinking *that*" rather than merely "thinking *of*" might then be regarded as a "mental sentence" rather than a "mental word." Since acts of *recognition* presumably also involve some "propositional" content, it might seem that we ought to regard their contents as well on an analogy with sentences rather than mere words. However, we have seen that insofar as the propositional content of some recognition is of the sort to be expressed by sentences of the form 'This is . . .,' the propositional function would seem to be performed by the very presence of a certain mental word in an act in the first place. An assertion of the sentence '*This* is the color red,' for example, might give expression merely to an intuitive act whose object is *this* color and whose content is the mental counterpart of 'red.' The (merely indirect) perceptual judgments which are merely "based upon" such acts of recognition, and the expression of which would not include the use of merely indexical expressions, would be regarded as separate acts possessing a content which is analogous to a complete sentence rather than a mere word.

These last remarks are significant, because while the notion of mental content, illuminated with the help of a certain linguistic analogy, cannot be explicated without some appeal to that of an object of immediate sensory apprehension, it may nevertheless be the case that the analysis of the claim that at least *certain* mental states are "directed toward" objects need appeal to nothing beyond the fact that certain contents are present in those states. While the claim, for example, that I am seeing the color red may imply that I am standing in some special relation of immediate psychological "acquaintance" with that color, the claim that I am merely thinking of the color red, or thinking that some particular object is red, requires no such supposition concerning special psychological relations. The former case simply requires the supposition that the content $\ulcorner red \urcorner$ (i.e., a · red ·) is present in my thought; the latter only that a content of the form $\ulcorner \alpha$ is red$\urcorner$ is present. Neither of these attempts to reduce the notion of a mental state's *object* in terms of its mere possession of *content* is incompatible with the claim that the latter notion requires an appeal to the notion of an object of a certain sort of mental state in the first place. What this shows is that a regulist theory of mental content, despite the way in which we have been forced to limit its claims, may provide a powerful tool for dealing with at least certain sorts of intentional phenomena.

It is also important to notice that the present account not only forces us to distinguish between propositions concerning the objects of immediate sensory apprehension and those concerning the objects of nonimmediate mental states, but it also requires us to distinguish between two different *sorts* of things that we say concerning the objects of the former. In particular, we may say both that (possibly uninstantiated) phenomenal *qualities* and (possibly non-actualized) *states of affairs* may be among the objects of immediate sensory awareness—and indeed both sorts of objects may always be among the objects of any *single* case of sensory awareness. Consider, for example, a perception of the color red. Insofar as it is impossible to apprehend the color red as an object without at the same time apprehending it as *being* something or other, the color which is the object of apprehension will always be apprehended as part of some state of affairs which might *also* be regarded as an "object" of apprehension. Thus suppose that I recognize the color in question as the color of my shirt; then there are really two distinct objects of my immediate sensory awareness. There is the possibly uninstantiated color red which I am seeing, and there is also the possibly unactualized fact of that color's being the color of my shirt. On the account which has been proposed here, that these two distinct sorts of objects *are* the objects of the awareness in question is a claim that is to be understood in two very different ways. That the color red is an object of immediate perception will involve a relation of direct acquaintance with that color; that I also immediately perceive the fact of that color's being the color of my shirt will simply involve the presence in the sensory act in question of the mental content ⌈the color of my shirt⌉.

It might *also* be argued that there must always be, among the objects of immediate awareness, at least one state of affairs which *is* in fact actualized. I must at least, for example, recognize that the color which I am apprehending is in fact the color red, or that it is a color, or that it is at the very least something that I am apprehending. It might then be argued that, in the case of *these* facts, my apprehension of them does indeed involve some sort of psychological relation with the state of affairs which is its object, and not merely with the phenomenal quality which that state of affairs involves. The only apparent reason for denying that awareness of states of affairs involves such a relation is the impossibility of formulating a satisfactory theory of non-actualized facts to serve as *terms* of the relation in question, but this difficulty does not arise in the present case. However, even if we do assume that at least some of the ways in which one perceives immediately apprehended phenomenal qualities necessarily involve verdical perceptions (and hence true judgments), it would still not follow that the apprehension of the states of affairs in question involves a special psychological relation. Veridically perceiving that some color is red might simply be regarded as being in a state which immediately apprehends that color and whose content is ⌈the color red⌉—where the color is in fact red. There is no need to suppose that some special relation is involved, over and above the relation of immediate acquaintance with red. Insofar as the *experiences* of veridical and non-veridical apprehensions may be identical, it would seem reasonable simply to *deny* any such relation is involved.

In the light of these conclusions, then, we may finally be in a position to present, in a somewhat more formal way, some specific suggestions for dealing with intentional phenomena, and for representing the logical form of propositions about them, in a way which does justice to the sorts of ontological issues that we have encountered here. First, we need to introduce a relational predicate in order to designate our relation of immediate, intuitive apprehension. However, it is convenient, in the light of our earlier discussions, to introduce such a predicate as one which will properly apply to a perceiver's *mental states*, and not merely to the perceiver himself. As our earlier discussions have shown, we will need to be able to distinguish between the case in which a *person* makes a certain judgment about what he is immediately apprehending and the case in which some particular apprehension *itself* "makes" such a judgment (only the latter involving a case of "direct apprehension"). Furthermore, we will also need to talk about the "contents" of *non-immediate* mental states, and this too can most conveniently be done only by quantifying directly over possible mental states. Thus we shall say that

> (1) *a* immediately apprehends the object *o* ≡ *a* is in a mental state *s*, such that *I*(*s*, *o*),

where the relational predicate '*I*' designates a basic psychological relation involving a person's mental states. Then we may proceed to distinguish several different *modes* of immediate apprehension, corresponding to the various sensory modalities, by distinguishing several determinate forms of the basic relation *I*. Thus for example,

> (2) *a* visually apprehends the object *o* ≡ *a* is in a mental state *s*, such that I_v(*s*, *o*).

Now the notion of visual apprehension was originally introduced, in Chapter 3, only in the case where the object *o* is a (possibly uninstantiated) property. In that case, we might simply identify visual apprehension with what we regard, in some cases at least, as "seeing." However, there are also senses of 'see' which cannot be identified with our notion of visual apprehension. Thus there is a sense of 'see,' and perhaps the most commonly-used sense, in which what we are said to be seeing are not properties at all, but rather individuals. We are said to "see an elephant" rather than the properties, for example, which are the various possible *shapes* of elephants. It seems, however, that any such notion of "seeing" will require, for its analysis, an appeal to the notion of visual apprehension.

Consider, then, the case in which a person is said to be "seeing an elephant," even though there may not in fact exist any particular object which the person can be said to see (in the sense in which he is "seeing an elephant"). Then there are two things which can be said about this case. First, the person in question must be visually apprehending *something*, hence, at least, some particular shape; and, second, he must be apprehending the shape in question *as* the shape of a (possibly non-existent) elephant. Thus we may suggest that

> (3) *a* sees₁ an elephant ≡ *a* is in a mental state *s*, such that, for some property *F*, I_v(*s*, *F*), and such that *s* tokens the content ⌈elephant shape⌉.[1]

We then may introduce a sense of 'see' in which a person cannot be said to be seeing an elephant unless there really *is* an elephant to see, that is,

> (4) *a* sees₂ an elephant ≡ *a* sees₁ an elephant, where *s* (his mental state) is such that (E*x*)(*x* is an elephant and *R* (*x*, *s*)),

where '*R*' designates certain relations, presumably largely causal, which need to obtain in order that a person can be said to be seeing some actually existing individual. Thus both the intentional and the nonintentional sense of 'see' may be defined with the help of our notion of "visual apprehension."

With regard to purely judgmental states, our problem is of course somewhat different. What we need to do here, as suggested in Chapter 4, is simply to find an appropriate interpretation for the notation which we introduced, borrowing from Kaplan, in order to represent the ascription of "content" to judgmental states. Given that notation,

(5) a judges that b is $F \equiv a$ j's $\ulcorner b$ is $F\urcorner$,

where judging is construed as "fully opaque," that is, resistant to substitution both with regard to b and to F. In the light of our discussion in Chapter 5, we may simply say that

(6) a j's $\ulcorner b$ is $F\urcorner \equiv a$'s mental state is of a kind K, such that K's are
     $\cdot b$ is $F \cdot$s.[2]

Now the antecedent of (6), we have seen, may be existentially generalized in a certain way, namely as

(7) $(E\alpha)(a$ j's $\ulcorner \alpha$ is $F\urcorner)$.

Using the notion of a mental word or sentence, this may also be accommodated:

(8) $(E\alpha)$ $(a$ j's $\ulcorner \alpha$ is $F\urcorner) \equiv$ There is an expression which, substituted
     for 'α' in $\ulcorner \alpha$ is $F\urcorner$, yields a sentence S which
     is such that K's are $\cdot S \cdot$s, where a's mental
     state is of kind K.[3]

We have finally an account of awareness which agrees in some respects with the views of certain philosophers, and disagrees in others. Like Bertrand Russell, for example, we have found it necessary to introduce a psychological relation of "direct acquaintance," but the present account does more justice than Russell's to our ordinary intuitions by restricting the occurrence of that relation to cases of immediate sensory intuition. The present account also agrees with Russell in denying that *judgmental* states are to be regarded as involving a psychological relation with the states of affairs which are said to be the "objects" of the judgments in question. However, unlike Russell's alternative appeal to many-termed psychological relations with the *constituents* of such would-be objects, the account that I have proposed does not fail to do justice to the *unity* which is always expressed on the "object" side of such propositions as 'Jones judges that a is F.' This unity would be accommodated, on the present account, by the fact that intentional propositions of this form do not merely express some relation between a judging subject and the individual objects designated by 'a' and by 'F.' They rather express the presence of a certain unitary *content* in some mental state of that subject. Nevertheless, it remains the case that the roles which these contents play in the life of the mind, and which define the semantical significance of these contents, could not be exhaustively explicated without an ultimate appeal to the notion of a relation of "direct acquaintance." In this (although extended) sense one might even agree with Russell that all apprehension of objects by mind "involves" such a relation. If there were not at least this much of a connection between merely "symbolical," non-intuitive thinking and the objects of possible intuition, then it is not clear how we could ever succeed in regarding our thoughts as thoughts *about* the very things which are also possible objects of intuition. To some philosophers (e.g., Sellars) this concession to a relational account of awareness will be too great; to others (e.g., Bergmann) it will not be great enough. Nevertheless I do not see how, in the light of the preceding investigations, we might be able to draw any closer connection between the mind and the world of its objects; nor is it evident how we can reasonably suppose that the human mind is not *even* this closely in touch with its world.

Notes

CHAPTER 1

1. Franz Brentano, *Psychologie vom empirischen Standpunkt* (Hamburg: Felix Meiner, 1925; rpt. 1955), 1:124. Translated by D.B. Terrell in Roderick Chisholm, ed., *Realism and the Background of Phenomenology* (Glencoe, Ill.: Free Press, 1960), p. 50.
2. Brentano, p. 125; Chisholm, p. 50.
3. Brentano, p. 138; Chisholm, p. 59. This point is also made by Linda McAlister, "Chisholm and Brentano on Intentionality," *The Review of Metaphysics* 28 (December 1974): 328–38.
4. I find that Chisholm's isolation of an "ontological thesis" in Brentano does not separate these two issues clearly enough, generating the mistaken impression that Brentano was centrally occupied with an attempt to provide some sort of positive ontological account of awareness, rather than merely with the polemical intent to reject certain views about the *objects* of awareness. Cf. "Brentano on Descriptive Psychology and the Intentional," reprinted in Harold Morick, ed., *Introduction to the Philosophy of Mind* (Glenview, Ill.: Scott, Foresman, 1970), pp. 130–49.
5. David Hume, *A Treatise of Human Nature*, ed. L.A. Selby-Bigge (Oxford: Clarendon Press, 1964), p. 191.
6. Ibid., p. 194. Italics added.
7. Ibid., p. 261.
8. Ibid., p. 194.
9. Cf. Alexius Meinong, "Über die Bedeutung des Weber'schen Gesetzes" (1896), in *Gesammelte Abhandlungen*, 2d ed. (Leipzig: Verlag von Johann Ambrosius Barth, 1929), 2: 323: "Extensiveness, on the contrary, is already assured its place among the facts of psychical life, through the fact that it quite essentially belongs to every presentation (*Vorstellung*) which grasps it, at least with respect to its content (*Inhalte*). If the presentation is a psychical experience, then so also is certainly that which is presented in it, as presented. In this sense, then, not only is the presentation of a spatial expanse, e.g., psychical, but also the presented spatial expanse." Meinong later came to reject this view. Cf. "Über Gegenstände höherer Ordnung" (1899), ibid., p. 383. For a relevant passage from Höfler's *Logik* (1890), cf. J.N. Findlay, *Meinong's Theory of Objects and Values*, 2d ed. (Oxford: Clarendon Press, 1963), p. 7. For an interesting treatment of the philosophical issues in nineteenth century psychology, see Gustav Bergmann, "The Problem of Relations in Classical Psychology," in *The Metaphysics of Logical Positivism* (New York: Longmans, Green, 1954), pp. 277–99, and "Intentionality," in *Meaning and Existence* (Madison: University of Wisconsin Press, 1960), esp. pp. 9–17.
10. Franz Brentano, *The True and the Evident*, ed. Roderick M. Chisholm (New York: Humanities Press, 1966), p. 78.
11. Ibid.
12. René Descartes, "Reply to Objections I," in *Philosophical Works*, trans. Elizabeth S. Haldane and G.R.T. Ross (Cambridge: Cambridge University Press, 1970), 2:10.
13. Descartes, "Preface to the Reader," "Meditations", ibid., 1:138.
14. Descartes, "Reply to Objections IV," ibid., 2:105.
15. Descartes, "Arguments Demonstrating the Existence of God and the Distinction between Soul and Body, Drawn up in Geometrical Fashion," ibid., 2:52.
16. Cf. Anthony Kenny, *Descartes* (New York: Random House, 1968), p. 114.
17. Cf. Timothy J. Cronin, *Objective Being in Descartes and in Suarez*, Analecta Gregoriana, Cura Pontificiae Universitatis Gregoriana edita (Rome: Gregorian University Press, 1966), 154:100: "The objective reality of ideas involves (1) the subject, (2) within the subject the object known by which the actual objects shall be ascertained, (3) the actual objects apart from the subject."
18. Descartes, "Reply to Objections V," *Philosophical Works* 2:231.
19. Cf. Brian E. O'Neil, *Epistemological Direct Realism in Descartes' Philosophy* (Albuquerque: University of New Mexico Press, 1974), Ch. 3; Thomas A. Lennon, "The Inherence

Pattern and Descartes' Ideas," *Journal of the History of Philosophy* 12 (January 1974):43–52; John W. Yolton, "Ideas and Knowledge in Seventeenth-Century Philosophy," *Journal of the History of Philosophy* 13 (April 1975):145–65.

20. Descartes, "Third Meditation," *Philosophical Works* 1:161–62.
21. Descartes, "Reply to Objections I," ibid., 2:11.
22. Descartes, "Preface to the Reader," "Meditations," ibid., 1:138.
23. For an interesting discussion of "representationalism" and its structural connections with idealism, see Gustav Bergmann, *Realism: A Critique of Brentano and Meinong* (Madison: University of Wisconsin Press, 1967), esp. Chs. 10 and 11.
24. Brentano is not, of course, the first to have attacked the classical theory along these lines. Cf. Thomas Reid, *Essays on the Intellectual Powers of Man*, ed. Baruch A. Brody (Cambridge, Mass.: M.I.T. Press, 1969), p. 197: "In perception, in remembrance, and in conception, or imagination, I distinguish three things, the mind that operates, the operation of the mind, and the object of that operation. . . . In all these the act of the mind about its object is one thing, the object is another thing. There must be an object, real or imaginary, distinct from the operations of the mind about it. Now, if in these operations the idea be a fourth thing different from the three I have mentioned, I know not what it is, nor have been able to learn from all that has been written about ideas."
25. Brentano, *Psychologie*, 1:111; Chisholm, *Realism*, p. 41.
26. Edmund Husserl, *Logical Investigations*, trans. J.N. Findlay (New York: Humanities Press, 1970), 2:572 ff.
27. This is done, for example, by Hubert Dreyfus, "*Sinn* and Intentional Object," in *Phenomenology and Existentialism*, ed. Robert C. Solomon (New York: Harper & Row, 1972), p. 207.
28. Brentano, *Psychologie*, 1:129; Chisholm, *Realism*, p. 53.
29. C. D. Broad, *Scientific Thought* (London: Kegan Paul, 1925; rpt. Paterson, N.J.: Littlefield, Adams, 1959), pp. 242–43.
30. Brentano, *Psychologie*, 1:139; Chisholm, *Realism*, p. 60.
31. Broad, p. 243.
32. Brentano, *The True and the Evident*, p. 42.
33. Ibid., pp. 15–16.
34. Ibid., pp. 77–78. Numbers have been added to the passages quoted.
35. Cf. Jan Srzednicki, *Franz Brentano's Analysis of Truth* (The Hague: Martinus Nijhoff, 1965), pp. 44–45. Cf. J.N. Mohanty, *The Concept of Intentionality* (St. Louis: Warren Green, 1972), p. 7. According to Mohanty, though Brentano later changed his mind, he had earlier held that "What the fact that there is an intentional act does entail is that there is an intended object, but not that this intended object is as such real" (p. 33). Since this view regards intentionality as neutral with regard to "real" existence, Mohanty describes it as "ontologically neutral," although this seems hardly appropriate in view of its commitment to non-real intentional objects.
36. Cf. Linda McAlister, "Brentano on Intentional Inexistence," *Journal of the History of Philosophy* 8, no. 4 (October 1970): 423–30; cf. Srzednicki, p. 32.
37. Brentano, *The True and the Evident*, p. 27; cf. Srzednicki, p. 32.
38. Brentano, *Psychologie*, 1:140; Chisholm, *Realism*, p. 60.
39. Roderick Firth, "Sense-Data and the Percept Theory," in *Perceiving, Sensing and Knowing*, ed. Robert J. Swartz (Garden City, N.Y.: Doubleday, 1965), p. 212.
40. Ibid., pp. 250 ff.
41. Brentano, *Psychologie*, 1:132; Chisholm, *Realism*, p. 55.
42. In this connection it is worth noting an important difference between Brentano's and Locke's approach to secondary qualities. Regarding secondary qualities as qualities apprehended in phenomena which yet have no real existence apart from our apprehension of them, Locke assumed that such qualities must nevertheless at least exist *in* that apprehension. Hence the Lockean distinction between primary and secondary qualities is not an instance of Brentano's distinction between actual and merely intentional objects. (A somewhat similar point is made by Douglas Odegard, "Berkeley and the Perception of Ideas," *Canadian Journal of Philosophy* 1, no. 2 (December 1971): 155–72. In Chapter 3 I discuss the possibility not taken seriously enough by Brentano, of regarding *properties*, rather than particulars, as the objects of a properly intentional perceptual relation.
43. Firth, pp. 250–51.

44. Ibid., p. 254.
45. G. E. Moore, "Some Judgments of Perception," in *Philosophical Studies* (London: Kegan Paul, 1922; rpt. Paterson, N.J.: Littlefield, Adams, 1959), pp. 236 ff.
46. Panayot Butchvarov, *The Concept of Knowledge* (Evanston, Ill.: Northwestern University Press, 1970), p. 248.
47. Ibid., p. 261.
48. Ibid., p. 253. The sense in which what I perceive "might" be a bodily surface cannot be construed as a case of mere epistemic possibility, where what I perceive might, *for all I know*, be a bodily surface. That is compatible with what I perceive not even being the *sort* of thing which could, in a non-epistemic sense, be a bodily surface. Hence what I sometimes perceive would be actual bodily surfaces, and at other times some other sort of entity entirely. But the sense-datum philosopher at least seems correct in maintaining that if we ever do perceive entities of the latter sort, then we must always be perceiving them.
49. The argument which follows is similar to one suggested by Romane Clark in "Sensuous Judgments," *Nous* 7 (March 1973): 45–56, and in "The Sensuous Content of Perception," in *Action, Knowledge, and Reality: Studies in Honor of Wilfrid Sellars*, ed. Hector-Neri Castaneda (Indianapolis: Bobbs-Merrill, 1975). I develop this view of the relation between conceptual and sensory aspects of perception in Chapter 4. Cf. also, for a discussion of Clark's papers, my "Perceptions and Perceptual Judgments," *Philosophical Studies* 28 (July 1975): 17–32.
50. Many commentators fail to distinguish clearly enough between sensation and sensible intuition in Kant. For Kant's view, cf. *Critique of Pure Reason*, B33–4, B377. I discuss the relation between judgment, sensation and perception in Kant in "Kant's Theory of Concepts," *Kant-Studien* 65 (1974): 1–19, and in "The Relationship between Pure and Empirical Intuition in Kant," *Kant-Studien*, forthcoming. That Brentano was prepared to make a parallel distinction to that between sensation and sensible intuition, though he tended to use a single term (*'Empfindung'*) to cover both cases, seems clear from *Psychologie*, 1:120 (Chisholm, *Realism*, p. 47).
51. Although she does not use the terminology which I have introduced, a similar point is made by G.E.M. Anscombe concerning the errors both of "ordinary language" and of "sense-data" approaches to sensation in "The Intentionality of Sensation: A Grammatical Feature," in *Analytical Philosophy*, 2d ser., ed. R.J. Butler (Oxford: Clarendon Press, 1965), p. 169.
52. Another interesting parallel between Brentano and Kant, as I interpret the latter, lies in the fact that "phenomenal objects" for Kant are *merely intentional* objects, though this point is sometimes obscured by Kant's suggesting that phenomenal objects really exist "in the mind." I argue for this interpretation of Kant in "Kant's Phenomenalism," *Idealistic Studies* 5 (May 1975): 108–26.
53. G.E. Moore, "The Refutation of Idealism," in *Philosophical Studies*, pp. 1–30, esp. pp. 17 ff.

CHAPTER 2

1. Roderick Chisholm, *Perceiving: A Philosophical Study* (Ithaca: Cornell University Press, 1957), pp. 169–70.
2. Roderick Chisholm, "Intentionality and the Mental," in *Minnesota Studies in the Philosophy of Science* (Minneapolis: University of Minnesota Press, 1958), 2: 510–13. The term 'intentionality' is often used simply to stand for a certain feature which linguistic contexts might exhibit. It may also be used, as I have been using it, and as Brentano originally used it, to stand for that feature in virtue of which a mental state might "refer to" or "intend" some object. The two uses are of course not unconnected, since the sentences describing intentional states, qua intentional states, do appear to possess certain special linguistic features. Nevertheless, it is important to keep the distinction in mind. I shall continue to use the terms 'intentionality' and 'intentional state' in the way that I have been, but also use the expressions 'intentional sentence' and 'intentional context.' The term 'intentional relation' will be used to designate any sort of relation, if there be such, which does not require the real existence of all its terms. Depending upon our criteria for intentional sentences, then, there need be no contradiction in denying that some relational sentences which are intentional sentences nevertheless do not express intentional relations.

The relation between Chisholm's linguistic approach and Brentano's approach to the problem of intentionality is discussed by J.N. Mohanty in *The Concept of Intentionality* (St. Louis: Warren Green, 1972), Ch. 2.

3. David M. Rosenthal, "Talking about Thinking," *Philosophical Studies* 24 (September 1973): 297 ff.

4. Chisholm himself has since modified his thesis in various ways, since it is clear that a number of non-psychological contexts, for example, modal contexts, would satisfy one of his conditions for intentionality. (It is not unreasonable to think that non-modal and non-psychological sentences which also happen to satisfy the conditions might simply be *translated* into sentences which do not satisfy them.) In "Brentano on Descriptive Psychology and the Intentional" he offers the following suggestion (reprinted in Harold Morick, ed., *Introduction to the Philosophy of Mind* [Glenview, Ill.: Scott, Foresman, 1970], p. 148):

> Consider the two formulae
> (1) (Ex) (Ey) (y = a&xRa)
> (2) (Ex) (Ey) (y = a&xRy)
> An expression which may occupy the place of "R" in such formulae could be said to be intentional if there is an individual term that may occupy the place of "a" with the results that (1) does not imply (2); (2) does not imply (1); and no well-formed sentence that is part of (1) is noncontingent.

This has the advantage of drawing our attention to the fact that the particular *sorts* of intentional contexts which psychological phenomena involve are at least apparently relational in character (unlike, e.g., modal contexts). In his article "Intentionality" in *The Encyclopedia of Philosophy*, ed. Paul Edwards (New York: Macmillan and Free Press, 1967), Chisholm simply employs the notion of a sentence prefix: "We may say that a simple sentence prefix *M*, is *intentional*, if, for every sentence *p*, *M(p)* is logically contingent." This also rules out modal prefixes such as "It is impossible that." Since we shall be primarily concerned with the relational, or apparently relational, character of intentional sentences about psychological phenomena, it is convenient to remain with Chisholm's original suggestion.

5. This distinction appears similar to Chisholm's distinction between an "ontological thesis" about intentionality, involving the notion of "intentional inexistence," and a merely "psychological thesis" (cf. "Brentano on Descriptive Psychology and the Intentional," Morick, p. 135). Chisholm's views about the "psychological thesis" are not entirely clear, however, since he sometimes presents his point by saying that "Living things have a funny kind of characteristic that ordinary physical things don't have" ("Intentionality and the Mental," p. 524). The claim that what distinguishes phenomena involving intentional reference from phenomena which lack it is a "funny kind of characteristic" is a claim which indeed appears to raise significant ontological issues.

6. Cf. Jaegwon Kim, "Materialism and the Criteria of the Mental," *Synthese* 22 (1971): 326–27.

7. Article "Intentionality," in *The Encyclopedia of Philosophy*.

8. A number of formulations of criteria for physical properties are considered by James W. Cornman, *Materialism and Sensations* (New Haven: Yale University Press, 1971), pp. 9 ff. The present formulation avoids an objection to one that Cornman considers and rejects on p. 11. On the latter, the fact that computers can think (if it is a fact) would automatically show that thinking is a physical phenomenon. On the present formulation, while the fact that computers can think might show that computers are capable of engaging in *psychological activities,* it would not automatically follow that these ativities involve purely physical properties. That would only follow if what it is for a computer to think could be *analyzed* solely in terms of properties which might be found, not simply exemplified by non-living beings such as computers, but in particular exemplified in the *non-psychological* activities of such beings. But the defect of the formulation that Cornman himself finally accepts (p. 12) is that it implies that thinking involves a *non*-physical property, quite apart from any concern with an analysis of what thinking is.

9. Cf. Kim, pp. 328–29.

10. It is worth distinguishing, in discussing the problem of mind/body identity, between the claim that any mental occurrence is identical with a physical one and the claim that the

same mental occurrence (e.g., "the same thought") is always identical with the *same* physical occurrence. It has been argued that this latter sort of identification is impossible by Bruce Goldberg, "The Correspondence Hypothesis," *The Philosophical Review* 77 (1968): 438–54. Since Goldberg's argument in effect turns on the fact that what we regard as the "same thought" always involves the *intentional* description we give to the thought, the argument might be taken to show how a consideration of the problem of intentionality might have a negative bearing on the claims of the identity theorist. But it is important to note that it does not bear on the *general* identity claim as I have formulated it.

11. Chisholm seems prepared to grant that relations of comparison may in fact provide the single exception to the principle that intentionality alone constitutes a relation between actual and non-actual entities: "There are sentences describing relations of comparison— for example 'Some lizards look like dragons'—which may constitute an exception to (1). If they are exceptions then we may qualify (1) to read: 'We do not need any intentional sentences, other than those describing relations of comparison, when we describe non-psychological phenomena'" (*Perceiving*, p. 172).

12. Chisholm, "Intentionality and the Mental," p. 512.

13. Franz Brentano, *Psychologie vom empirischen Standpunkt* (Hamburg: Verlag von Felix Meiner, 1925; rpt. 1959): 2:136–37.

14. Ibid., p. 134.

15. Cf. Gustav Bergmann, *Realism: A Critique of Brentano and Meinong* (Madison: University of Wisconsin Press, 1967), p. 252.

16. Chisholm, "Intentionality and the Mental," p. 524.

17. This principle is rejected by Reinhardt Grossmann, "Non-existent Objects: Recent Work on Brentano and Meinong," *American Philosophical Quarterly* 6, no. 1 (January 1969): 32.

18. Ibid., p. 21.

19. Brentano, 2:247.

20. Ibid., p. 232.

21. Ibid., p. 216.

22. Cf. Franz Brentano, *The True and the Evident*, ed. Roderick M. Chisholm (New York: Humanities Press, 1966), pp. 82ff.

23. Brentano, *Psychologie*, 2:215–16.

24. Ibid., p. 218.

25. Chisholm, "Brentano on Descriptive Psychology and the Intentional," Morick, p. 144.

26. Ibid., p. 145.

CHAPTER 3

1. Cf. J.N. Findlay, *Meinong's Theory of Objects and Values*, 2d ed. (Oxford: Clarendon Press, 1963), ch. 6.

2. Cf. Herbert Hochberg, "Universals, Particulars, and Predication," *Review of Metaphysics* 19, no. 1 (September 1965): 87–102.

3. Cf. Reinhardt Grossmann, *The Structure of Mind* (Madison: University of Wisconsin Press, 1965), p. 164: "To talk about actual and possible states of affairs is to talk about what *there is* and what *there could be*."

4. This notion of a fact, or state of affairs, as a complex entity of a certain sort is developed by Gustav Bergmann in many of his essays and most recently in *Realism: A Critique of Brentano and Meinong* (Madison: University of Wisconsin Press, 1967).

5. Some philosophers appear to have confused the two senses of 'fact.' Russell, for example, often assumes that an object which is referred to in any proposition must actually occur as a *part* of that proposition. Cf. "On Denoting," in *Logic and Knowledge*, ed. Robert C. Marsh (New York: Macmillan, 1956), pp. 45ff.

6. Bergmann, p. 9. Bergmann uses roughly the argument which I use above in order to introduce the special connectors which he calls "nexus," although I have used that argument only to distinguish states of affairs from mere collections of entities.

7. Whether a state of affairs is distinct from the mere collection of its constituents is of course independent of the question whether there are any such entities as collections over and above their constituents taken individually. That there are no such entities as collections is maintained by Bergmann, pp. 9ff. Cf. also Russell, p. 191.

8. I have in mind Sartre, who appears to regard an awareness of some intentional object as a

state of affairs which contains only that object itself as its constituent. This at least is one interpretation of Sartre's claim that awareness is "nothing." Sartre describes, for example, consciousness as an "internal negation" and claims that "the term-of-origin of the internal negation is the in-itself, the thing which *is there*, and outside of it there is nothing except an emptinesss, a nothingness which is distinguished from the thing only by a pure negation for which *this* thing furnishes the very content." *Being and Nothingness*, trans. Hazel E. Barnes (New York: Washington Square Press, 1968), p. 245. Cf. my "Two Problems of Being and Non-Being in Sartre's *Being and Nothingness*," *Philosophy and Phenomenological Research*, forthcoming.

9. Cf. Bergmann, pp. 366ff.

10. Alexius Meinong, *Über Annahmen*, 2d rev. ed. (Leipzig: Verlag von Johann Ambrosius Barth, 1910), p. 31.

11. Ibid., pp. 44–45.

12. Findlay, p. 87.

13. Meinong, p. 69.

14. Ibid., p. 59.

15. Alexius Meinong, "Über Gegenstände höherer Ordnung" (1899), in *Gesammelte Abhandlungen*, 2d ed. (Leipzig: Verlag von Johann Ambrosius Barth, 1929), 2:382–83.

16. Meinong, *Über Annahmen*, p. 79. Cf. "Über Gegenstandstheorie" (1904), in *Ges. Abh.*, 2:492; translated in Roderick Chisholm, ed., *Realism and the Background of Phenomenology* (Glencoe, Ill.: Free Press, 1960), p. 85.

17. Ibid.

18. Ibid., p. 80. Commentators are not agreed on the question whether *Aussersein* is a genuine mode of being for Meinong. Leonard Linsky denies that it is in *Referring* (New York: Humanities Press, 1967), pp. 14–15. His interpretation is criticized by M.S. Gram, "Ontology and the Theory of Descriptions," in *Essays on Bertrand Russell*, ed. E.D. Klemke (Urbana: University of Illinois Press, 1971), pp. 124ff.

19. Cf. Meinong, *Über Annahmen*, p. 234: "if I think about untroubled human happiness or about the *perpetuum mobile*, my thoughts are as surely directed to "something," i.e., directed to an object, as if it were thereby a matter of the most everyday piece of reality."

20. Cf. Nicholas Wolterstorff, *On Universals* (Chicago: University of Chicago Press, 1970), p. 207.

21. Russell maintains, for example, that the technique of the theory of descriptions allows us to substitute for an expression such as "Julius Caesar" some description which shows that propositions containing the original expression were only "nominally about" Julius Caesar in the first place ("Knowledge by Acquaintance and Knowledge by Description," *Mind* 11 [1910–11]:120).

22. Meinong, *Über Annahmen*, pp. 34ff., 52, 59.

23. Meinong, "Über Gegenstandstheorie," *Ges. Abh.*, 2:493; translated in Chisholm, p. 85.

24. This in turn involves the three Objects *a*, *b*, and *R*. At one time Meinong used the word *Relation* to designate the third of these objects ("Über Gegenstände höherer Ordnung," *Ges. Abh.*, 2:389ff.), but he later reserved that term for the designation of relational Objectives, and he used the word *Relat* for such entities as *R* (*Über Annahmen*, p. 283).

25. Every relation generates such a complex for Meinong. At one time he called it a *Komplexion* ("Uber Gegenstände höherer Ordnung," *Ges. Abh.*, 2: 388ff.), but later he used the term *Komplex* instead and reserved the original term for the designation of certain Objectives (cf. *Ges. Abh.*, 2, editor's note 17, p. 474).

26. Cf. *Ges. Abh.*, 2:390: "The complex (*Komplexion*) is the relation and its members taken together. Only this ought not to be understood as if the complex were *only* the relation *and* its members: that would indeed be fundamentally nothing but the previously rejected objective collection (*Kollektiv*) of *a*, *b* and *r*. Rather *a* and *b* stand in the relation *r*, which can only signify that *a* and *b* also must each stand in a relation to *r*, say *r'* and *r''* respectively, although both these relations may also be the same. It becomes immediately evident that what was just asserted in connection with *a*, *b* and *r* can now also be repeated in connection with *a*, *r* and *r'*, or also in connection with *b*, *r* and *r''*, and that in this way new and ever new relations must appear without end."

27. Cf. F. H. Bradley, *Appearance and Reality* (1930) (Oxford: Clarendon Press, 1966), ch. 3. The Bradley argument and some responses to it are discussed by M.S. Gram, "The Reality of Relations," *The New Scholasticism* 44 no. 1 (Winter 1970): 49–68.

28. Findlay, p. 146. Meinong claims that the regress poses no more difficulty than the infinite divisibility of a line segment: "Über Gegenstände höherer Ordnung," *Ges. Abh.*, 2:390.
29. Meinong, "Über Gegenstände höherer Ordnung," *Ges. Abh.*, 2:391.
30. Cf. Findlay, p. 138.
31. Cf. Grossmann, p. 157: "In general, what ties objects and relate together into complexes are objectives." Cf. Findlay, p. 141.
32. Linsky, p. 15.
33. Meinong, "Über Gegenstandstheorie," *Ges. Abh.*, 2:493; Chisholm, p. 86. I have departed somewhat from the translation in Chisholm.
34. Meinong, "Über Gegenstandstheorie," *Ges. Abh.*, 2:494; Chisholm, p. 86.
35. Meinong, "Über Gegenstände höherer Ordnung," *Ges. Abh.*, 2:382–83.
36. Meinong, *Über Annahmen*, pp. 59–61.
37. Ibid., p. 70.
38. Meinong, "Über Gegenstandstheorie," *Ges. Abh.*, 2:493; Chisholm, p. 86.
39. Kant, *Kritik der reinen Vernunft*, B 626–27.
40. Meinong, *Über die Stellung der Gegenstandstheorie im System der Wissenschaften* (Leipzig: Voigtländer, 1906), p. 17.
41. Gustav Bergmann, *Logic and Reality* (Madison: University of Wisconsin Press, 1964), p. 270. Some qualifications are in order. First, the sort of ontological tie which intentionality involves is, according to Bergmann, a "nexus" rather than a "relation." Second, the tie in question is not, strictly speaking, a tie between a mental act and its intended object, but rather between the act's "content" and its object. These points do not affect the argument which I pursue.
42. Ibid., pp. 307–8.
43. Ibid., 308. Cf. *Realism*, pp. 214–15.
44. The example presupposes a distinction between particulars and universals. The point does not affect the argument, however, as our earlier discussion of states of affairs should show.
45. Bergmann, *Realism*, p. 9.
46. Ibid., p. 42.
47. Ibid., pp. 43–44. The introduction of nexus in order to avoid an infinite regress of constituents in a complex is criticized by Gram in "The Reality of Relations."
48. Cf. Nicholas Wolterstorff, "Bergmann's Constituent Ontology," *Nous* 4, no. 2 (May 1970): 122–23.
49. For Hintikka, 'a believes that b is F' is (roughly) equivalent to 'b is F in all possible worlds compatible with what a believes.' This shows, according to Hintikka, that expressions such as 'b' occurring in intentional contexts have a "multiple reference," referring to all those objects in various possible worlds which are the same object as b. Cf. "Semantics for Propositional Attitudes," reprinted in Jaakko Hintikka, *Models for Modalities* (Dordrecht: D. Reidel, 1969), pp. 106ff.
50. Though Hintikka denies (ibid., pp. 94–95) that his views commit him (ontologically) to merely possible entities, it is difficult to see how he avoids such a commitment, so long as he regards the terms which occur in intentional predicates as having genuinely referential occurrences there. Perhaps he only means to suggest that the *terms* that occur in such contexts are to be regarded as possessing a genuinely "multiple reference," but not that they are *used*, in such contexts, in a referential way.
51. Bertrand Russell, *The Problems of Philosophy* (London: Oxford University Press, 1943), p. 196.
52. Ibid., p. 197.
53. Ibid.
54. Cf. Findlay, p. 100.
55. Russell, *Problems*, p. 201. Emphasis added.
56. Peter Geach discusses some problems posed by relations for Russell's account of judgment in *Mental Acts* (London: Routledge & Kegan Paul, 1957), pp. 49ff.
57. The distinction has of course been frequently used in recent years. If we could allow ourselves, at this point, the notion of a "proposition," then we could regard ascription of judgment *de dicto* as the assertion that a believer *judges a certain proposition to be true*, and ascription of judgment *de re* (with respect to some particular) as the assertion that a believer judges something *to be true of that particular*. The notion of a "proposition," however, will be clarified in the next two chapters.

160 NOTES

58. Cf. Bertrand Russell, "On Denoting," in Robert C. Marsh, ed., *Logic and Knowledge* (New York: Macmillan, 1956), p. 55: "One interesting result of the above theory of denoting is this: when there is anything with which we do not have immediate acquaintance, but only definition by denoting phrases, then the propositions in which this thing is introduced by means of a denoting phrase do not really contain this thing as a constituent, but contain instead the constituents expressed by the several words of the denoting phrase."

59. Cf. Edmund Husserl, *Logical Investigations*, trans. J. N. Findlay (New York Humanities Press, 1970), 2:784–802.

CHAPTER 4

1. David Kaplan, "Quantifying In," in Donald Davidson and Jaakko Hintikka, eds., *Words and Objections: Essays on the Work of W. V. Quine* (Dordrecht: D. Reidel, 1969); reprinted in Leonard Linsky, ed., *Reference and Modality* (New York: Oxford University Press, 1971), pp. 112–43.

2. A similar point is made by W.V. Quine, "Quantifiers and Propositional Attitudes," in *The Ways of Paradox* (New York: Random House, 1966); reprinted in Linsky, pp. 101–11. There (p. 109) Quine points out that "believing a sentence true" of something does not even require *knowing the language* in which the sentence occurs: "We may treat a mouse's fear of a cat as his fearing true a certain English sentence. This is unnatural without being therefore wrong." Of course, this move requires *distinguishing* the occurrence of 'believing' in 'believing a sentence true' from its occurrence in, say, 'believing *a* to be *F*.'

3. This bears some similarity to Quine's notion of "believing a sentence true" of some particular. Cf. Quine, p. 109.

4. This again follows a suggestion of Kaplan's, extending the suggestion, however, beyond the issue of singular terms in intentional contexts. *R* is supposed to be an extensional relation (of "representation") between expressions and entities which they denote. That the relation must involve *more* than mere denotation is made clear by Kaplan, pp. 220–21. For our purposes it is not necessary to consider the particular line of analysis that Kaplan goes on to suggest for the representation-relation. That analysis rests mainly on an appeal to certain sorts of *causal* connections between Jones' use of a certain expression and the entity which that expression denotes. (For convenience, I have transformed Kaplan's three-term relation into a two-term one. Strictly, a term that denotes some particular entity might "represent" that entity *to Jones* without representing it to someone else.)

5. For a criticism of Kaplan's view concerning conditions for inferences of the sort in question (and hence of Kaplan's whole program), cf. Ernest Sosa, "Propositional Attitudes de Dicto and de Re," *The Journal of Philosophy* 67 (5 November 1970): 883–96. Sosa, in turn, is criticized by Jaakko Hintikka, and replies to Hintikka, in the same journal, 68 (19 August 1971).

6. Cf. Robert Swartz, "Seeing and Substitutivity," *The Journal of Philosophy* 70 (20 September 1973): 526–36.

7. Jaakko Hintikka, *Knowledge and Belief* (Ithaca: Cornell University Press, 1962), Ch. 6; "Semantics for Propositional Attitudes," in *Models for Modalities* (Dordrecht: D. Reidel, 1969), reprinted in Linsky, pp. 146–67. The "possible worlds" in question, on Hintikka's view, are just those possible worlds that are compatible with the particular propositional attitude that is in question.

8. In "Three Types of Referential Opacity" (*Philosophy of Science* 39 [June 1972]: 153–61), Richard Sharvy also emphasizes the need for distinguishing substitution-opacity from quantification-opacity. Sharvy, however, sanctions quantification into an opaque context only in cases of what he calls "small-scope opacity." These are cases where a sentence, such as (1), is *ambiguous* as between two readings on which the psychological verb has either a shorter or a longer scope; thus (1-short) Jones believes (the proposition) that *a* is *F* and (1-long) Jones believes of *a* that it is *F*. Here, *the short-scope reading* of (1) is unambiguously resistant to substitution, and hence is "substitution-opaque" (thus making (1) itself "small-scope opaque"), even though (1) itself is not necessarily resistant to quantification. But I have tried to show, contra Sharvy, that even *unambiguously* substitution-opaque contexts may permit quantification. Thus (11), *unambiguously un-*

derstood as equivalent to (12) is substitution-opaque (not just small-scope opaque) and yet not quantification-opaque.

9. Alexius Meinong, "Über Gegenstände höherer Ordnung," *Gesammelte Abhandlungen*, 2d ed. (Leipzig: Verlag von Johann Ambrosius Barth, 1929), 2:382.
10. Arthur O. Lovejoy, *The Revolt Against Dualism*, 2d ed. (La Salle, Ill.: Open Court, 1960), p. 21.
11. Bertrand Russell, *The Analysis of Mind* (London: Allen and Unwin, 1921), pp. 233–34.
12. Cf. Reinhardt Grossmann, *The Structure of Mind* (Madison: University of Wisconsin Press, 1965), p. 120.
13. J.N. Findlay, *Meinong's Theory of Objects and Values*, 2d ed. (Oxford: Clarendon Press, 1963), p. 24. Emphasis added.
14. Ibid., p. 23.
15. Ibid., p. 24.
16. Meinong, 2:384.
17. Cf. Gustav Bergmann, *Logic and Reality* (Madison: University of Wisconsin Press, 1964), p. 31.
18. Meinong, 2:384.
19. Ibid., p. 385.
20. Franz Brentano, *Psychologie vom empirischen Standpunkt*, vol. I (Hamburg: Felix Meiner, 1924; rpt. 1955), p. 124. Translated by D.B. Terrell in Roderick Chisholm, ed., *Realism and the Background of Phenomenology* (Glencoe, Ill.: Free Press, 1960), p. 50.
21. Cf. Findlay, p. 6.
22. Meinong, 2:381ff.
23. Franz Brentano, *The True and the Evident*, ed. Roderick M. Chisholm (New York: Humanities Press, 1966), pp. 82ff.
24. Meinong, 2:384n.
25. Findlay, p. 12.
26. Grossmann, p. 121.
27. Bergmann, p. 97.
28. The view presented in this section develops some suggestions made by Romane Clark in "Sensuous Judgments," *Nous* 7 (March 1973): 45–56, and in "The Sensuous Content of Perception," in *Action, Knowledge and Reality: Studies in Honor of Wilfrid Sellars*, ed. Hector-Neri Castaneda (Indianapolis: Bobbs-Merrill, 1975). For a discussion of Clark's view, cf. my "Perceptions and Perceptual Judgments," *Philosophical Studies* 28, no. 1 (July 1975): 17–31.
29. G. E. Moore, "The Refutation of Idealism," in *Philosophical Studies* (London: Kegan Paul, 1922; rpt. Paterson, N.J.: Littlefield, Adams, 1959), p. 25.
30. This distinction may be useful in dealing with G.E.M. Anscombe's distinction between a "material" and an "intentional" object of perception. Cf. "The Intentionality of Sensation: A Grammatical Feature," in R.J. Butler ed., *Analytical Philosophy*, 2d ser. (London: Basil Blackwell, 1965), esp. pp. 158–68.
31. I have attempted, in some recent papers, to argue that such a view of concepts and of their relation to thought and perception was held by Immanuel Kant. Cf. "Kant's Theory of Concepts," *Kant-Studien* 65 (1974): 1–19; "The Relationship Between Pure and Empirical Intuition in Kant," *Kant-Studien*, forthcoming.
32. This way of regarding "direct preception" also avoids another difficulty confronting the alternative approach. For the latter, namely, there is no reason why certain presumably highly unusual, if not (at least physically) quite impossible, direct perceptions should in fact be experiences which are at all out of the ordinary. Thus on the causal theory, *sounds* should be as easy to see directly as colors are, so long as it is no more difficult (as it presumably is not) for visual sensations directly to occasion thoughts or judgments about sounds than is it for them directly to occasion thoughts or judgments about colors. But on the account that I have offered, *more* is required for directly seeing colors in the first place than just the occasioning, by means of visual sensation, of certain thoughts and judgments about colors. What is required is that those very sensations undergo a certain *transformation*, in virtue of coming to exhibit the concept of color. That it is no more difficult for those same sensations to exhibit the concept of *sound* at least hardly follows from the fact that it is not at all difficult for them directly to *cause* the occurrence of mental states which exhibit that concept, and even though there may be no *analytical* impossibility in their

doing so, hence in someone's directly seeing sounds (as indeed some persons in "altered states of consciousness" claim to have done).

33. The view in question can also be extended beyond perceptual acts proper to any acts which involve, as essential ingredients, "sensuous content." The most fruitful extension of the view is in the case of at least certain (occurrent) *emotional* states. Cf. my "Causes and 'Constituents' of Occurrent Emotion," *The Philosophical Quarterly* 25 (October 1975): 346–49, and "A New Look at Kant's Aesthetic Judgments," *Kant-Studien*, forthcoming.

34. Gottlob Frege, "On Sense and Reference," trans. Peter Geach and Max Black in *Translations from the Philosophical Writings of Gottlob Frege* (Oxford: Basil Blackwell, 1960), p. 61. The original essay is reprinted in *Kleine Schriften*, ed. Ignacio Angelelli (Hildesheim: Georg Olms, 1967), pp. 143–62.

35. Husserl, p. 290.

36. Frege, p. 57.

37. Husserl, p. 293.

38. Frege, p. 62.

39. Husserl, pp. 280–81.

40. Frege, p. 59.

41. Husserl, p. 327.

42. Thus Herbert Spiegelberg's terse observation: "Here Husserl utilized and developed some of Frege's ideas," *The Phenomenological Movement* (The Hague: Martinus Nijhoff, 1965), 1:105. Cf. J.N. Mohanty, *Edmund Husserl's Theory of Meaning* (The Hague: Martinus Nijhoff, 1964), p. 17: "It is at once obvious that the distinction runs closely parallel to Frege's, though the terminological departure must be noted: Frege's *Sinn* = Husserl's *Bedeutung*, while Frege's *Bedeutung* = Husserl's *Gegenstand* (the named or the referred)."

43. I do not of course suggest that the difference is unknown to the above-mentioned commentators. But the fact that it is ignored indicates an insufficient attention to the *ontological* issues with which Husserl was clearly concerned. The difference between Husserl's conception of *Bedeutung* and Frege's theory of meaning has been recently discussed, though in the context of a very different issue from the one which I am pursuing, by Dallas Willard, "The Paradox of Logical Psychologism: Husserl's Way Out," *American Philosophical Quarterly* 9, no. 1 (January 1972): 94–100.

44. Husserl, p. 330.

45. Bernard Bolzano, *Theory of Science*, trans. Rolf George (Berkeley and Los Angeles: University of California Press, 1972), pp. 61–62. This edition contains selections from Bolzano's *Wissenschaftslehre* (Sulzbach, 1837).

46. Cf. the passage reprinted in Jan Berg, *Bolzano's Logic* (Stockholm: Almqvist & Wiksell, 1962), p. 48, in which Bolzano equates judging that some state of affairs obtains (dass eine Sache so oder anders sey) with thinking *an einen Satz*. The passage is from Bolzano's manuscript "Einleitung zur Grössenlehre."

47. Cf. Bergmann, pp. 31–32.

48. Frege, p. 59.

49. Gottlob Frege, "The Thought: a Logical Inquiry," trans. A.M. and Marcelle Quinton, *Mind* 65, no. 259 (July 1956): 307. The original essay is reprinted in Angelelli, pp. 342–62.

50. Ibid.

51. Husserl, p. 332.

52. Frege, "The Thought," p. 300. I have slightly modified the translation.

53. Ibid., p. 301. Elsewhere, Frege distinguishes between a subjective and an "objective" notion of content, and allows that Senses may be contents in the latter sense: "On Sense and Reference," p. 62n.

54. Gottlob Frege, "On Concept and Object," Geach and Black, p. 54. The original essay is reprinted in Angelelli, pp. 192–205.

55. Frege, "On Concept and Object," pp. 45ff.

56. Frege, "On Sense and Reference," pp. 67ff.

57. For a discussion of the issue, cf. Gustav Bergmann, "Frege's Hidden Nominalism" and Reinhardt Grossmann, "Frege's Ontology." These are included, together with E.D. Klemke's reply "Professor Bergmann and Frege's 'Hidden Nominalism'" in *Essays on Frege*, ed. E.D. Klemke (Urbana: University of Illinois Press, 1968).

58. Gottlob Frege, "Function and Concept," Geach and Black, p. 24. The original essay is reprinted in Angelelli, pp. 125–42.
59. Frege, "On Sense and Reference," p. 63. Cf. Reinhardt Grossmann, *Reflections on Frege's Philosophy* (Evanston, Ill.: Northwestern University Press, 1969), pp. 181ff.
60. Frege, "On Concept and Object," p. 54.
61. Cf. Gottlob Frege, *Nachgelassene Schriften*, ed. Hans Hermes, Friedrich Kambartel, and Friedrich Kaulbach (Hamburg: Verlag von Felix Meiner, 1969), p. 192.
62. Ibid., p. 209. (Cf. "On Sense and Reference," p. 62.)
63. Ibid., p. 299.
64. Ibid., p. 262.
65. Frege, "On Sense and Reference," p. 65. Emphasis added.
66. Ibid., p. 64.
67. Cf. Husserl, p. 795.
68. Cf. Dagfinn Føllesdal, "Husserl's Notion of Noema," *The Journal of Philosophy* 66, no. 20 (16 October (1969) : 680–87; David Woodruff Smith and Ronald McIntyre, "Intentionality via Intensions," *The Journal of Philosophy* 68, no. 18 (16 September 1971) : 541–61. Robert Solomon compares Husserl's notion of "essence" (*Wesen*) with Frege's notion of *Sinn* in "Sense and Essence: Frege and Husserl," reprinted in *Phenomenology and Existentialism*, ed. Robert C. Solomon (New York: Harper & Row, 1972), pp. 258–82. Husserl's notion of *Wesen*, however, is something very different from his notion of the "noema," and the comparison is not a satisfactory one.
69. Edmund Husserl, *Ideas: General Introduction to Pure Phenomenology*, trans. W.R. Boyce Gibson (New York: Collier Books, 1962), p. 238. The original work is reprinted as vol. 3 of Husserl's *Gesammelte Werke* (The Hague: Martinus Nijhoff, 1950).
70. Ibid., p. 271.
71. Ibid.
72. Ibid., p. 240.
73. Aron Gurwitsch, "On the Intentionality of Consciousness," reprinted in *Phenomenology*, ed. Joseph J. Kockelmans (New York: Doubleday, 1967), p. 135.
74. Smith and McIntyre, p. 561.
75. Husserl, *Logical Investigations*, pp. 287–88.
76. John E. Atwell, "Husserl on Signification and Object," *American Philosophical Quarterly* 6, no. 4 (October 1969) :316.
77. Ibid.
78. Ibid., p. 317.
79. A.J. Ayer considers this argument in *Thinking and Meaning* (London: H.K. Lewis, 1947), p. 3.
80. Husserl, *Logical Investigations*, p. 555.
81. Ibid., p. 558.
82. Bergmann, pp. 33–34, recognizes this fact by insisting not only that an act's intentional character involves the presence of a non-relational "content" in that act, but in addition a unique "nexus" connecting that content to the state of affairs intended by the act. An act's intentional character is thus due to a certain fact about the *content* of the act. Bergmann's relational approach to such facts has been criticized in Chapter 3.

CHAPTER 5

1. Wilfrid Sellars, "Intentionality and the Mental," in *Minnesota Studies in the Philosophy of Science* (Minneapolis: University of Minnesota Press, 1958), 2: 525, 534–35, and 535, respectively, for the three passages, Cf. ibid., p. 527.
2. Ibid., p. 531.
3. Wilfrid Sellars, *Science, Perception and Reality* (New York: Humanities Press, 1963), pp. 354–55.
4. Willard Van Orman Quine, *Word and Object* (Cambridge, Mass.: M.I.T. Press 1960), Ch. 2; "On the Reasons for Indeterminacy of Translation," *The Journal of Philosophy* 67 (26 March 1970): 178–83.
5. Sellars, "Intentionality and the Mental," p. 532; *Science, Perception and Reality*, p. 55. In "Intentionality," *The Review of Metaphysics* 26 (June 1973): 716–17, Julian Young suggests, on the basis of this difficulty, that Sellars may not in fact be endeavoring to find

logically equivalent substitutes for semantical sentences in the first place. One possibility is that Sellars regards semantical discourse as involving the ascription of *unanalyzable* semantical properties (pp. 709–10). Some confirmation of this seems to be found in Sellars' "Reply to Marras,"*Canadian Journal of Philosophy* 2 (June 1973) :485–93. Cf. Ausonio Marras' original paper and his counter-reply in the same volume.

6. Wilfrid Sellars, *Philosophical Perspectives* (Springfield, Ill.: Charles C. Thomas, 1967), p. 311; *Science and Metaphysics* (New York: Humanities Press, 1968), p. 95.
7. Sellars, *Philosophical Perspectives*, p. 311.
8. Sellars, *Philosophical Perspectives*, p. 314. Cf. Gustav Bergmann, *Logic and Reality* (Madison: University of Wisconsin Press, 1964), p. 33.
9. Sellars, *Science, Perception and Reality*, p. 315.
10. Ibid.
11. Cf. *Science and Metaphysics*, pp. 80, 87.
12. Sellars, *Philosophical Perspectives*, p. 316n.
13. Sellars, *Science and Metaphysics*, p. 89.
14. Peter Geach, *Mental Acts* (London: Routledge & Kegan Paul, 1957), pp. 52ff. For Sellars on the possibility of dispensing in general with separate parts of a judgment corresponding to predicate expressions, cf. *Science and Metaphysics*, p. 121.
15. Ibid., pp. 99–100. I have slightly modified the symbolism.
16. Ibid., p. 99.
17. Sellars, *Philosophical Perspectives*, p. 317.
18. Cf. Ibid., p. 315n.
19. W.J. Ginnane, "Thoughts," *Mind* 49 (July 1960): 389. A similar claim is made by Jean-Paul Sartre, *Being and Nothingness*, trans. Hazel Barnes (New York: Washington Square Press, 1968), p. 23.
20. Ginnane, p. 387. A similar argument also leads Zeno Vendler to the conclusion that "Speech needs a language; thought does not" in *Res Cogitans: An Essay in Rational Psychology* (Ithaca: Cornell University Press, 1972), p. 51. Cf. pp. 66, 134. In fact, however, Vendler's own view seems to be an undeveloped form of the linguistic theory. He speaks, for example (p. 142), of concepts and thoughts being "encoded" in the nervous system in just the same way that the same word can be encoded in various sorts of symbols.
21. The distinction was presupposed in Chapter 4, although we were only concerned there with the "content" of an act. The distinction is defended, as one between the "quality" and the "matter" of an act, by Edmund Husserl, *Logical Investigations*, trans. J.N. Findlay (New York: Humanities Press, 1970), pp. 586ff. It is also defended by Bergmann, pp. 33ff.
22. Husserl devotes considerable attention to this difficulty, although he concludes, not that the distinction between the content and the mode of an act cannot be analogous to that between the shape and the color of some spot, but rather that the former quality is not what we designate by such predicates as 'presents that *p*.' But what sorts of predicates are appropriate for designating the contents, or "matters," of acts, Husserl does not indicate. Cf. pp. 598ff.
23. Cf. Geach, p. 12: "in general there is no established usage for a sentence as a whole. . . . It is words and phrases that have an established usage."
24. Ibid., pp. 52ff.
25. Sellars, *Science, Perception and Reality*, p. 329.
26. Ibid., pp. 178ff.
27. Roderick Chisholm, "Sentences about Believing," reprinted in *Minnesota Studies in the Philosophy of Science*, 2:511.
28. Sellars, *Science, Perception and Reality*, pp. 321ff.
29. This "inner language" cannot, of course, literally be identified with *any* public language, such as English or German. Public languages can only provide either languages into which one's inner language may be *translated*, or languages which, in the form of images in thought, merely *accompany* inner speech proper. Thus Zeno Vendler goes too far in inferring (p. 143) that "one's own thoughts are not in any specific language." His arguments at most establish that one's own thoughts are not in any specific *public* language.
30. Sellars, *Science and Metaphysics*, pp. 75–77.
31. Sellars, "Reply to Marras."

32. Sellars, *Science, Perception and Reality*, pp. 324ff. Some issues raised by Sellars' notion of "pattern-governed" behavior are discussed by Ausonio Marras in the papers mentioned in n. 5 above and also in "Sellars on Thought and Language," *Nous* 7 (May 1973): 152–63. The whole issue is unnecessarily complicated, in my opinion, by Sellars' failure to be clear about the precise bearing on the notion of pattern-governed behavior of his distinction between two kinds of *rules*: ought-to-do and ought-to-be rules. For the latter distinction, cf. Sellars' "Language as Thought and as Communication," *Philosophy and Phenomenological Research* 29 (June 1969): 506–27. So far as I can see, the discussion which follows brings out the basic thrust of Sellars' program, though it does not appeal to that distinction at all; and it thereby avoids the charge of circularity that Marras develops out of some of Sellars' claims concerning that distinction.

33. Ibid., p. 326.

34. Ibid., p. 327.

35. Perhaps it is worth noting (contrary to Marras' suggestion in "Sellars on Thoughts and Language," p. 157, n. 3) that Sellars' view is not at all incompatible with recent developments in psycholinguistics pointing to the existence of *innate* linguistic structures. These, on Sellars' view, can simply be regarded as determining certain innate patterns of correct behavior.

36. Sellars, *Science, Perception and Reality*, pp. 328–29.

37. Ibid., p. 339.

CHAPTER 6

1. This formulation itself allows of two possibilities, depending upon just what one takes the content ⌐elephant shape⌐ to be; that is, depending on just what one means by apprehending some shape "as an elephant shape." Taken one way, we might have in mind the content ⌐shape of the sort that elephants usually exhibit⌐. Taken another way, we might mean the content ⌐shape actually exhibited by some elephant in my presence⌐. Only the latter case provides a sense of "seeing an elephant" in which seeing is, in the usual sense, *believing*.

2. On this interpretation, "indirect quotation" of a person's thoughts involves the specification of "synonyms" of that person's thought. In actual practice, of course, one might legitimately "quote" another person without producing synonyms. In actual practice, in other words, what we do, in saying that a judges that b is F, is simply report that a is in a mental state of some kind K, such that K's are as *close* to being ·b is F·s as our interests in the present context require. How close that is will of course vary with the context.

3. This of course involves the supposition that there *is* a particular expression which may not in fact occur as part of any actual overt language. This might be avoided, however, by complicating matters a little more: a is in a mental state of kind K, such that K's are mental sentences which would be ·S·s, if S *were* a sentence produced by substituting for α in ⌐α is F⌐ an expression which is "synonymous" with that part of a's mental state which is *combined* in that state with that part which is an ·is F·.

Index

Judgment—*Continued*
    intentional relations, 57, 78–85; in per-
    ception, 21–24, 48–49, 52–53, 93–94,
    103–7, 148–50, 151

Kant, I., 23, 72, 156
Kaplan, D., 88, 91, 152

Language, Ch. 5 *passim. See also* Meaning
Locke, J., 155
Lovejoy, A.O., 96

Meaning, 58, 107–18 *passim*, Ch. 5 *passim*
Meinong, A., x, 50, 62–73, 77–78, 96–101,
    108, 115, 154
Mental act, defined, ix
Mind/body identity, 1–2, 28–32
Mode (vs. content) of mental acts, 109–10,
    132–34
Moore, G.E., 20, 24, 103

Non-existent objects, ix, 2, 6, 12–13, 14–18,
    19, 21, 24–25, 43, 44–45, 48, 49–57, 64–
    66, 79–80, 90, 95, 96–97, 151. *See also*
    Fiction, State of affairs (possible)

Objectives (Meinong), 62–64, 66–67, 69–73,
    77–78, 99–100
Opaque contexts, 91–95, 105. *See also* In-
    tentional sentences

Percept theory, 18–19
Perception, 21–24, 85–86; as intentional,
    13–21, 25, 48–57, 85, 93–94, 103–7, 148–
    51; as involving intentional relations, 48–
    57, 85, 151; direct, 18, 107, 149, *see also*
    Sense-datum theory; in Brentano, 13–20
Phenomenal reality: in Brentano, 14–20; in
    Kant, 156
Phenomenology, ix, 20, 106–7, 116
Physical phenomena (in Brentano), 1–2, 14–
    15, 18–20, 24
Physicalism, 29–30
Possible: particulars, 79, *see also* Non-
    existent objects; states of affairs, 35, 49,
    57, 62, 73–78, 85, 99, 102, 104, 118–19,
    120, 150

Presentation, 109, 111, 132–33
Primitive qualities, 146. *See also* Intention-
    ality as primitive property
Properties. *See* Universals
Propositions, 35–36, 57–59, 61–63, 67, 70,
    73, 90–91, 99, 102, 109–10, 118–19, 132,
    149, 160. *See also Gedanke,* Objectives
Pseudo-existence. *See* Intentional existence
    in Meinong

Qualities. *See* Universals
Quine, W., 124

Recognition. *See* Judgment in perception
Reference, 91–95, 110–15 *passim,* 145–46,
    148; to the non-existent, 44–45, 64–67,
    95, 144
Reid, T., 155
Relational theories of awareness, x, 97–98,
    103–4, 119, 152–53. *See also* Intentional
    relations, Sense-datum theory
Relations, 39–43, 67–70. *See also* Inten-
    tional relations
Representationalism, 11–12, 24
Russell, B., x, 72, 78–85, 90, 96, 152–53

Sartre, J.-P., 158–59, 165
Sellars, W., x, Ch. 5 *passim,* 153
Sensation, 142–46. *See also* Perception,
    Sense-datum theory
Sense (vs. reference). *See* Meaning
Sense-datum theory, 14–15, 18, 20, 24–25,
    49, 51, 55–56
States of affairs, 35, 42, 49, 57–62, 67–69,
    72–79, 83–84, 85, 99, 101–2, 104, 113,
    115, 118–19, 120, 150, 152
Subsistence (Meinong), 71

Thought. *See* Judgment, Propositions
Truth, 46, 70, 120–21

Universals, 34, 35, 51–57, 59–62, 79, 83–84,
    85, 90–93, 146–51; *de re/de dicto* distinc-
    tion applied to, 84, 90–93; in Frege, 110–
    15
Unsaturated entities (Frege), 111–14